Why the Cross?

For if by one man's offense death reigned through one, much more they who receive abundance of grace, and of the gift, and of justice, shall reign in life through one, Jesus Christ. Therefore, by the offense of one, unto all men to condemnation, so also by the justice of one, unto all men to justification of life.

—ROMANS 5: 18–21

EDWARD LEEN, c.s.sp.

Why the Cross?

SCEPTER PUBLISHERS
Princeton, New Jersey

First published in 1938 by Sheed & Ward

Imprimi potest: D. Murphy, C.S.SP., D.D.

Nihil obstat: Lucas Willems, O.S.B., PH.D.
                   Censor deputatus

Imprimatur: Canon S. Banfi
                   Vicar General, Southwark
                   April 19, 1938

This edition published in 2001 by
Scepter Publishers
P.O. Box 1270, Princeton, NJ 08542

ISBN 1–889334–28–6

Typeset in ITC New Baskerville
Composition by Shoreline Graphics, Rockland, Maine

PRINTED IN THE UNITED STATES OF AMERICA

CONTENTS

PART TWO — THE TREE OF LIFE

ACKNOWLEDGMENTS

My sincere thanks are due to
Rev. J. Murphy, C.S.Cp., D.D.,
and
Rev. B. Fennelly, C.S.Cp.,
for several useful emendations
and many valuable suggestions

INTRODUCTION

WHY THE CROSS?

A EUROPEAN politician once stated that Christianity had failed. It did not seem to him that his assertion needed proof. The actual condition of things in his own country and in other countries appeared to him to be ample justification for what he said. Yet the statement, so far from being indisputable, can be shown, on analysis, to betray a gross confusion of thought.

Christianity has not failed, for the simple reason that it has scarcely been tried. It certainly has not been tried on any extensive scale. It could be branded with failure, if having been guaranteed by its founder to be able to achieve certain definite results, it had been, when put to the test, found wanting. But if Christianity is but imperfectly or incompletely applied to the task of reducing to order the confused issues of human existence, it cannot be blamed for the relative chaos that results. If Christianity in its integrity was accepted by all and its principles were applied in efforts to solve the practical problems of life, peace and comparative happiness would be the result. If Christianity were put in practice for one entire day by all people throughout the whole world, then for that day the woes that afflict mankind would in great part have ceased.

Though all suffering and sorrow would not have ended (Christianity does not guarantee that it will put an end to distresses inherent to mortality and the fallen state of mankind), yet the earth would bear a not-too-remote resemblance to the Garden of Paradise. To dream of bringing about this happy state of affairs without applying the principles of Christianity to the unraveling of the tangled issues of human existence is to dream a dream that can never be realized. Many world leaders indulge this idle dream. It is not astonishing that the result of the political efforts of such dreamers is but to intensify the existing disorder and to make confusion worse confounded.

As has been said, Christianity cannot be accused of failure: it is mankind that can, with strict justice, be accused of failure, because, on the whole, man has failed to respond to the appeal of Christianity. It is more than doubtful if it can be maintained with any truth that, at any time, since the beginning of the Christian era, any body politic wholeheartedly accepted and applied the full Christian program in the organization and regulation of its life. Doubtless such an application has been made partially and, on occasions, even to some considerable extent. But the Christian philosophy of life, in its political and social aspects, was never given full and unhampered play in molding the public life of modern nations. There was a time when things were shaping toward this, more or less remotely. The condition of public affairs was satisfactory or unsatisfactory according to whether there was an approach to, or a falling short of, the Christian ideal.

What has been said of social groups is not universally true of individuals. There have been individual men and women who have given a wholehearted trial to Christianity and have not found it wanting. In their hands it has been a complete and triumphant success. These persons are known as saints. They have illustrated the annals of the Church in all ages. They understood Christianity to be what it actually is, a divinely fashioned instrument, made for the express purpose of transforming human nature. Christianity guarantees this result—this divine transformation of humanity—if it is applied to the work. It asserts that it is equipped with ample resources to bring this process to a successful issue. It does not guarantee this result if inadequately used, or if ill used; and ill used it must be if it is not wholly accepted or if it is badly understood.

The saints accepted Christianity wholeheartedly. In their case there was no failure. They became exactly what Christianity guaranteed to make them, super-men in the highest sense of the term. They became transfigured with a transfiguration symbolized by that of Christ on the Mount. They became human beings—more human than the others, and yet human beings who diffused rays of the divinity. They are people who have permanently benefited mankind. Their spirit and their works survive them and serve as an enduring leaven in the mass of humanity. The good they did was not interred with their bones. They were eminently great, and Christianity was the source of their greatness. In others, be they individual persons or groups of persons, Christianity succeeds in a measure that corresponds exactly with the degree in which it is accepted. Unfortunately, to subscribe to Christianity is not the same thing as being integrally a Christian. To be this latter, one must accept the Christian standard of values. If this is not done fully, elements of disorder and distress necessarily invade the life of the individual and of society. The failure to achieve an existence that is satisfying must not, in these circumstances, be laid at the door of Christianity, but of those who profess Christianity, while forgetting Christian values in practice. This is not the failure of Christianity, but the failure of men to be Christians.

The life of the follower of Christ is bound to be filled with contradiction and inconsequence, unless he is clearly aware of what Christianity is for, what it guarantees to do, and what promises it holds out. Amid the clamor and tumult arising from social and economic disorders, the real message of the Gospel of Christ can, with difficulty, be heard. The enemies of Christianity—and many of them, very likely, are enemies only of what they conceive Christianity to be—attack it, either as being the cause of evils from which the nations are suffering or, at least, as not playing its due part in striving to remedy these evils. There is a certain amount of tragic irony in seeing Christianity blamed for those evils that have arisen from the abandonment of Christian principles. For from the corruption of the Christian social structure, resulting in the great schism of the sixteenth century, emerged those germs of economic theory and practice that have been in subsequent times so prolific in fruits of economic evil. Men were not aware at the time that, in replacing the living authority of Christ by private judgment, they were actually abandoning Christianity. They were not aware of the logical implications of their revolt. Retaining much of what materially belonged to Christianity, they believed themselves to be formally Christians. The logical consequences of their premises, derived from their revolt, are becoming perfectly clear now. Their errors in doctrine reacted on the organization of human life in a way they could scarcely have foreseen. The economic, social, and political principles that formed from their dogmatic positions contained, in germ, the social, economic, and political evils that afflict civilization today.

When man has declined in spirituality, it is natural that he should find his material needs to be the most insistent and the most important. People feel far more intensely their economic than their spiritual distress. Aristotle acutely remarks that a person is prone to make happiness consist in a condition of things that is the direct opposite to a misery from which he happens to be, at the moment, suffering. To a man suffering from dire poverty, wealth is happiness.[1] To the dispossessed multitudes cut off from the sources of wealth by the operation of modern industrialism, happiness appears to lie in free access to the world's goods and secure possession of them. They are taught by their guides to believe that Christianity blocks the path to economic security and are roused to fierce anger against it. The folly and injustice of this attitude have just been pointed out. It is the extreme of perversity to blame Christianity for what has followed from the abandonment of Christianity. It is not Christians who are responsible for the

[1] Arist., *Nich. Ethics,* bk. 1, ch. 2.

woes that afflict humanity. It is men, who, whether they call themselves Christians or not, apply to the solution of life's problems and to the regulation of life's conduct principles that deviate from the principles taught by Christ. They are responsible to the exact degree of that deviation.

But this is not the only point to make. The defenders of Christianity in the ardor of their defense are prone to be drawn away into a position dictated by their adversaries. When, for instance, the Church is bitterly assailed for not remedying the economic evils, the Christian apologist hastens to point out all that the Church has done in this sphere of action. What the Church has done and is doing is immense, undoubtedly. But it must not be forgotten that her primary concern is with spiritual and not with temporal values. Very willingly she leaves the sphere of temporal interests to be regulated by man's own thought and by man's own inventions. Social, political, and economic problems can be solved by the exercise of human reason and by the right use of human will. The Church, the living voice of Christianity, does not wish to supersede, but to stimulate, human activity. She contents herself with giving directions that will prevent the activity from taking courses she knows, with her divinely infused wisdom, will ultimately militate against man's good. She desires that man should himself exert his faculties to the full to secure, by human designing, a satisfactory arrangement of human affairs, and such a measure of temporal well-being as is feasible.

This attitude is not one of haughty aloofness from, or cold indifference to, men's earthly cares. It is dictated by a sovereign respect for those inborn possibilities of development, which can be evolved by man's use of his own powers. She has a notable precedent for it in the attitude of her Divine Founder. A contemporary of the Savior urged Him to leave aside for the moment His labors for the establishment of the Kingdom of God, and devote Himself to something more immediately practical, the settlement of an economic dispute.

"Master," he said, "speak to my brother that he divide the inheritance with me." Here there is a very characteristic situation. When things go to men's satisfaction, they are quite willing to dispense with the guidance of God. But when, left to their own resources, they have thoroughly mismanaged their affairs, then they turn to Him, that is, to His living voice on earth, to put order into the confusion they have created. More likely than not, they upbraid the Church and assail her as being responsible for the existing disorder. The Church could reply to the appeal and to the calumny in the words of Jesus: "O man, who hath appointed me judge and divider over you?" [2]

For men, as a rule, have but shown themselves too eager to manage their own temporal affairs. They resent what they call the Church's interference. This resentment culminates in a deliberate exclusion of the Church from the councils of peoples. Even at the best of times, when States were not yet professedly secularist, what jealousy was always manifested with regard to the action of the Church in secular matters! How slow men were to take her advice! How her efforts for procuring the temporal welfare of men were hampered, thwarted, and positively resisted!

The gradual silencing of the voice of Christianity in the councils of the nations is the evil cause of the chaotic conditions of modern civilized life. This issue was inevitable. For though the Church's wisdom is primarily in the domain of things of the world to come, yet she is wise, too, with regard to the things of the world that is. She is not for the world, and yet she is able and even ready to act as if she were equipped specially to procure the temporal good of men.[3] She is able and willing to give men directions in temporal matters, which, if followed, will result in temporal prosperity. She is too wise to promise unrealizable Utopias, from which all suffering and toil will be

[2] Lk 12: 13–14.
[3] See Maritain, *St. Thomas Aquinas*, p. 134.

banished. She can give prudent directions how to devise measures for the mitigation of inevitable hardships and the elimination of unnecessary evils. If rulers and ruled alike listened to her voice, the authentic voice of Christianity, what a change would come over the world! It would not cease to be a vale of tears but would cease to be a vale of savage strife. It would not become an earthly Paradise but would become an earth where man's dreams of a satisfying order of things could be realized.

But when all this has been said, it remains true that the sphere of activity in which the Church's efficacy is to be tested is not the sphere of economics. That is not her proper province. There, nothing more than relative success can attend human efforts, whereas, in that work which it properly belongs to Christianity to accomplish, no failure can attend on its efforts. The function of Christianity is not to reform or devise economic or social systems: her function is to reform and to transform the economists themselves. The Church, the organ of Christianity, is well aware that a change in social conditions, unaccompanied by a change in the dispositions of people, will only result in the substitution of one set of wrongdoers for another. "And the last state of men is made worse than the first."[4] The Church undertakes to change people, not systems. She knows that if individuals become what they ought, systems will become what they ought. The dictum of her Divine Founder remains her own and voices her wisdom as well as her experience. "Seek first the kingdom of God and His justice and all these things shall be added unto you."[5]

There is so much clamorous abuse of the Church for not remedying social evils, that both her friends and her enemies gradually have their minds dulled to the apprehension of what the Church's essential function is in the world. But it must be repeated that the creation of satisfactory social conditions is far from being the primary, much

[4] Mt 12: 45.
[5] Mt 6: 33; Lk 12: 31.

less the only, aim of Christianity. What that aim is—what promises Christianity holds out to people—what it guarantees to effect for them—what means and processes it offers for the realization of these hopes—what is the reason that these means and processes take the form that they actually assume—and finally, what a wondrous life, satisfying every desire and aspiration, it infallibly provides for all, if people will only consent to make use of the resources it puts at their disposal. In short, to set forth the real message of Christianity, its promises, its methods, and its guarantees, is the purport of the following pages.

In Christendom today, conflicts regarding particular points of the Christian dispensation have come to an end. The battle in the realm of the spirit is now waged on a narrow front. It is the value itself of the Christian notion of human character and of the Christian ideal of life that is challenged.[6] The world is dividing itself rapidly into two hostile camps, one combating that ideal *à outrance*, the other defending it with what might be accurately termed a dogged tenacity. The protagonists of the Christian theory of human existence are rapidly shrinking in numbers. They know that they are not fighting a losing battle, but they undergo all the agony of mind of men who feel that they are fighting against overwhelming odds. The fight cannot be lost, but the losses can be very heavy.

In this strife, where all Christian values are called in question, the best vindication of the Christian ideal is its bold, uncompromising expression. Such an expression may not be without its effect on the enemies of Christianity, and may not be without its utility for those who are loyal to Christianity. It is possible that the sincere among the former have but a distorted idea of what they attack, and that many among the latter have an imperfect view of what they defend. Many are the misguided who in their revolt against the Christian ideal of human character and

[6] See A. E. Taylor, *The Faith of a Moralist* (Gifford Lectures, 1926–1927), pp. 10–11.

WHY THE CROSS?

the Christian rule of life are in revolt not against that ideal itself, but against what they conceive it to be. It is hard to say how far Christians themselves are responsible for this state of affairs. Not only inadequacy in the practice of Christianity, but also a faulty presentation of its values, is apt to rouse antagonism in the sincere and the reflective. The Christian theory of life is so coherent, so logical, so simple yet so mysterious, so accommodated to the average person as well as to the most highly gifted, and finally so soul-satisfying that, when adequately presented, it must readily recommend itself to all people of sincerity and good will. It alone among all other theories faces the problems offered by human existence and gives an answer to them. Contrasted with the Christian theory of life and life's experiences, all the theories that conflict with it and set themselves up in opposition to it must appear barren, ignoble, and utterly incapable of satisfying the ineradicable aspirations of the human spirit. On the other hand, for those who rally to the standard of Christ, a clear and explicit notion of what Christianity essentially means must have the effect of strengthening their hands and confirming their resolution in the defense of the values to which they give their allegiance.

PART ONE

THE TREE OF DEATH

CHAPTER ONE

*We have looked for peace and there is no good, and for a
time of healing, and behold trouble.*

—JEREMIAH 14: 19

*The characteristic of human life that in a special way forces
itself on the attention of the thoughtful is its feverish
restlessness.*

IN THE HOMERIC POEMS, "unvintaged" was one of the
common, conventional epithets applied to the ocean. It is
a word that is not without its aptness to convey the impression that the consideration of the mighty, restless energy
of the vast expanse of waters generates in the spirit of
the thoughtful. The "wine-dark" waves put forth much
movement and exert great force, and yet this output of
activity is barren of result. No fruits are garnered from its
strivings. It is difficult for the reflective to sit by the great
sea and contemplate it, even in its least feverish moods,
without catching something of the haunting pathos that
prompted the well-chosen adjective of the Greek verse.
This is, perhaps, the explanation of the vague, indefinable
melancholy that gradually envelops the spirit even of lov-
ers of the ocean if they sit long by its waters and permit
their souls to absorb, more or less passively, the message
conveyed in the hoarse murmurs of the waves. In the
depths of one's being is sensed what was sensed by the
penetrating and keenly analytic spirit of the Greek epic
poets, namely, that human life, for the majority of men,
finds itself imaged in the fretful restlessness and ever-
changing moods of the great waters. For how many
(whether we consider groups or individuals) does life

resolve itself into the expenditure of huge effort that yields no harvest—effort that oftentimes is perpetuated only in the ruins that it has caused.

Man instinctively feels that he must be in movement. Modern man tends to understand this more and more in terms of mere locomotion.

The unrest, so characteristic of the lives of many, is universal, not merely in the sense that it is widespread, but also in this, that it belongs to all ages and generations of mankind. It is not more a feature of our age than it has been of those that have preceded. If there be a difference between former and modern times, it lies only in this, that the incessant endeavor, to which men feel themselves committed, tends more and more to express itself in violent and rapid motion, in which they hurl themselves from one end of the earth to the other with vertiginous speed. They do this as though they had some secret hope that life would discover its purpose and achieve its utmost expression in compassing the greatest distance in the shortest possible space of time. Life is in movement, it is true, but not in movement of this kind. Because the earth is round, the more rapidly men can propel themselves mechanically, the more quickly they will arrive at their starting point! What a barren achievement!

The craze for ever-greater speed in transport gives this generation an appearance of being more feverish and restless than those that have gone before. This is only an appearance. The unrest has, probably, been as profound during any period in the last four centuries as it is now. Yet there is a difference that can be detected by the thoughtful. An unwonted note is discernible in the utterances that voice the discontent of humanity as—dissatisfied with and relinquishing what it has attained—it presses forward toward a more alluring future. A tone of hopelessness is making itself audible in the words of those who express the strivings of the modern man. The efforts, directed along the lines of what was regarded as human progress, were buoyant and optimistic. A goal, worth man's endeavors and an adequate compensation for actual present sacrifices, was deemed ultimately attainable. This note of hopefulness, of confident expectancy, of moral certainty of achieving eminently satisfactory conditions has gradually, but in recent times more rapidly, grown fainter. Mankind's efforts after "progress" are becoming less assured; they are obviously becoming more haphazard; they have come to be almost despairing. There is a growing misgiving, hardening into a certainty, that the confident, swinging march of post-medieval man along the road of "progress" has brought him, not to the borders of the looked-for Utopia, but to the verge of a howling waste peopled by nameless powers of evil. The toilsome struggle onward of the last four centuries has brought man nowhere. It has left him exhausted, disillusioned, bewildered, and too dispirited to retrace his steps. To do this to some purpose, he would need to be able to discover where he had taken the wrong turning. He has no assurance from his prophets that this would be possible for him.

Two great evils followed the revolt in the sixteenth century of the greater part of Christendom against the authority of Christ, living in His Church. The portions of the Christian world that were affected by the revolt (and what part wholly escaped its influence?) lost, first, the true sense of the supernatural life, and then became vague and hesitant even with regard to the natural. Blindness as to the meaning of that transformation of man's being which it was the Redeemer's task to achieve was followed by blindness as to the constituent elements of the true human good on which that transformation was to work.[1]

---

[1] "If I were to set forth my thought in full, I should say that, to my mind, the greatest benefit the Church owes to the Angelic Doctor, the most urgent intellectual task that he had to accomplish, was to fix, by absolutely firm and definite principles, the theological distinction between the natural and the supernatural order, a distinction that cannot he bridged over and is deeply cherished by the Catholic faith; a

A loss of the right sense of eternal values was immediately followed by a progressive darkening of the sense of temporal values.

The supernatural good of man is the elevation and sublimation of the natural good of man. Having ceased to understand the real meaning of the supernatural, the men of the revolt rapidly lost firmness in their grasp of the scheme of nature. Europe suffered grievously from this loss. Owing to the political power and wealth and wide influence of the countries that broke away from the unity of Christendom, the literature of the peoples of these countries came to mold and to fix the thought of vast masses who once formed part of the true Church. And what is more, the minds of the faithful themselves have been seriously tainted by the prevailing errors concerning questions of a social, economic, artistic, and political kind. Clear ideas as to the manner in which the domestic, economic, and civil life of man should be organized so as to yield true temporal prosperity and well being have been lost for those who have abandoned the true faith, and have become obscured for those who have maintained contact with the source of unity. Christians, in vast numbers, have lost the knowledge of how to live, not only the divine life of grace, but even the life of reason. "The good for man," says St. Thomas, "is to live according to reason." This is what is truly natural for him. Now, as things are, it is only by striving to live a supernatural life that man will succeed in living a truly natural life. Grace, in perfecting nature, keeps nature true to itself. It is only by living as supernatural men that we shall succeed in living as natural men.

---

distinction that is as important for the commonweal as for the Church, as important for a *sound understanding of the things of nature and of the things of grace* and the complete rational theory of which had to be elaborated during the course of centuries in a long process, full of vicissitudes, until it attained its full maturity in the thought of St. Thomas" (Jacques Maritain, *Réflexions sur l'intelligence*).

Fallen man, to be humanized, must be, by grace, in a sense, "divinized." [2]

Men, having wandered from the city of God in search of a city of their own making, are beginning to awake to the fact that they have become homeless. The naturalistic civilization that they have labored to build up after plans of their own devising is crumbling into ruins. They should have known that "unless the Lord build the house, they labor in vain that build it. Unless the Lord keep the city, he watcheth in vain that keepeth it." [3] How aptly do the secret misgivings, gnawing at the hearts of the men who sense that the civilization they have known is trembling to its fall like a dead leaf, find their expression in the words of the inspired writer of the Book of Wisdom. "Therefore we have erred from the way of truth, and the light of justice hath not shined upon us. We wearied ourselves in the way of destruction and have walked through hard ways, but the way of the Lord we have not known. What hath pride profited us? Or what advantages hath the boasting of riches brought us? All these things have passed away like a shadow, and like a post that runneth on, and as a ship that passeth through the waves, whereof when it is gone by, the trace cannot be found, nor the path of the keel in its waters." [4] What bitter deception

---

[2] The meaning of the supernatural life will be set forth in a later chapter. For the moment it suffices to say that it is the specific life of man taken and elevated by divine grace to have a range and amplitude and power such as it could never attain to, even were its powers indefinitely strengthened and perfected along the lines of their own natural development. Grace gives to the will and the intellect of man an energy and vitality that are not contained in the natural possibilities or exigencies of these faculties. This vitality spreads to the lower faculties and ultimately to the body. The sensitive nature of man participates in the perfection bestowed on his higher nature by grace. The "supernature" is, as the word implies, what is essentially beyond the capacities and the exigencies of nature. By divine grace alone man becomes a "super-man."

[3] Ps 127: 1.

[4] Wis 5: 6–10.

breathes through these words, *ergo erravimus* (and so we have gone astray)? How perfectly they express the icy despair that, in moments of deep reflection, grips the souls of millions caught in the inextricable tangle and pathless chaos of modern life! For the words "what hath the boasting of riches brought us?" substitute the paraphrase, "whither has our much vaunted 'progress' conducted us?" Europe is a prodigal son that some centuries ago left the Father's house, to enjoy untrammeled freedom of thought and will. It has fed on the husks of swine and finds itself devoured by a spiritual hunger, of which the material want from which it suffers is but a faint symbol.

> *Movement implies tendency toward a definite goal;*
> *knowledge of what is the right goal of human endeavor is*
> *needed if human movement is to be rightly directed.*

The mistake of mankind is not to be attributed to eagerness for progress and for that incessant movement which is the natural consequent of this eagerness. Movement is not a bad thing in itself. It leads to disaster only when ill-directed or wrongly directed. The impulse onward—the impatience with what has already been gained—is but a manifestation of man's deep-seated instinct that he is incomplete and that the law of existence is that he should press forward toward completion. That men are in movement would not of itself imply that they have missed their way; it might signify that they have not reached their goal. The root of the dissatisfaction that is the motive force in all struggle is the keen recognition that the life one experiences is far from satisfying the inextinguishable aspirations of the human spirit. This insight is accompanied by an ineradicable conviction that a perfect life is destined for man and that the energies of society are to be pooled and coordinated in order that it may be achieved. "To live excellently" is the object of all human endeavor.[5] The

---

[5] Aristotle, *Nich. Ethics*, bk. 1, ch. 2.

profound sense of not being perfectly living is what goads the generations of men into activity. They feel the irresistible urge to be ever up and doing, never resting in the positions gained. But this searching and groping and striving are doomed to futility unless there be a clear and universally accepted idea of the elements that go to constitute the ideal life for man.[6] The idea of human happiness must be the correct one. To live ideally and to be happy are expressions that are synonymous. Furthermore, what is thus clearly conceived, at least in outline, as the right goal of social and political effort must be understood as something the attainment of which depends in some measure, at any rate, on the due exercise of man's powers. It is because there is an almost universal confusion of thought as to the very meaning of human existence here on earth that there is such chaos in human strivings. Incidentally, it is the ruthless clarity in the communistic idea, false though it be, of the fundamental purpose of life's activity, that gave communism its force.[7]

Movement that is nothing but movement is meaningless. It becomes mere restlessness. To have a meaning, it must have an ending. Men toil to be at rest. Movement has, as its object, repose in a term. And inasmuch as men, in great numbers, in the countries once Christian, have no clearly defined objective in their minds, their movement has become but a feverish tossing to and fro in the delirium of a mortal sickness. They are journeying but getting nowhere, because they know not where to go. They thirst for life and cannot taste it, because they are ignorant of the ingredients of a true life. The prophets, to

[6] See ibid., bk. 1, ch. 1. The knowledge of the *Summum Bonum* (i.e., the perfect life for man) has a mighty influence on the conduct of life; and if we have it before us as a mark, at which, like archers, to aim, shall we not the more readily attain to what is meet and right?

[7] Hence it is clear that the only effective opposition to the communistic ideal will be offered by that Body which has the firm certitude that it infallibly knows what man is for and knows, too, by what steps he can reach his goal.

whom they look for inspiration and guidance, fail them. The oracles not only are mutually contradictory, they are, as often as not, self-contradictory. Deaf to the voice of their true guide and unheeding His directions, they wander blindly and stumble through stony places. The words of Scripture can be aptly applied to them: "And seeing the multitudes He had compassion on them; because they were distressed and lying like sheep that have no pastor."[8] To a thoughtful spirit gazing on our planet from outside, our world would in a great measure appear like a huge cage in which men pace to and fro with the futile restlessness of wild animals behind their bars.

> *The preservation of human existence, on which so much humanitarian attention is bestowed, is desirable if, with health, can be given a right notion of the meaning and purpose of life.*

The thoughtful ones of earth contemplating the scene presented by a human activity that continually changes its purpose and is powerless to assign itself any purpose that human reason cannot instantly question must feel the pathos of much well-meaning and humanitarian effort. Great generosity is shown and real kindness is spent in praiseworthy attempts to arrest the ravages of mortality, especially among the young. "Save the children" is an appeal that finds a ready response in the hearts of the humane and kindly. Not with cynicism, but with real sympathy, one may ask, "Save them for what?" Is it for the adult life that frets itself away in vain endeavors to assign itself an adequate reason for living? Is it worthwhile to preserve children for what any person would logically confess to be not worthwhile?[9] Is this charity of the kindhearted dictated by the hope that somehow life for these children may prove different from what it has been for

[8] Mk 6: 34.

[9] Therse are questions only for those who have not the view of the aims and objects of life as furnished by the true faith or even by sound philosophy.

WHY THE CROSS?

those who have tried to save them from death and disease? Are there grounds for hope that the little ones, when come to adult age, will light on, by chance, a solution of the problem of existence that has evaded their grown-up benefactors? What is the use of bestowing health unless there can be given with it the key to such a use of life as will issue in happiness? Life is a precious gift when it is accompanied by the knowledge of how to live rightly and the means to exercise this right living.

Catholics are frequently, though wrongly, not less at a loss than those without the Church, as to how life's ordinary activities are to be used so as to result in an ever fuller life.
Were this loss of the art of making life's earnest efforts issue in an ever fuller life confined to the millions plunged in the darkness of paganism, or to those other millions wandering in the deceptive obscurity of heresy and infidelity, the case would be pitiable but understandable. But what is tragic in the extreme is that souls entering at birth into the full light of revelation should suffer, in large measure, from the same blindness as those so much less favored than themselves. Those who enter into the inheritance of the Catholic faith should experience no hesitation as to what direction they are to impose on life's ordinary activities. They, with the unerring word of God to instruct them, should know in what human happiness consists and how it is to be gained. But how many of them, like those outside the true fold, are tormented in the depths of their souls with the uneasy feeling that they are not getting the best or the most out of their lives! They too are perplexed with the practical problem of how to make their actual pursuits, operations, determinations, enterprises, and activities bring them toward what they know full well to be the objective of life's doings and undertakings. Even deeply religious souls find themselves faced with the difficulty of making their hourly activities yield them up the sense of growth in real life and of the happiness that should spring from such a growth. Very often,

when the day's doings are ended, they ask themselves: What has it all meant? They are persuaded that they *should* have arrived somewhere, and they have an agonizing suspicion that they have arrived nowhere. They have no difficulty in solving for themselves, by the light of their faith, questions of right and wrong. They can find God in formal prayer, yet they seem unable to handle their lives in such a way as to secure by such handling the progressive satisfaction of the deep yearnings of the human heart and soul.

Obscurity in all these matters is, as may be expected, greater among the ordinary run of Christians. In a true sense, it can be said of them that they do not know how to live. That means that they do not know how to organize their deliberate activity so as to secure from it something permanent, abiding, soul-satisfying. They can aim at immediate, temporal objects and results, and that is all. As a rule, even the conscientious among them aspire no higher in their acts and decisions concerning temporal matters than to avoid displeasing God and running counter to His laws. They do not concern themselves with making these very acts instrumental in bringing them closer to the Source of Life. "The aim of most men, esteemed conscientious and religious, or who are, what is called, honorable, upright men, is, to all appearance, not how to please God, but how to please themselves without displeasing Him. . . . They make this world the first object in their minds and use religion as a corrective, a restraint, upon too much attachment to the world." [10]

If exception be made for a certain number of actions that are concerned with the cultural observances imposed by their religion and a certain clear-sightedness with regard to moral issues, Catholics, in vast numbers, differ little in their experiments at life from those who hold differing religious views. Apart from these experiences, which spring from acts that are specifically and directly

[10] John Henry Newman, *Parochial and Plain Sermons.*

WHY THE CROSS?

acts of their religion as Catholics, such as the reception of the sacraments, attendance at Mass, and the like, they resemble others in their reactions to things. In their views, their aims, their worldly ambitions, their judgments, their tastes, their appreciations, their amusements, and their pursuits, they do not present any striking contrast to those who profess a false religion or no religion at all. This is not true universally, of course, but the number for whom it is not true is relatively inconsiderable. For the considerable portion of them, there is no clear line of demarcation between *their* way of dealing with the ordinary interests of life and that of the votaries of this world. If one were permitted to penetrate into the inner sanctuary of the soul, where is developed the real drama of human existence with all its secret doubts, resolves, conflicts, and tragic vicissitudes, one would discover in the case of a multitude of Christians the same unrest, the same dissatisfactions, the same haunting fear that something of permanent value is being missed, as that which torments the spirit of the worldly.

> *Catholics do not utilize life properly, because they do not allow themselves to be enlightened by their faith in many of the ordinary issues of social, political, economic, and aesthetic life.*

It is a strange thing that Catholics so frequently, in their quest after a satisfying life here below, do not allow themselves to be guided by their faith. They do not instinctively apply the principles of faith to the so-called "secular" aspects of life. For the most part—though this conclusion they would not admit—they treat their faith as though it were useful to secure happiness only in the world to come, not in the world that is. The faith is not only considered (practically, at least) as being of no positive help to the realization of ideal life-conditions here below, it is looked upon rather as a hindrance. The followers of Christ are, unfortunately, prone to be deeply influenced in what may be called their instinctive judgments of concrete realities, by the world in which they live. The art and literature of that world, with the exception of a very small and unobtrusive part, is the expression of the soul of unregenerate humanity and of that soul's ideals. They are the aspirations and the appreciations of unregenerate humanity, which find loud and imperious utterance in the works of human genius. This utterance, in a thousand varied tones, seeks to interpret entirely in its own fashion the fundamental yearnings of the human spirit.[11] Because all people, with the two exceptions known to us by faith, are a prey to the instincts generated by the original prevarication, the voice of this literature-tainted-with-falsehood finds an echo in every human heart. It is easy, then, for Christians to have their understanding of temporal problems profoundly modified by the prevailing trends of thought. While retaining a firm hold on dogmatic truths, they can be swayed by the world in those questions, the connection of which with dogma is not apparent.

This influence of the unregenerate spirit is felt especially in those problems that deal with the ways and means of compassing man's temporal well-being. Those who have the faith, like those who have it not, too often find contact in their social, political, and economic views. They can, alas, approximate one another in their notions of the constituent elements of human happiness in this world.

---

[11] It cannot be otherwise; human nature is in all ages and all countries the same, and its literature therefore will ever and everywhere be one and the same also. "Man's work will savor of man; in his elements and powers, excellent and admirable, but prone to disorder and excess, to error and to sin. Such, too, will be his literature; it will have the beauty and the fierceness, the sweetness and the meekness of the natural man, and with all its richness and greatness, will necessarily offend the senses of those who, in the Apostle's words, are really exercised to discern between good and evil. . . . Natural literature is, in a parallel way, the movements of the reason, imagination, passions, and affections of the natural man, the leapings and the friskings, the plungings and the snortings, the sportings and the buffoonings, the clumsy play and the aimless toil, of the noble lawless savage of God's intellectual creation" (John Henry Newman, *Idea of a University*).

WHY THE CROSS?

The inconsequent Christian, like the non-Christian, tends to judge the ideal life to be that which would result from the elimination of all the evils grouped under the headings of pain, ignorance, and want, and in the presence of everything that ministers to the taste for pleasure, culture, and ease. The absence or nonattainment of these desirable things is for him synonymous with human unhappiness. When his efforts at counteracting what he regards as the forces hostile to human well-being prove unavailing, he may accept the situation with resignation and seek in his religion a safeguard against misery in the world to come. His religion, seeming to him to oppose itself to his ideas of temporal happiness, will be regarded as offering a post-temporal happiness at the price of present unhappiness. To many, religion appears to demand actual misery as a condition of future well-being. This is a totally mistaken view of things.

God means earth to be a preparation for, or—rather—the vestibule of heaven.

God does not demand unhappiness as the price of happiness. He plans happiness here as a prelude and foretaste of happiness hereafter. Such a statement sounds paradoxical to the average person. This is not surprising, considering the manner in which Christianity is ordinarily presented. A little reflection should suffice to dispel the difficulties that the proposition just enunciated finds in minds fixed in the unreal, conventional attitude toward life's realities. It is not the way of God to give things at a price. For Him to do so would be inconsistent both with His infinite generosity and with His Fatherhood of men. He created man not only for an existence that should endure always, but for an existence that should be a veritable life throughout its whole duration. His plan might involve that this life should be incomplete for a while, but not that it should be, at any instant, lacking in the elements of a true and real life. Happiness for men and the true life for men are identical motions. To live perfectly is to be perfectly happy. To live incompletely is to be incompletely happy, but it means to be happy, at any rate, in a certain measure. Man is blind to this truth because of his inveterate tendency to identify suffering and unhappiness. If man were, once for all, to rid himself of that false prejudice and allow himself to see the truth, that suffering and happiness are not mutually exclusive terms, he would be well on the way to the solution of the chief problem of life. The great problem for man is, How is he to realize for himself a happy life on earth?

Unhappiness has its cause in whatever impedes the realization of a full life—in what militates against man's well-being. God could not but intend man's well-being in creating him. What is more, this idea involves the direct intention, on the part of the Creator, to provide His creature with the means to attain this well-being—and that from the very beginning of the creature's existence. Submitted, like all living things, to the law of growth, the soul cannot have from the start the whole of its final reward. But in God's design, every movement of that process of growth is meant to be a partial entering into, a gradual acquisition of, the ultimate wealth of life. A man, while becoming rich, enjoys a measure of affluence though not all the affluence that is yet to be his. If God's purposes were realized—that is, if men met God half way—each soul could be at every moment happy with the happiness proper to that stage of development which it then has reached. What is more, the happiness it would experience would be essentially the same as the felicity that is final.

Human happiness, being of a specific kind, must be essentially the same throughout the entire duration of human existence.

There is always continuity in God's plan. He could not have meant that the life of man in time and the life of man in eternity should be of two distinct patterns artificially joined together: a bar of gold riveted to a bar of iron. The soul is simple. Its existence must present a unity, a sameness of texture through its whole length. The happiness of man must be based on the same principle. As long as man is man, what makes him happy *as man* must always be the same thing essentially. If a rational creature in bliss is judged to be living a life that makes it supremely happy, it follows that the same creature, while on earth, must live something of the same life or be unhappy. Man cannot be happy in two specifically distinct ways. He is certainly happy in heaven. There is, then, no possibility for him of achieving happiness on earth unless he can anticipate in time the conditions of eternity.[12]

It is through failure to recognize this truth that Christians in the vast majority are involved in contradictions and inconsistencies in the practical handling of life. They plan their own well-being and that of others on the practical assumption that the happiness of time is essentially different from the happiness of eternity. The logical consequence is that they seek the satisfaction of the human soul on earth in ways, and make it consist in objects, that are not the ways and objects in the life after death. If their faith teaches them that the blessed are happy because they enjoy a certain kind of vital activity, they should conclude that the road to happiness on earth is to strive to exercise the same activities—practice the same way of living. Beatitude consists in a certain life of thought and love. As the human soul finds its ultimate satisfaction in the life of thought and love in the world beyond, so, of necessity, will it find contentment and the quieting of its desires in the present world only in living the same life of thought and love, as far as that may be done.

The great tragedy lies in this, that Christians will continue to experiment in ways and means of happiness as if it could be attained in any other way or made up of any other elements than those just referred to. Taking action at variance with the beliefs they profess—for in the light of the faith they could not question what has been

---

[12] As will be seen later, God enables man to do this to a certain degree and thus to taste a real, though incomplete, beatitude while on earth.

stated—their measures to promote temporal beatitude will be of the same kind as those of the unbelieving world in the midst of which they live. They will pursue wealth, position, and pleasure with an eagerness similar to the eagerness of those who are wholly surrendered to the material and the transient. The worldly Christian divides in two the existence that God has planned as one. He will have life before death governed by one set of ideals; he will allow life after death to be governed by another and different set. The attempt does not meet with success. In spite of everything, the life to come will urge its claims and press its values on the life that is present. The unfortunate Christian is drawn in diverse ways, and his every deliberate choice is tainted with a contradiction to which he is keenly sensitive in the depths of his Christian consciousness.

It is mortifying that the faithful in such great numbers do not, in spite of the advantages they enjoy, rise to the lofty ideal of human life formed by the great pagan philosopher who lived three hundred years before Christ. Aristotle, seeking to discover what constitutes for man the "Supreme Good" or the "Ideal Life" or, simply, "Happiness," rejects with a certain disdain the views that place it in pleasure, in honor, in unsocial and inactive virtue. His tone becomes contemptuous when he refers to the view that makes the pursuit and acquisition of wealth the *Summum Bonum*. His investigations lead him to the noble conclusion that "the happiness proper to man resides in a virtuous activity of all the powers within the soul, consisting in the regulation of moral actions according to virtue, and in a contemplation of the Supreme Truth and in a love of the Supremely Perfect." [13] There is a remarkable grandeur and nobility in the words with which he brings his philosophic enquiry to a close. He writes: "The happiness proper to man dwells in activities according to virtue; and if there be among such activities any preeminent

---

[13] Aristotle, *Nich. Ethics*, bk. 1, ch. 8, and bk. 10, ch. 7.

WHY THE CROSS?

one, that will be the special seat of happiness. For happiness is preeminent and the crown of all things, and our crowning activity is that of the best among our powers ... that power which, by nature, rules and guides us toward truth and the good.... It is that part in us which comprehends things honorable and divine.... The activity of this power, well and fitly developed, and in accordance with its special virtue, must be perfect Happiness. If, therefore, intellect is divine relatively to man, then the life which is conformable to intellect will be divine relatively to the life of man. But, for all that, we ought not to follow the advice of those who bid us think only of human interest, as proper to our human life, and of the mortality that all men share. *Rather should we, so far as may be conceivable and possible, enter upon immortality and shape our very thought with the aim of living by the standard of the highest principle within us....* No man can live a life like this so far as he is merely man, but in so far as there is a divine element in his nature." [14]

> *The life that Aristotle, with the astonishing intuition of genius, perceived as the ideal for man, is made accessible, in an incomparably more perfect form, to the Christian.*

What the great Stagirite dreamed of is a reality within the reach of the humblest followers of Christ, and in a manner that surpasses the most exalted visions of philosophy. If the Christian would make use of the forces and powers generated in him by divine grace, he would, even already here on earth, "enter upon immortality" and inaugurate that life which, in its complete evolution, brings absolute felicity. The supreme vital activity, which means life at its highest—and, therefore, perfect happiness—consists in giving the fullest play to the faculties of intellect and will on the most perfect objects with which these faculties can deal. *Intellect* at its utmost energy of action, *will* at its supreme energy of loving—that is human life at its best.

[14] Ibid., bk. 10, ch. 7.

The Reality, source of all reality, the True, source of all truth—that seen in its inmost nature by man's intellect raises his intellect to its highest power, to its final activity. Beyond that Reality, there are no fields for it to range over, no possible world for it to conquer. The Supremely Attractive—source of all attractiveness—the Supremely Desirable—the source of all desirableness—with its inmost Beauty unveiled and offered to the human will, fully extends and exhausts the will's energy of loving. Grace brings this life within the range of man's faculties. By it, man can arrive at knowing, contemplating, loving, and enjoying God, the Supreme Truth and the Supreme Good. The life of glory is but the final development of the life of grace. Hence the life of glory is meant to be enjoyed here below in an inchoate form. As God planned things, life was to be an unbroken line, beginning at birth and continuing everlastingly. Death is not a break but a stepping stone by which one passes from one stage to another in the same existence. But man will perversely and blindly strive to effect a cleavage in that line and persuade himself that the good of the human life that *precedes* death can be different from the good of human life that follows death. The result is that he is necessarily at cross-purposes with God. It is not surprising that the creature, seeking to gain the goal of life—namely, happiness—by a use of life's powers and energies at variance with the design of the Creator, should be continually frustrated in his main object, should enjoy no peace, and should be involved in contradiction and become a prey to perpetual dissatisfaction. What is the way out of this impasse? The way out is through a thorough understanding of the religion of our Lord and Savior, Jesus Christ, and a practice based on such understanding.

In the foregoing pages was analyzed the dissatisfaction with life that torments modern man. Mankind has a despairing sense of having lost its way irretrievably. This powerlessness to give ultimate reality and meaning and purpose to life's activities affects those who once believed and have lost the faith. Those who have been born to the inheritance of the faith are not untouched by it. Even these have lost the secret of living humanly. It is only a thorough understanding of Christianity, what it means and what it holds out to men, that will enable mankind to recover the secret of happiness.

CHAPTER TWO

Seek not death in the error of your life; neither procure ye destruction by the works of your hands.

—WISDOM 1: 12

Happiness, of a relative kind, is obtainable in this world.

HAPPINESS, real, though limited, is within the reach of man even on this earth. In the actual order of things, where mortality, along with its attendant conditions, is the fate of all the children of men, attainable happiness cannot be without the alloy of suffering. Yet, in spite of this drawback, it will be capable of giving a zest to life and tranquility to the restlessness that devours the hearts of the vast majority of mankind.

The chief cause of unhappiness is not suffering, but a certain intangible fear, which casts a dark shadow on almost all human enterprises.

There is something that people fear more than death itself. It is not easy to give it a name. It is what might be called "moral annihilation," though the description would be somewhat inaccurate. Every being, animate and inanimate, shrinks desperately from disintegration, but the shrinking that is here in question is of a different nature. There is in all reasoning beings an instinctive desire that what they actually make their life to be, should continue everlastingly. The Valhalla of the old Norsemen was a place of repose, where were continued eternally in a more excellent manner those gratifications which for them constituted the ideal of earthly bliss. Every man desires his life to endure without end. St. Thomas, following in this Aristotle, says that pursuits to which a man gladly surrenders his vital energies may be, figuratively, described as his life.[1] The Vikings conceived Paradise as a place in which there was to be a perpetual round of those festivities in which they used to take their delight.

No reflective person, born under the Christian dispensation, pictures the life after death in this gross manner. When such a one allows his thoughts to dwell on the hereafter, he has little difficulty in forming to himself a notion, vague perhaps, but nevertheless true, of the interests of the blessed. Life expresses itself in activity. Now, it comes home to Christians, in those moments in life in which they are brought face to face with ultimate realities, that most certainly those activities in which they take their greatest pleasure and to which they devote themselves assiduously cannot possibly survive the test of death. They realize, in the depths of their souls, that what they are making "their life" to consist in cannot endure beyond a fixed and limited number of years. Through their own choice, their "life" is made a thing of inevitable death. There is, then, constantly hanging over them the dread of nothingness—a nothingness worse than the mere cessation of existence. The notion of end is impressed upon all to which they passionately cling. "Insofar as a man takes life seriously, his aim is to find and enjoy a good that is never to be left behind and never to be superseded."

Man naturally desires the permanence of any good he possesses.[2] He therefore desires permanence of what he is actually making his life to consist in. For any man, a present good, to be a real good, must be one that does not become past. A really "good time" is a time that is tempered with eternity. But if a man be a Christian, deep down in his being is the inextinguishable sense that the materials out of which he is weaving his life and constructing his personality can as little endure the light of eternity

---

[1] *Summa theologiae*, I-II, q. 179, a. 1.

[2] Ibid., q. 5, a. 3, c. See also Professor Taylor, *The Faith of a Moralist*, pp. 88–89, 98.

as the frail gossamer the heat of the risen sun. This inner realization of the ephemeral nature of those experiences which mean life for so many, robs every enterprise, every fulfilled ambition, every pleasure, of its power to procure unqualified gratification. The dark shadow of this fear of inevitable loss attends on all elements of life that men seek to construct for themselves out of earthly resources. Men desire passionately to live what St. Paul, in an untranslatable phrase, calls a life that is truly life.[3] Abidingness is a necessary quality of a veritable life. What so frequently causes a sudden chill to descend on the soul in the very act of taking part in worldly entertainments is the unwelcome thought that what one is surrendering oneself to cannot last. The heart is weighed down by the reflection that the life one is making for oneself is but a death— an inevitable nothingness.[4]

It is not death itself that is so feared. If it were, as it is meant to be for us, but a mere modification of the conditions of our actual existence, it would carry no terrors with it. But if a man knows perfectly well that his mode of living here and now, his thoughts, his ideals, aspirations, affections, pursuits, tastes, have nothing in common with what must be the tastes, ideals, aspirations—in a word—with the mental outlook characteristic of the blissful world beyond the tomb, then he is naturally filled with fear. For fear is the passion stirred up by the imminence of an evil that one feels powerless to grapple with and overcome.[5] Is this fear a necessary accompaniment of the rhythm of life? It would appear not. It is a striking thing that in the canticle of Zechariah the removal of fear from human life is stated to be one of the objects that the Redeemer sets

[3] 1 Tim 6: 19. *Tēs ontōs zōēs* in Greek—where the word qualifying life is an adverb formed from the present participle of the verb "to be."

[4] This horror we have of death, writes Bossuet, has a deeper source than the warnings of our reason, that we have grounds for dreading what follows death. The horror arises from this, that we received life so as not to die (Bossuet, *Sermons*, 4:158–160).

[5] *Summa theologiae*, II-II. q. 41, a. 2.

WHY THE CROSS?

before Him to accomplish. "Blessed be the Lord God of Israel because he hath . . . raised up an horn of salvation to us . . . that being delivered from the hand of our enemies, we might serve Him *without fear*." [6]

*Happiness is found through putting an element of
permanence into what is of its own nature fleeting.*
The dark shadow of inevitable nothingness can be dispelled, if it becomes possible to endow the passing moments of existence with the quality of everlastingness—if it becomes possible to seize the instants in their rapid flight and eternalize them.[7] If each deliberate act could be stamped with the seal of eternity, then the sense of life slipping away, like water through a man's fingers, would disappear. If it were possible to make each day yield a good that would survive the day's passing and would coalesce with a similar good to be derived from the days that succeed, then life would become a reality perpetually growing, instead of a shadow continually passing. The art of making life become a life truly life, and not a continual dying, consists in transmuting time into eternity. But does not this involve a seeming impossibility? The religion that Jesus Christ came on earth to give to men confers on them the means of realizing what appears so obviously impossible.

The Savior, describing the purpose of His divine mission, said: "I have come that they may have life and may have it more abundantly." [8] His coming was to destroy death—not the ordinary natural separation of soul and body—but that moral nothingness which has been spoken of in the preceding paragraphs. Jesus has given men the power to achieve an eternal life, not in eternity only, but already in time. The life He bestows is not an ephemeral

[6] Lk 1: 68–74.
[7] St. Augustine writes: "Do not expend so much effort in striving to die a little later: aim at making a supreme effort in order never to die" (*Sermons*, 302).
[8] Jn 10: 10.

life but an eternal one. He enables men to live so as not to die, by transferring the conditions of eternity into time.

The activity in which the true life[9] after death expresses itself consists in the soul's knowing intuitively the Supreme Reality and loving the Absolute Good. To live, for a rational creature, is to know and to love.[10] To live most perfectly is to know most intimately and to love most intensely the Supreme Object of knowledge and love. Happiness and the ideal life for man are synonymous terms. To live fully—to live to man's utmost capacity as man—is to be supremely happy. Pleasure or gratification, whether of sense or spirit, is not to be confounded with happiness, though intense gratification is the natural resultant of every conscious vital activity healthily exercised about its appropriate object. "The most pleasurable activity is that which is most perfect, and the most perfect activity is that of a man who, being perfectly balanced, exercises his vital activity on the noblest object that can come before it." [11] Pleasure follows in the wake of every process of reasoning or play of thought.[12]

The supreme form of conscious activity for man is the exercise of his intellect and will on Supreme Truth and on Supreme Beauty, in contemplation and love. That experience is, in a certain limited measure, offered by our Savior to men while still on earth. Through His grace and the life communicated to the human soul by grace, man is empowered to have a personal knowledge and love of God. Grace enables him to live a life of supreme vital activity. To live excellently, that is, to put forth the highest vital activity, is the very definition of happiness. Divine grace imparts the faculty to exercise this activity, which contains no element of mortality. The vital activity that has its origin in grace does not die in its birth, as does all merely natural activity. Grace gives, here and now, an *eternal* life.

[9] The existence of the reprobate is not life but eternal death.

[10] See Aristotle, *Nich. Ethics*, bk. 1, ch. 6, and bk. 10, ch. 7.

[11] Ibid., bk. 10, ch. 4.

[12] Ibid.

Jesus, lifting up His eyes to heaven, said: "As Thou has given Him [Thy Son] power over all flesh, that He may give *eternal life* to all whom Thou hast given Him. Now *this is eternal life* that they may know *Thee the only true God,* and Jesus Christ, Whom Thou hast sent."[13] From these words it is clear that the Savior has power to initiate those who believe in Him into a life that is not transient but eternal. This is the very thing that man in the inmost depths of his being is craving for, namely, a life that will endure. Furthermore, it is clear from the context that this excellent life is not envisaged by the Redeemer as one from which man is separated by the abyss of death. This ideal existence, in its commencement (and, therefore, happiness, in an inchoate form), is made accessible to man here and now. Those who have trusted Christ completely have verified in their personal experiences the truth of His words. They have tasted on earth a bliss that was a foretaste of the ravishing life of heaven.

If their religion were real, men would be happy.
There are, however, many who will say that they practice their religion reasonably well and yet get little comfort out of it, much less happiness or ideal life. Hence it is that when the practice of the faith does not, for them, fulfill its promise of yielding an existence of tranquility and contentment, they are tempted to renounce religion altogether. If they do not yield to this temptation, they drag their faith with them through life as a galling encumbrance. They chafe under it as something that is the constant obstacle to their happiness.

It may be remarked that those who rail at religion as disappointing them are not accustomed to inveigh with equal bitterness against those things of the world which prove illusory in their promises of bliss.

If the religion that Jesus Christ has given to men proves ineffective in satisfying men's thirst for "a life that is truly

[13] Jn 17: 2–3.

life," it is not because it is inadequate to the task, but because it is not the religion men practice. Religion fails them only because the gospel by which they regulate their existence bears a very inadequate resemblance to the original. If Christians in considerable numbers are not happy, it is not because they are followers of Jesus Christ, but because they follow Him very far off, very hesitatingly, and with many detours along the way. Happiness (not, however, unattended by suffering) is for those who "believe in" Him, and of the many who subscribe to His teaching theoretically, there are relatively few who adhere to it practically.

The belief in Jesus Christ that yields a full life is not a mere notional assent to certain dogmatic truths.
The belief in Jesus Christ that stirs up the dull embers of time and sets them ablaze with the flames of eternity is not a mere facile and cold assent of the intelligence to certain truths bearing on God's redemptive dealings with mankind and on the mysteries of God's inner life. A faith in certain truths, which is not vitally linked to action consequent to these truths—a faith that does not seize upon all the deliberate acts of a man's day and invest them with a higher significance—a faith that does not link up these acts with an objective far beyond the immediate one aimed at—a faith that does not set up order in men's doings and elevate them to that high plane where they shall be in harmony with that exalted condition which the Christian knows by his faith to be his—such a faith is not a living one and cannot, in consequence, be a vitalizing one. Such a faith is powerless to transfigure life and to burn away the elements of mortality. The living faith that Jesus looks for and that is invariably the object of His special commendation is something far different from this dead assent, without vital influence on a man's judgments, decisions, and acts.

To *believe in* Jesus Christ is not the same thing as *believing Him*. Belief in Him is something more than accepting His statements as true, on His word; it is even more than yielding assent to certain mysterious propositions relative to His origin, His life, and His dual nature. *Belief in* a person is not equivalent to believing a person or believing things about that person. It means a complete going over, and a wholehearted surrender of ourselves, to the man in whom we place our belief. It is to substitute His principles and views for our own. Hence, to believe in Jesus Christ is to subscribe to His entire theory of life and to accept it as our own. It means to make His values ours. Life for such a believer has that inner meaning, that significance, that purpose which it has for the Divine Master.[14] If He, with His insight into things, declares that the ideal human life is such and such, His true followers must warmly embrace that ideal, as being the only one. In a word, to believe in Jesus Christ is to accept His guiding principles of life, to renounce all theories of the "good life" that are in opposition to His, and to submit not only our whole conduct but our judgments as well to His ruling. It is to make His mind ours in those matters that pertain to the working out of our life on earth. "For let this mind be in you, which was also in Christ Jesus," writes the Apostle in his letter to the Philippians.[15] It is to be noted that we do not rise to this transforming belief by merely holding that the

[14] The Venerable Francis Libermann, C.S.Sp., commenting on the text in St. John (3: 16)—"That whosoever believeth in Him may not perish, but may have life everlasting"—writes: "It is to be noted that our Lord says, that all who believe *in* Him and not believe in His name, for the latter expression signifies but a belief in the Person of our Lord, or in the doctrine which He preaches—a belief which can coexist with very indifferent conduct. Those who have this kind of belief should not place a false confidence in the Cross of our Savior: it will condemn instead of saving them. There is required a faith in Him (*in eum*, not *in ipso*—in Latin it is the accusative, not the ablative, case)—a term which signifies union and adhesion of the soul to our Savior. This implies an estrangement from sin and the putting of a supernatural principle and motive into one's activity. For if the soul is truly united to our Lord by this perfect and real faith, then its action is united to His and the Savior is the principle of that action."

[15] Phil 2: 5.

Savior's theory of life is, indeed, praiseworthy, admirable, sublime, and incomparable if at the same time we regard it as one that admits of more humble alternatives. We do not *"believe in"* the Savior wholly unless we have the practical conviction that His theory of life and life's conduct is the only one admissible.

There is only one gospel for all mankind.
All Christians freely admit Christ's teaching to be a program of perfection. They will not quarrel with any of the principles of that program considered abstractly. They acknowledge that these principles can be reduced to practice and have been in fact reduced to practice by numbers of persons called saints, but they assume that the strict application to life of the Gospel precepts may be left to exceptional persons in exceptional circumstances. The vast majority act on the persuasion—a persuasion for which it is difficult to find any justification in the pages of the New Testament—that there are other roads to eternal life than the one chosen by those who take Christ at His word. They accept His teaching as regulative of their conduct, but with many reservations. They will confess that the full evangelical program, if carried out, is capable of raising men to the highest perfection; but they think themselves entitled to exercise a certain eclecticism in that program if they do not personally aspire to these dizzy heights with their rarefied atmosphere. Their ideal is more modest. From the Lord's statement that in His Father's house there are many mansions, they deduce, with facile but faulty logic, that there are various routes leading thither. They hold, without exactly formulating it, the belief that the gospel is susceptible of a multitude of applications, and capable of accommodating itself, with marvellous flexibility, to the cherished imperfections of the diverse categories of human creatures who are not tainted by spiritual ambitions.

Such persons, finding it hard to accept the gospel as anything more than a lofty ideal of life, which admits others of a less-exacting standard, and not looking on it as a practical program for all people in its preceptive injunctions, proceed to lop and prune it until it fits their individual tastes, aptitudes, and shortcomings. Few, comparatively, are they who bring home to themselves how uncompromising the Lord's teaching really is. *He is very tender toward the imperfect, but relentless toward imperfection.* For His followers He will not be satisfied with a conduct that falls short of the flawless ideal. It must not be thought that the severe and extremely exacting precepts are addressed only to a limited number—to the more heroic among men as a test of higher achievement. There are two types of Christians who dishonor God's law and are content with a low standard of duty. One type, believing that Christ in His own person has done all, thinks that He has taken the yoke of the Law off the shoulders of His followers by obeying the Law in their stead. The other type of Christian, by far the more common, presuming to decide for himself "that God does not require much, brings down the Law to his own power of obeying it." [16]

The Christian is not free to leave aside the difficult injunctions of the Law and confine his efforts to those he finds easier to fulfill. There is no one exempt from the observance of the two commandments that synthesize all the prescriptions of the Christian moral code. "Thou shalt love the Lord, thy God, with thy whole heart and with thy whole soul, and with thy whole mind, and with thy whole strength: and the second is like to this: Thou shalt love thy neighbour as thyself." [17] The fulfillment of these two precepts, "on which dependeth the whole law and the prophets," demands a readiness to suffer any loss, even that of life itself, rather than to fail in the moral obligations to God, to oneself, and to one's fellow men. St. Luke notes that the Savior, in positing the necessity of the constant and rude sacrifices that this adherence to the law of Christian righteousness involves, addresses Himself to *all.* "And

[16] Newman, *Parochial and Plain Sermons*, 5:141.

[17] Mt 22: 37–39; Mk 12: 30–31.

He said to *all*: If any man will come after Me, let him deny himself and take up his cross daily and follow Me." [18]

Christ's theory of life is one. If a single element of it be subtracted, the whole crumbles to pieces. It is true that His teaching admits various degrees of perfection in the practice of it, but it admits of no variations, no adaptations, no essential modifications. Failure to recognize this truth carries with it a misreading of the Gospels. In its practical teachings on the Christian ideal of conduct, the text of the Evangelists is sufficiently clear. Our Lord's instructions on morality can be grasped by the most ordinary intelligence, and yet there is no text that encounters such difficulty in being understood by men. After the lapse of so many centuries, the meaning of the gospel, as a whole, is clearly grasped only by the few. For the many, the textbook of Christianity is still a sealed book.

Men on the whole have not had ears to hear the good tidings of great joy.

The Redeemer's message to mankind, unequivocal as were the terms in which its main principles were conveyed, has, for the most part, fallen on deaf ears. He knew, when delivering His message, that this would be its fate: hence He reiterates His appeals for close attention: "He that hath ears to hear let him hear." [19] Men, on the whole, have caught phrases here and there; they have not pieced together the stray syllables that have fallen on their ears into an intelligible word. "Christianity," writes Newman, "has raised the tone of morals and enforced external decency and good conduct on the world at large; it has advanced certain persons in virtuous or religious habits, who otherwise might have been imbued with the mere rudiments of truth and holiness.... Still, on the whole, the great multitude of men have, to all appearance, remained, in a spiritual point of view, no better than before. The state of great cities now is not so different as to make

[18] Lk 9: 23.
[19] Mt 11: 15; 13: 9, 43; Mk 4: 9, etc.

WHY THE CROSS?

it appear that the main work of Christianity has lain with the face of society, or what is called the world. The highest class in the community and the lowest are not so different from what they would be respectively without the knowledge of the Gospel."[20] In what sense can the words of the angels on the night of the Nativity be said to have been fulfilled? They proclaimed themselves the heralds of good tidings of great joy. The Savior has come, and where is the joy for the Jews and for all the people?[21]

The angels did not stir up false hopes. The joy came to men, and they refused to embrace it.[22] Men hear the words of Christ and strive to crush them into their own systems of thought. They cast aside what does not admit of adjustment. To use another figure, the pure light of His mind falls on the distorting mirror of man's intellect and, in its reflection, becomes deformed and fragmentary. Hence it is that the Christian religion is very inadequately grasped and very incompletely applied to life by great numbers.

Many Christians take a purely self-interested view of religion, making of it a mere machinery for the getting rid of sins.

"Christ," says St. John, "hath appeared to take away our sins."[23] Too many Catholics understand this in a negative sense. They do not advert to the truth that the taking away of sins means not only the absolution from guilt, but also the provision of the means to grow in spirituality. Persons with a narrow and self-interested view of religion may have faith enough to recognize the grave consequences of wrongdoing and to dread God's judgments, and yet have no inclination to use the spiritual resources of their faith with a view to noble living. They tend to use their religion as a mere means to escape the penal consequences of

[20] Newman, *Parochial and Plain Sermons*, 4:154.
[21] Lk 2: 10.
[22] Jn 1: 11.
[23] 1 Jn 3: 5.

wrong living and not as an aid to the acquisition of habits of upright action. For such persons, religion is not so much an instrument of doing rightly in this world as an assurance against faring badly in the next. *To live* has been defined as "the laying hold of that good which is capable of perfecting us."[24] Christ came to put such a good in our power, and that is His positive way of taking away sins. His object is to furnish men with the means of becoming perfect, and not merely with the means of escaping the painful consequence of being imperfect. What the Savior intended should effect man's emancipation from sinfulness, man strives to turn into a mere means of emancipation from sin.

Too many use their religion as medicine and not as food. They make of it a remedy for evil and not a means to good. This attitude leads, inevitably, to a sectioning of life, in which only a small part is set aside for Christian practice. There is a disproportionate outpouring of activity on objects and pursuits that are judged to constitute the real stuff of life, while religion is kept as a standby to serve to undo the evil consequences that attend conflict with God's law.[25]

Christ's communication to mankind was something to enable man to shape his life according to God's will and to profit by it; man uses this communication to enable him to follow his own will and not suffer by it. There is too pronounced a tendency to fix attention only on those passages in the Gospels that set forth the Savior's practical sympathy for the moral and physical ills of His fellows. There is not sufficient balance given to the reading of

[24] *La Vie spirituelle*, 1:74.

[25] Ibid, 1:79. We tend to regard the Christian life as one of earth in its actual course, reserving for the world to come what is divine in it. From this arises the temptation in so many Christian souls to effect a duality in themselves. One part, the only one that counts in practice and is regarded as real and tangible, consists in pursuing the objects and pleasures of this world. There is another which must be taken into account in view of the future. That future, however, is so remote that it is quite sufficient to think of it later on.

such parts of the Gospels by dwelling with equal emphasis on the Lord's positive teaching and His calls to a life of nobility and self-sacrifice. There is more in the inspired word than the record of the mercy and condescension of Jesus toward sinners.

> *It is just and reasonable for the sinful and suffering to have confidence in the mercy and kindness of God; but the gospel is not wholly taken up with inculcating this confidence.*

It is scarcely necessary to call attention to the mutilation that the gospel suffers through being dealt with in this manner. Far be it from anyone—conscious of the frailty of human nature, its proneness to evil, its sluggishness for good—to touch lightly on the measureless sympathy of the heart of Jesus for the miseries of fallen man. All are sinners and have sore need of the mercy of God, and all have to draw heavily on the riches of that mercy. Great sinners would fall into despair, because of the enormity of their crimes, had they not the explicit assurance that no iniquity can exhaust the mercy of the Redeemer.

Besides, apart from all moral considerations, the trials of life are crushing, and for every child of Adam the earth is a vale of tears. If God appeared utterly insensible to human sorrows, pain, and grief, men would be tempted to sullenness and a querulous anger against their Maker. It would be difficult for them to see a beneficent purpose in their sufferings had they not set before them the portrait of a God actively and compassionately engaged in relieving human misery. From this they can learn that if their cares are not alleviated, it is not because of a want of sympathy or want of power on the part of God.

> *But the mission of Jesus was not one of mere benevolence. His purpose was not to secure for men merely material well-being.*

But when all this has been conceded, it still remains true to say that the undue stressing of the "humanitarian" aspects of the Savior's life is apt to create a very false impression of His mission and His work. To overemphasize certain features is to produce a caricature. The portrait of Jesus as presented to us by a certain type of spiritual literature has not escaped this fate. It is suffering that seems to most men to conflict most effectively with their well-being. Humanity tends to be awed by its presence, distressed by its mystery, and rebellious to its inevitableness. Hence it is that nothing in the New Testament makes such a strong appeal to the pain-stricken as the Savior's encounters with suffering and His victories over it. The passages that reveal Jesus in the exercise of works of mercy, in healing disease, in consoling grief, and in overcoming death are given an undue emphasis. In this way the central truth is obscured, namely, that the conflict of the Redeemer was primarily with spiritual evil and only incidentally with physical evil. His purpose was to banish from earth the ills that appear to God as such, not those that appear so to the pain-dreading nature of man.

The horizons of Jesus were not bounded by this world. His *role* was not to create a revolution in economics, hygiene, and politics. The conquest of disease, though He wept bitterly for the death of His friend, and the banishment of want, though He compassionately fed the hungry multitudes in the desert, would not appear to Jesus to constitute the redemption of mankind. The gospel is not a record of a more or less successful philanthropic mission.

The writings of the Evangelists will violently resist all efforts to crush them into a mental category of this kind. The attempt to adapt the teachings of Jesus to the conceptual molds of humanitarianism results simply in there being left in one's hands broken fragments of evangelical thought, which cannot be formed into any intelligible pattern. The inescapable facts of life will obstinately refuse to adjust themselves to this idea of things. To Christians, who persist in thinking that the function of Christianity is to provide men with good things and banish from their life evil things—understanding by "good" and "evil" what appear such to fallen human nature—life will

WHY THE CROSS?

speedily prove unintelligible. To men with such views, the mystery of pain becomes insoluble. In face of the harsh realities of existence, their belief stands condemned. They have no answer to give to the ever-recurring question: if God is kind and good and tender toward human suffering, why does suffering continue to be not only for those that deserve it but also for those who do not?

That Jesus, in His power and goodness, did not put an end to all human suffering shows that, in His eyes, suffering is not the real source of human unhappiness.

Jesus frequently, with a word, on a sorrowful avowal of guilt on the part of the sinful person, forgave sins, but His action never ended at that. He did not content Himself with removing the load of guilt from the sin-burdened soul and giving it the peace that follows on this release. The forgiveness of sin was accompanied by a pressing call to immediate moral and spiritual effort directed toward the Christian ideal. His pardon was not a dispensation from, but a stimulus to, moral struggle.

It is true that the Son of man had compassion on sorrow, soothed pain, expelled disease, and dispelled the gloom that death brings to human hearts. He dried the tears of woe, He restored vigor to the wasted frame, and He raised the dead—but those He recalled to life, ultimately returned to the grave; those He consoled, suffered fresh sorrows; those He fed, again endured want; and those He healed, once more contracted illness. All the ills of mortality remain. Of the vast numbers of human beings stricken with disease, how few were those who were cured! How few were those who, through His power, cheated death for a little while! If His mission had as object the banishment from earth of physical and mental anguish, then His mission was a dismal failure.

It is clear that in the Redeemer's conflict with human woes, it was not want of power that limited His action. For disease and death could not resist His might. Neither was it want of goodness or sympathy that restricted the range of His benevolence. If He could, and did not, end material distress, it is evident that He judged this not to be His work. When He healed disease and raised the dead, He aimed at a good beyond the immediate effects of His acts. Every exterior dealing of the Savior with men carried with it an interior grace that drew the soul to aspire after something higher than the material advantage first desired and prayed for.[26] Much as Jesus pitied the sufferings of mankind, He evidently did not regard pain as the one and only evil; neither did He regard ease, luxury, comfort, and material "progress" as the only good. He did not consider it as the chief object of His mission to pander to the self-indulgence of men. The "good news" brought by the angels of the Nativity was not the advertisement of salvation on easy terms, nor the unfolding of a scheme by which a working compromise could be effected between the demands of the present world and the exigencies of the world to come.

There is something that men dread more than physical death. It is that moral nothingness which awaits a life's activities devoid of eternal significance. This fear poisons all the satisfactions of life. Men ardently desire to live "so as not to die." The religion of Jesus Christ gives this power: it enables men to put the stamp of eternity on their actions. But to achieve this life and to banish fear from their existence, men must embrace the gospel in its integ-

---

[26] Libermann, concerning John 1: 31, writes: "All contact with men, and all actions in reference to them on the part of the Savior, brought with them an interior grace bearing a certain analogy to their outward acts. Bodily vision bestowed was the exterior sign of an inward vision given. The ill-disposed did not profit by these graces but became more blind and perverse by resistance to them." See also *La Vie spirituelle*, 5:38. St. Thomas Aquinas writes: "The end aimed at by Christ in these external cures was the healing of the soul. It did not, therefore, become Christ to heal the body unless at the same time He should heal the soul" (*Summa theologiae*, III, q. 44, a. 3, ad. 3).

rity. It will not do to follow Jesus partially. One must believe in Him wholly. Few do this. Men tend to adapt the gospel to their self-seeking lives. They seize on the merciful traits in the portrait left by the Evangelists and glide over the sterner ones. They overlook the fact that the salvation wrought by Jesus is to rescue men not only from their sins, but from their sinfulness. The mission of Jesus was not a purely humanitarian one.

CHAPTER THREE

He came unto His own: and His own received Him not.
—JOHN 1: 11

Jesus, kind to the wayward, was inexorable toward sin.

ST. PETER, speaking to the household of Cornelius the Centurion, described the earthly career of Jesus of Nazareth as that of one "who went about doing good."[1] The description is touchingly apposite. Yet the attitude of the Savior was no mere kindly, good-natured indulgence to human weakness, nor an easygoing, tolerant concession to human waywardness. He never deviated a hair's breadth from His principles out of consideration for men's failings or prejudices or even their good will. He never met men halfway. Gentle in His dealings with them, He was inflexible in His demands on them. The ideal of conduct He traced for them was of a forbidding austerity, yet He never showed any tendency to mitigate its requirements when faced with the protestations of human frailty. He never yielded in the slightest when His hearers strove to win Him over to their own views of what was feasible, expedient, and properly religious for men.

Man, persisting in regarding life from his own standpoint,
puts himself at cross purposes with his Creator.
The gospel has two aspects. It is a historic document relating actual events, localized and temporal, that took place some centuries ago. These external events have, however, an inner significance not limited to a particular

---

[1] Acts 10: 38.

epoch or a particular place. They are the vivid portrayal of the conflict of invisible spiritual forces independent of any rigidly defined space and time; they dramatize a conflict coextensive with time. The scenes of the Gospels show forth the habitual reactions of fallen human nature to the advances of the supernatural or, in other words, the reactions of man to be redeemed to the action on him of his redeeming God. Tragic misunderstanding seems at all times to be the result—at least for the majority—when God, answering the cries of distressed humanity, hastens to its deliverance. The misunderstanding always arises from the fact that "Redemption" is understood differently by the creature and the Creator. For the Creator it means the restoration to mankind of the power to bind itself anew to God in terms of intimate friendship; for the creature it means merely an emancipation from the galling disabilities of life on earth.

Man understands salvation as a change in the state of things external to himself. God understands it as a change in the internal state of the human soul. "Unless you be *converted,* you cannot enter into the kingdom of heaven,"[2] and "Unless a man be born again he cannot enter the kingdom of God,"[3] are the formulas in which God conveys His message of hope to men. From God's point of view, to save man is to offer him the means of this change of heart and this new birth. Man obstinately persists in attaching his happiness to other things than this power to be made a child of God and enter into the inheritance of God's own life and bliss.[4]

> *The acceptance and rejection of Jesus follow laws valid not only for the period of His earthly career but for all time.*

The Jews, at the coming of the Redeemer, were an extremely religious people. Jesus Himself bears testimony to their intense, extravagant zeal for the observances

[2] Mt 18: 3.
[3] Jn 3: 5.
[4] Jn 1: 12.

of their faith. They bore the heavy ceremonial burdens of the Law with fortitude and fidelity. They worshiped God diligently and with punctilious exactitude according to the prescriptions God Himself had laid down. At a chosen moment in time the divine object of their adoration presented Himself in visible form to His people, and an extraordinary thing happened. The Jews rejected decisively the God Whom for ages they had, apparently, worshiped assiduously. What was more, this dramatic rejection of their God took place at the very time when the nation had gathered together for, and were actually engaged in, the most solemn of their acts of worship of their God. How account for such a strange anomaly?

All purely rational explanations of the rejection of the Son of God by the Jews are wholly unconvincing. It was not the result of purely accidental and transient circumstances. It is impossible to read the Gospels in a spirit of faith and not find oneself intimately persuaded that in the story told by the Evangelists a glimpse is given of a world where actions and reactions are guided by laws that differ much from those of the moral world known to mere reason. As the pages are turned over, one after the other, and the narrative pursues its course to its dénouement, that dénouement is, by some mysterious instinct in the soul, sensed to be inevitable. The conviction is gradually formed that the death of God is no accident, but the outcome of laws that run in this mysterious realm glimpsed by faith.

The great catastrophe is perceived to be inevitable if we consider what man is and what God must be when He becomes man and mingles in human concerns. This means that—certain moral dispositions being presupposed—the Jews being what they were and God becoming man being what He is, no other issue was to be expected from their meeting face to face. Jesus of Nazareth, true God, consubstantial with the Father, was rejected by the Jews, who prided themselves on being the only people

WHY THE CROSS?

who worshiped the true God. Jesus continues to be rejected down along the ages by those who are not Jews and for the same fundamental reasons. The laws that govern the acceptance of God and the rejection of God are valid for all times, all regions, and all men.

Each epoch finds man crushed beneath the burden of misery laid on his shoulders by his own errors and his own wickedness. Again and again, the cry for salvation ascends to heaven. "See, O God, the affliction of thy people and send whom thou wilt send; send forth the lamb, the ruler of the Earth that he may take away the yoke of our captivity. We have sinned and we are all become as one unclean; we have all fallen as a leaf, and our iniquities, like the wind, have taken us away."[5]

In answer to this appeal, God has come and is ever coming with salvation in His hands, and those who explicitly or implicitly long for His coming, in vast numbers, reject Him. They turn from Him and the plan of salvation that He traces for them. The consequence is that history is a record of catastrophes that recur with monotonous regularity.[6]

This is the case because men consistently refuse to recognize their salvation in the program of life that God traces for them.

---

[5] Hymn for Advent—*Rorate Coeli*. Its verses are taken from the prophecies of Isaiah. It is an almost despairing search in every direction for some power that will ward off the ruin that menaces civilization. Believers know well, and unbelievers will be forced to acknowledge, that no merely human power can save the world from the ruin toward which it is rushing with vertiginous speed.

[6] As a particular and topical instance of what is here asserted can be noted the world's attitude toward the papal instructions on economic and social problems. Vast masses of men are clamorous for the establishment of conditions that will place a reasonable human life within the grasp of the millions who, at present, are in a state worse than slavery. Christ's Vicar on earth outlines in clear terms a plan of economic and social reform that would effectively remedy human misery—and, for the most part, his words pass unheeded. Men prefer to be led to destruction by false messiahs.

The Jews rejected Jesus because He pointed out that in rescue from slavery to their sins and their false ideas of religion, and not in mere political emancipation from the Roman yoke, lay their salvation.

Although the Jews sighed for redemption, they in reality had little understanding of that redemption of which they stood in need. They chafed against their political subjection to the Romans. Their national pride revolted against this yoke. They conceived that it would be altogether well with them were it shaken off. The Redeemer was for them one who would strike it from their necks and make them masters of the earth. This would be their redemption. This would constitute him redeemer. Jesus roused their hopes for a while, but, as the months passed and He was making no move to use His undoubted power to gratify their aspirations, their early enthusiasm cooled. A questioning of His claims to be the Messiah followed. When He made it clear that in His eyes salvation for them was primarily to be sought in an inner revolution of a spiritual nature, and not in an external revolution of a political nature, their disappointment gave place to anger. Anger, finally, yielded to open revolt. When He revealed that the purpose of His coming was to save them from slavery to themselves and not from slavery to the Romans, they refused to recognize Him as their redeeming God.

It is only on a superficial view that the issue between Jesus and the Jews would appear to be political.[7] It is true that in Him their messianic dreams suffered a cruel disappointment, but the opposition arising from this immediate source was the symptom of an inner spiritual attitude

---

[7] In a strikingly parallel manner at the present day, Christ, living in His Church, tells the toiling world that mere economic reforms will not bring them happiness unless based on a change of heart and the acceptance and practice of the Christian ideal of life. He meets with the same anger and revolt. As in the time of the Jews the political conditions were the occasion of conflict, so now the economic slavery fulfills the same *role*. In both cases the cause of the conflict, between God and man, lies deeper.

not peculiar to the Jews of their age, but to be found in men of all races and of all times.

All God's relations with man are controlled by a supernatural objective. Everything, in God's point of view, is subordinated to and directed toward man's supernatural good. He is interested in natural things only as they are a means to this. The contacts between God and His creatures are usually established through happenings that outwardly appear to sense and to reason as differing in nothing from ordinary human happenings. But, nevertheless, when God approaches men, He always approaches with the intentions of God. He comes with a supernatural purpose to fulfill—never to gratify men's unsupernatural ambitions.

If man, on his side, meets God and does not meet Him on the supernatural plane, the encounter issues only in misunderstanding. Great numbers crossed the path of God, as He walked on earth, and they profited nothing from the meeting. What was worse, instead of a help, He proved a stumbling block for many—for practically the whole—of His compatriots! The Savior constantly stressed the necessity of approaching Him in faith and not under the influence of human prejudices. Any beneficent effect to come from contact with Him was conditioned by faith.[8] To trace to its source the opposition of men to God is to penetrate into the supernatural world. It is in that sphere that the conflict is knit. The issue between the Prophet of Nazareth and His compatriots was religious, not political. In the matter of religion, they differed profoundly and radically. It was from this difference that sprang all the other differences. In fact all the important divisions that set men fiercely at variance with one another will be found, in ultimate analysis, to have a theological basis. Men differ because they have different views of the meaning of existence.

[8] "And He wrought not many miracles there, because of their incredulity" (Mt 13: 58).

*Unregenerate man in his religious aspirations tends to
frame for himself a religion that differs from that which
accords with the views of God.*

The Jews, obeying purely human instincts—following the
traditions of men as Jesus expressed it[9]—had brought
deformations into the religious ideas that God had communicated to them in the early days. Yet, secure in the
belief that they held without blemish the true faith that
was theirs, they had no misgivings about their religion.
The idea that their views on the relations that should exist
between God and His chosen people needed modification and reform appeared blasphemous to them. They
could not, therefore, think of salvation in terms of such a
reform. And yet, having wandered from the way of "wor-
shiping in spirit and in truth,"[10] they had plunged into
error as to the meaning and purpose of human life. Having ceased to understand life, their minds were incapable
of grasping the ideal of life when outlined for them by the
Savior. Jesus strove to make them understand that the real
obstacle to their happiness was not presented by the irksome external conditions of social and political life under
which they chafed, but by their erroneous views on the
fundamental issues of life itself.

The error under which the Jews labored is not confined
to their race. It is rooted in tendencies as universal as
human nature itself. Man is a being instinctively religious,
but he tends to seek a religion that will allow him to gratify
the instincts of his fallen nature, or at least some of these
instincts, and yet secure him the favor of God. He looks
for a formula or a code that will permit him to please
himself without displeasing his Maker. The Sovereign Lord
knows that such a formula cannot be found. When He
reveals to men that this is so, the creature's instinct is to
question the incompatibility of satisfying God and satisfying the corrupt inclinations of fallen nature. Man will
strive to persuade himself that he can, "by burnt offerings

[9] Mk 7: 8.
[10] Jn 4: 23–24.

and sacrifices" (that is, by certain concessions to his Creator), secure himself against the disfavor of Heaven. He persuades himself that the divine favor has its price—short of the price of a total surrender of life to the divine ruling. Following the traditions of men, that is, the promptings of his natural desires, he is tempted to indulge the vain hope that he can enter into a sort of "concordat" with the Creator. He is prepared to make concessions to God and expects that God on His side will leave man free to follow his own devices in some respects. Religion, with the Jews, had come almost to this. The same tendencies are to be observed at all times—both in those who profess the true faith and in those who adhere to a false worship.

"What must we do to be saved," is a question that shows an incomprehension of the meaning and conditions of salvation.

Religion, with men of religious inclinations who do not labor to keep their minds and wills subject to God's views, tends habitually to degenerate into "formalism." This "formalism," though most pronounced in the Pharisees of our Lord's time, was by no means confined to them. The people of Israel regarded God as a sovereign who had unquestioned rights over them. He was their Sovereign Lord, and they were His subjects. As such they readily paid *tribute* to Him. Their devoted service to their Lord consisted in the punctilious acquittal of the rites, ceremonies, and sacrifices of the Law and in the payment of the regular contributions to divine worship. God's friendship was God's return for this faithful observance. The Jews believed that the "works" of the law secured for them the promises of God for time and eternity. That this was the current view of religion appears clearly from many a passage in the New Testament. When Nicodemus came by night to question the Savior on divine things, he was clearly nonplussed by the notion of an access to God depending on a new birth of a spiritual kind, involving an inner revolution of mind and heart. Progress in holiness, for him, as for the Jews generally, meant an increase in the number of observances and in a more minute attention to the prescriptions of the Law. This was a very convenient form of religion because it left man to follow the desires of his heart and demanded only the accomplishment of "works" prescribed by the religious code.[11] One could live as one desired, and one could "be" as one wished, on condition of paying a certain fixed tribute to God. The renouncement of such a comfortable view of man's obligations to his Maker met with much opposition even in the case of a worthy man, such as Nicodemus undoubtedly was.

This rooted prejudice meets the Lord's instructions constantly. A very well-behaved young man came to the Savior and, bowing respectfully to Him, asked: "Good Master, what should I *do* that I may have life everlasting?" He looked to Jesus to specify some additional devotional practice that should infallibly guarantee his salvation. He is disappointed. The question was based on the usual false assumption, that a man's salvation depended on certain things he did, rather than on what he was. The Divine Master, much taken by the earnestness of the young Jew,[12] delicately strove to disabuse his mind of the false views of religion that he entertained, by pointing out that God Himself was "the good" for man—and God, He insinuated, was to be won, not by bribes, but by a personality modeled on that of Jesus. "Go, sell whatsoever thou hast, and come, *follow Me*." On another occasion, the same question, inspired by the same preoccupation, was put to the Savior by a doctor of the Law. The interrogation was couched in the customary terms: "Master, what must I *do* to possess eternal life?"[13] Again, no direct reply is given. The Divine Master wished to save the learned man the humiliation of being told that his question proceeded from an inadmissible assumption—that he was, in asking

[11] Ven. Libermann, *In Jo. C.*, III, v. 4, p. 82.
[12] Mk 10: 21.
[13] Lk 10: 25.

WHY THE CROSS?

it, guilty of what the logicians call an *ignoratio elenchi*. The "lawyer" is asked to state what he thinks to be the fundamental prescription of religion. On the reply being given, in the words of Deuteronomy, that the chief commandment was to love God with all one's heart and mind and soul and strength,[14] Jesus approved of the answer. He said: "Thou hast answered right: *this* do, and thou shalt live." [15] The doing that brings one near to the kingdom of God consists in loving God, and loving the neighbor for the sake of God.

The rooted prejudices of the Jews prevented them from seizing the import of the Savior's teaching. His words suffered distortion in their warped and formalistic minds. To the end, they sought salvation in "works of the Law." Their hopes rose high after the multiplication of the loaves, and they were in a mood to admit the messianic claims of Jesus of Nazareth. The latter seemed, if with some qualification, to encourage their aspirations. He said: "Amen, amen, I say to you, you seek me, not because you have seen miracles, but because you did eat of the loaves and were filled. Labor not for the meat which perisheth, *but for that which endureth with life everlasting, which the Son of Man will give you. For Him hath God the Father sealed.*" [16] In spite of their implicit rebuke, these words were of fair promise. They seemed to imply that a messianic millennium was within their reach—at a price. Straightway there sprung to their lips the inevitable: "What shall we *do,* that we may work the works of God?" [17] The answer this time is decisive and final, leaving no further room for illusion. "This is the *work* of God, that you *believe* in Him, whom He sent." [18] Salvation for them consists, not in the perfunctory accomplishment of some legal prescriptions, but in an acceptance of the Savior's

[14] Dt 6: 5.
[15] Lk 10: 28.
[16] Jn 6: 26–27.
[17] Jn 6: 28.
[18] Jn 6: 29.

theory of life with a consequent abandonment of their own views and theories. The Savior implies that it is a question of "being" rather than "doing." [19]

The Apostles themselves had to be warned against allowing themselves to labor under the illusions that darkened the religious understanding of their compatriots. Their greatness, they were told, as well as their ultimate good, depended, not in the lofty positions at which they aimed, but in an inner change of heart, which, at the time, made little appeal to them. "Unless you be converted and become as little children, you shall not enter the kingdom of heaven." [20]

The characteristic tendencies of unregenerate nature do not change with the passage of time. Men who do not wish to break definitely with God (or who strive to cheat themselves into the belief that they have not broken with Him) will still look for a religion that will not demand the complete renouncement of their ungodly inclinations. They consent to give God a certain regard and to consecrate to His service a certain amount of their time and their possessions, provided He leaves them the sovereignty over certain defined portions of their life, with its own purposes, determinations, and ideals. Many of those who profess the true faith now, as in the time of Christ, can be accused of believing that they can secure and retain the friendship of God by clinging to the routine usage of the ceremonial rites, bequeathed by Christ to His Church, without imposing on themselves the necessity of

[19] It is scarcely necessary to remark that the Savior does not discredit "works." What He stresses is that only "right *being*" issues in right "*doing*." If a man *is* what God wishes him to be, he will do what God wishes him to do. The Scholastic philosophers express this truth pithily, saying: *Omne agens agit secundum quod est actu.* "Deeds are only prized as having intrinsic and absolute worth so far as they can be taken to be effects revelatory of a character or quality of the doer. The supreme moral imperative is not '*do* this,' but rather '*be* this.' A good tree brings forth good fruit" (A. E. Taylor, *Faith of a Moralist*, p. 68).

[20] Mt 18: 3.

bringing their minds into harmony with the mind of Christ.[21]

Unfortunately, in many cases, there is only too much justification for such an accusation. Nothing causes the name of God to be so blasphemed as the union of the punctilious observance of the holy forms of religion with conduct that conflicts with the basic principles of religion.[22] Men tend to pervert good and holy things in their usage of them. Many a superficial Christian looks upon salvation in the same material fashion as the Jews; they think of it in terms of a change of place rather than a change of heart. They look upon the sanctifying rites instituted by Christ as things that give them a kind of official passport for heaven, rather than a means to make them fit to be in heaven. They recognize the necessity of repentance and absolution from the guilt of sins by the sacramental rite, but they do not so readily recognize the necessity of conversion in order to have access to eternal life. They judge "that any man, whatever his habits, tastes or manner of life, if once admitted into heaven, would be happy there. Men think they can reconcile themselves to God when they will, as if nothing were required in the case of man in general but some . . . strictness, during our last sickness. . . . An opinion like this, though commonly acted on, is refuted as soon as put into words. . . . Here every man can do his own pleasure, but there he must do *God's* pleasure. . . . If we wished to imagine a punishment for an unholy reprobate soul, we perhaps could not fancy a greater than to summon it to heaven. Heaven would be hell for an unreligious man. . . . God cannot change His nature. Holy He must ever be, but while He is Holy, no unholy soul can be happy in heaven."[23] True religion does not exist to dispense man from holiness of life but to mold him to it.

---

[21] See Phil 2: 5.

[22] See Rom 2: 24 ("For the name of God through you is blasphemed among the Gentiles") and Is 52: 5.

[23] Newman, *Parochial and Plain Sermons*, 1:1.

The world plunges from one crisis to another, and in its powerlessness to extricate itself from its miseries it has the need of a Savior forced on its notice. But it will persist in looking for a Messiah formed to its own notions. When the Redeemer comes and warns men that the real cause of the evils with which they are afflicted is found in the evil dispositions of their hearts: when He tells them, in consequence, that before they can hope for a change for the better in outward circumstances they must first set up a change in themselves: then, "they find this a hard saying and they go back and walk no more with Him." [24] Those who, though finding Christ's teaching unpalatable, still elect, like St. Peter, to cleave to Him, will always be the few. The many will murmur against the teachings of Christ and His Church, will grow discontented with Him and her, and will ultimately reject Him and her, saying, "Away with Him, crucify Him." Every age witnesses these practical rejections of Christ. They are not confined to the avowed enemies of God. In a measure, they take place on the part of very many who outwardly appear passable Christians. Compromise leads to quarrel. So the Christian, in whom religion has degenerated into formalism—in whom the religious rite is divorced from its living foundation, that is, from a concept of a Christian life as a preparation for a future divine destiny—will inevitably find himself at variance with the Divine Master. Such a Christian will not experience the peace that comes of a resolute walking in the way of salvation. Disappointment and misery await the religious-minded who willfully will not understand the gospel of Jesus Christ, aspire to what it promises, and accept without demur its solution of the problem of human existence.

The tenderness of Jesus for human distress in all its aspects should not lead one to judge the mission of the Savior to be a purely humanitarian

[24] Jn 6: 66.

one. To Jesus, the spiritual transformation of mankind is the main object to be achieved. Failure to recognize this intent will lead to misunderstanding between the Savior and those He comes to save. Misunderstanding leads to rejection. The Jews, the worshipers of the true God, rejected the true God when He came to them. The conflict between the Messiah and His people was on religious, not political, grounds. They persisted in viewing salvation as a change in their circumstances and not in themselves. He took the opposite view. Hence the clash. They thought they could purchase the Kingdom of God at a price short of the renouncement of their views in favor of the views of God; their religion had degenerated into formalism. The same thing happens in the case of many Christians, with the same results. The way to happiness is a wholehearted acceptance of the gospel of Jesus Christ. What is the gospel?

CHAPTER FOUR

*As many as received Him He gave them the power to be
made the Sons of God.*

—JOHN 1: 12

*The Savior traces for His adherents a moral code that
prescribes conduct of flawless perfection. The model after
which they are to form themselves is God Himself. "Be you
perfect as your heavenly Father is perfect."[1] The Gospel is
not merely a sublime ethical code, nor yet a mere substitution
of new and simpler forms of worship for the ancient and
more elaborate ones. Much less is it a system of inhuman
restraints.*

THE RELIGION REVEALED to mankind by Jesus comprehends a number of exterior rites and ceremonial observances. Its ritual, though not so elaborate, complex,
and extensive as that of the Old Law, is sufficiently rich
and varied. It is simple and harmonious, yet it makes

---

[1] Mt 5: 48. Christians are bidden to imitate the life of God in its two
aspects. The inner life of God consists in the knowledge and love of the
infinite divine reality. By the divine infused virtues of faith, hope, and
love, the human soul is empowered to exercise this divine activity, an
activity, in its nature, exclusive to God. The external life of God consists
in His relations to His creatures. These relations are characterized by
unwearying kindness and forbearance. God never loses patience with
men or fails in charity toward them. "He maketh His sun to rise upon
the good and bad, and raineth upon the just and the unjust" (Mt
5: 45). In the context it is this manner of acting on the part of God that
Jesus invites His followers to imitate. They are told that they must never
fail in goodness toward men, however hardly they may be treated by
men. Obedience to this injunction demands the utmost self-sacrifice
and the sublimest perfection of character.

considerable inroads on man's time. From birth to death, every important incident in the life of the faithful is laid hold of by a Church ceremony and invested with the significance of an act of divine worship. But for all that, Christianity is not merely a splendid protocol, regulating the procedure to be observed in the relations between the creature and the Creator.

Jesus reiterates the prohibitions of Mount Sinai. As formulated by Him they are made still more stringent, and their scope is widened. Hence to many the gospel appears as a system of stern restraint, opposing itself relentlessly and cruelly to the most imperious instincts of human nature. To these people its positive aspect appeals as a promise of a superhuman happiness after death on condition of submitting to a series of inhuman restrictions during life. The religion of Christ does impose restraints, but what it restrains is not human nature as such, but human nature that is tempted to be faithless to its true self. It curbs only those instincts which menace ruin to human personality; as a consequence, it remains essentially a law, not of self-repression, but of self-expression.

The gospel, as the word implies, is the announcement to mankind of good news—namely, the news that happiness is placed within its reach.

What, then, is the gospel if it is not the formation of a code of morality more exacting than that of the Old Law, nor the substitution of spiritual forms of worship for ones more material, nor, finally, the imposition of a number of galling restraints on self-expression? The import of the gospel is conveyed by the very name it bears. It is, above all else, "good tidings," for it is the announcement to mankind that a degree of happiness is placed within its reach—even here on earth; it is a revelation of the content of that happiness; and, finally, an unfolding of the means placed at the disposal of men for its attainment. The whole theme of the gospel was set forth in one short sentence to be found in the inaugural address of Jesus to the Multitudes—"*Blessed* are the pure of heart," He said to them, "for they shall see God."[2]

The utterance of these words marks a dramatic moment in human history. It was some thousands of years since man had become estranged from his God and had embarked on the vain enterprise of being for himself the author of his own happiness.[3] He had set out with high hopes to find in the wealth of earth and in his own inner resources the materials of his beatitude. He had suffered tragic disillusionment. A crushing sense of inescapable misery must have weighed upon the spirits of the most thoughtful at the peak point of ancient civilization. It was felt that man was powerless to satisfy himself, and a vague longing for the intervention of a superhuman power stirred the depths of pagan consciousness.[4] The people of God had clearer vision than their pagan neighbors. They had the assurance from their prophets that a Savior was to come and that the time of expectation was drawing to an end. In the meantime, they had the Law to guide their conduct. But they too shared the general distress of mankind. The Law did not satisfy the aspirations of the human heart or adequately solve the great problem of existence. Much as the Jew differed from the Gentile, he resembled him in this, that he yearned for a light that should reveal to him how he could make his life on earth yield that happiness for which his soul craved. Even a careful and blameless observance of the Law failed to yield contentment of heart.[5]

[2] Mt 5: 8.

[3] The significance of this statement will he developed in a subsequent chapter.

[4] "The whole Jewish world was then expecting a Messiah, and this expectation had, on the showing of pagan historians, overflowed through all the East and beyond" (L. de Grand Maison, *Jesus Christ*, 2:17; see also 1:287–291).

[5] The young man who won the regard of Jesus, avowed to the Divine Master that, though he had observed the Law from his youth, he still found existence unsatisfactory. "All these I have kept from my youth, what is yet wanting to me?" (Mt 19: 20).

WHY THE CROSS?

The great longing in the heart of all men is to discover a theory of existence that can make life on earth an experience that brings happiness.

At length, such a light as was looked for seemed to be dawning. A remarkable Prophet had made His appearance in Galilee: He exercised a marvelous ascendancy over those with whom He came in contact, if these latter were of good will. He had given proof of superhuman power. The most inveterate diseases yielded to His healing influences. The demons fled, cowed, from His presence. His utterances, as yet few, were, nevertheless, full of glowing promises. In the synagogue of His native town, He had appropriated to Himself the words of the prophecy of Isaiah. He had stated that He was come "to preach deliverance to the captives and sight to the blind, to set at liberty them that are bruised, to preach the acceptable year of the Lord and the day of reward." [6] Clearly He set before Himself the task of rescuing men from the weariness that oppressed them—the *taedium vitae* that crushed their spirits.

Expectation was stirred to the highest pitch. So that when Jesus, having selected His immediate followers, prepared to make His first important address to the multitudes gathered about Him on the mountainside, all felt they were to listen to a pronouncement of the utmost moment.

The gathering was vast, as St. Luke affirms. "And coming, He stood in a level place and the company of His disciples and a *very great multitude* from all Judea and Jerusalem and the seacoast of Tyre and Sidon." [7] It was a throng representative of many classes of men. They varied in culture, in rank, in condition, in age, and in outlook, but all were in one respect alike. If they were to voice their inmost aspirations, they would confess that they looked for some theory of existence that could guarantee them happiness. How were they to handle life so as to make it a

[6] Lk 4: 18–19.
[7] Lk 6: 17.

satisfying experience for the soul? That was their thought. And as Jesus looked into their expectant faces, He beheld not only that multitude gathered from Judea and Galilee and the seacoast; His gaze passed beyond them, and He saw in spirit all humanity ranged before Him in serried ranks, generation after generation, down to the very end of time. For His words were to concern all.

Jesus thought in terms of humanity. His heart was wrung with anguish at the pageant of human misery before Him, as He beheld the wanderings of man estranged from God. Having espoused men's nature, He loved them all intensely. He pitied them as His lost brethren. Loving them, He yearned to procure their good—to secure their happiness. He had the secret of it.

Jesus was a "man of joy as well as a man of sorrows."
We are so habituated to think of Christ as the Man of sorrows that we are prone to lose sight of a truth of vast importance for the right apprehension of Christ's message. This truth is that Jesus lived an intensely happy human life. He suffered grievously, but He did not know an instant's unhappiness or dissatisfaction. He possessed all that a human heart could desire, and nothing could snatch His treasure from His possession. Nor was the bliss He enjoyed of an unearthly sort, too rarefied to satisfy the longings of a creature, part spiritual, part material, like man. Jesus enjoyed life as man was meant to enjoy life. His soul, being human, was happy with the happiness proper to a human soul. There was immeasurably more satisfaction crowded into a single moment of the Savior's earthly life than was enjoyed by all the saints taken all together in the ravishing experiences of the mystical life. For Jesus, the problem of existence had been solved from the beginning. He longed to communicate that solution to all men. To reveal His secret, He sought for those phrases that should be most expressive, most effective, most persuasive. He knew what a happy revolution His message, if accepted, would make in men's lives, and He desired with

a great desire that they should allow themselves to be persuaded to its acceptance. To accept would mean the power to enter into His experience, to share His life, and to partake of His happiness.

It was not a happiness deferred that Jesus promised to men. He guaranteed to alleviate the burdens of the human heart and bring it peace, even here and now.

Christ's solution of the problem of existence was communicated to His hearers in a few words. The main theme of "the gospel" was compressed into one short sentence. All His spiritual teaching was crystallized in the statement: "Blessed are the pure of heart, for they shall see God." This communication, so concise, and yet so pregnant with meaning—for the rest of the ascetic and spiritual instructions of Jesus are but an amplification and exposition of it—falls into three divisions. The opening term, "Blessed," is already an assurance that if men would give ear to Him, the dream they always cherished of a happiness, attainable on this earth, would be a dream no longer. He could make it come true. This was the "good news," the *evangelium*, which He was commissioned to announce and also to bring to pass.

"I have come," He said later on, "that they may have life and may have it more abundantly."[8] The dream could become a reality for all who would trust His word and share His theory. "He that believeth in the Son hath life everlasting: but he that believeth not in the Son shall not see life, but the wrath of God abideth on him."[9] The promise is not solely for the future, as is signified by the present tense "hath." The concern of Jesus is not exclusively centered on the life to come. He was profoundly interested in the problems of the present moment and in their solution. He proposed to Himself the relief here and now, and not merely the deferred relief, of actual human unhappiness. "Come to me," He said, "all you

[8] Jn 10: 10.
[9] Jn 3: 36.

that labor and are burdened and I will refresh you." [10]
These words were not lightly or inconsiderately spoken.
They were no idle boast that He could not justify. He
meant exactly what He said. His power was equal to His
word. What is more, He could not make men happy were
He Himself unhappy. What illuminates must itself be luminous. The living source of communicable happiness
must itself be happy.

> *Jesus was happy because He saw God. He makes men happy
> by bestowing on them the power to share His vision.*

In what consists this beatitude that Jesus enjoyed and that
He came to share with men? The third part of that statement, which I have called a compendium of the gospel,
sets it forth in outline. Bliss springs from the vision of
God. "Blessed are the pure of heart, *for* they shall see
God." Jesus is happy without ceasing, because He enjoys
the vision of God unceasingly. He will make man happy by
making that vision possible for him in turn. Man's own
experiments at happiness had failed. He had sought contentment in the resources of his own nature, in the free
play of his own powers, and in the exploitation of creatures—and his search had proved vain. He had dug himself fountains in the earth and, having drunk at them,
found his thirst not slaked but become more violent. The
disillusionment of humanity finds utterance in the words
of the Samaritan woman by Jacob's Well: "Sir," she said to
Jesus, "give me this water, that *I may not thirst,* nor *come
hither to draw."* [11] Jesus has the power and the will to dispense men from this wearisome return to the waters (that
is, the pleasures of earth) which ever fail to satisfy. He can
replace them by those which do allay the thirst of the soul
and satisfy all its cravings. "Whosoever drinketh of this
water" (that is, earthly satisfactions) "shall thirst again: but
he that shall drink of the water that I will give him *shall not
thirst for ever.* But the water that I will give him shall be-

[10] Mt 11: 28.
[11] Jn 4: 15.

come in him, a fountain of water, springing up into life everlasting."[12]

God is the source of all reality. He must, therefore, be the source of happiness. Happiness exists, as in its native abode, only in Him; it can be found only in Him; it can be derived only from Him. To seek it elsewhere is to embark on an adventure doomed to failure. The mission of Jesus on earth was to guide men to the living waters of the Divinity, ever gushing up in streams that satisfy all desire. To see God is to drink at these Sources. The term "see" poorly conveys all that is enjoyed by the soul when God is revealed to its gaze. The word "see" expresses primarily an act of the bodily faculty of vision. By analogy it is employed to describe an act of the intellect. What is contemplated by the bodily eye, if beautiful, gives pleasure but remains external to the beholder. The artistic masterpiece, picture or statue, does not become the possession of the person who looks upon it, no matter how appreciative and discerning may be his contemplation.

In a similar way, what the mind sees or grasps does not become the property of the mind unless in a purely ideal way. The word "grasp" as applied to the act of intellect, in knowing the object of thought presented to it, is clearly metaphorical. But in the vision of God, made possible for men by Jesus, things are wholly otherwise. To "see God" means literally to have or to possess God.[13] It implies the power to enter into and to make our own those infinite resources of life and happiness which are in God—or rather, which are God. We can enter into them, needless to state, only in that limited measure which is permitted us by our condition as finite creatures.

Man can be made happy, not by things, but by life. Mere existence cannot give him beatitude. He becomes happy when existence is transformed into veritable life by

[12] Jn 4: 13–14.
[13] The expression is from St. Thomas Aquinas, who says that when it is given to the soul to see God, the soul can be said to have God as its own belonging, to use and to enjoy (*Summa theologiae*, I, q. 43, a. 3).

being brought into contact with Life itself. Without the Savior, man would exist, but he would not live. Hence Jesus states that the purpose of His coming is that man might have life and have it in ever-increasing measure.

Life expresses itself in appropriate activity. Satisfaction or delectation is the result of the normal play of every vital faculty, exercised on an object that fully extends the powers of that faculty, without, however, unduly taxing them. "In fact, pleasure follows in the wake of every sensation, and in like manner also of every process of reasoning or play of thought, and the more pleasurable activity is that which is most perfect, and the most perfect activity is that of the man who is in a normal state when the activity is brought to bear upon the noblest object that can come before it."[14] Perfect beatitude is the concomitant of the output of supreme spiritual energy.

The most perfect activity is the expression of the most perfect life. God is infinitely happy because He has the experience of infinite life. Jesus, by giving us access to the vision of God, introduces us to the divine life and empowers us to share in the vital experience of God Himself. That is what is implied in the words: "As many as received Him, He gave them power to be made the Sons of God."[15] To see God perfectly and, in consequence, to possess Him perfectly does not belong to the condition of the life on earth. Yet it is something not wholly deferred until the abyss of death has been traversed. While in the body, the soul can gaze upon God only through a glass, darkly: "We see now through a glass in a dark manner."[16] God is enveloped in the thick veils of faith, but imperfect though the vision of faith be, yet it is vision. By it God is beheld and possessed in a manner that is a beginning of the final vision and the final perfect possession. This vision of faith proper to the time of exile can go on constantly increasing in perfection. The more perfect it becomes, the more

[14] Aristotle, *Nich. Ethics*, bk. 10, ch. 4.
[15] Jn 1: 12.
[16] 1 Cor 13: 12.

WHY THE CROSS?

happiness it imparts. The deep contentment that at all times, and the positive transports that occasionally, mark the lives of the saints, reveal the beatifying effects of the higher degrees of faith. This real though incomplete happiness is offered to all men: it will be experienced by them in proportion to the degree in which they respond to the designs of the Savior and accept the conditions He traces for the vision of God here and hereafter.

The gospel of Jesus Christ is not a negation of human aspirations. It is the glad tidings that man's perennial dream of immediate happiness can be realized. Jesus outlines for His hearers the nature of this happiness and tells them that He has the power and the will to lead them to it. He says that He can create the Source of it in the depths of their own souls, if they will believe in Him and follow His directions. To see God is to be happy. He undertakes to make that vision possible for men, if they consent to tread the path of life He traces for them.

CHAPTER FIVE

Whosoever shall seek to save his life, shall lose it: and whosoever shall lose it, shall preserve it.

—LUKE 17: 33

It was only in a veiled manner that Jesus, in the beginning of His ministry, put before His hearers His plan for human happiness.

WHAT ARE THE CONDITIONS that man must fulfill if he is to enjoy the happiness promised him by the Savior? They are insinuated in the clause that, in the text of the beatitude, immediately follows the opening words. Those who are pure of heart will enjoy that vision of God. For the moment, the Divine Master does not enlarge on all the implications of this purity of heart. He contents Himself with sketching in outline the exigencies of the pure morality that His adherents are expected to practice. Jesus, knowing intimately the perversity of the human nature that He aimed at reforming, observed a prudent economy in the presentation of His theory of life. If He were to develop clearly from the beginning all that was required of men in order to attain to purity of heart, He knew His message would be met with instant rejection. He allowed men to be drawn to Him by the prospect of having their dreams of happiness realized through His instrumentality.

Of what was meant by the vision of God that the Prophet of Nazareth promised, they could have no clear idea, but, instinctively, they identified it with the satisfaction of all their aspirations. Very likely it was connected in their minds with those manifest interventions of God on behalf of their race, so frequent in the course of their history. But when the minds of His hearers had been sufficiently prepared, Jesus proceeded to trace for them more clearly the course they should follow if they were to gain the salvation for which they sighed.

> *The vision enjoyed by Christ is participated in by those who share His Cross.*

One day Jesus "said to *all*. If any man will *come after me*, let him deny himself and take up his cross *daily* and follow me."[1] These words must have profoundly startled and disquieted men whose expectations of an earthly paradise had been roused to the highest pitch. The words seldom fail to send a chill to the heart of all who recognize that in them is traced the program of Christianity. Jesus had won Himself adherents by promises of beatitude. He had claimed to be able to give rest to their souls and to take away the crushing burdens of life, and now, as they eagerly reached out for what He had bidden them hope for, He spoke of the Cross, and a cross not to be shouldered once only but every day of their lives. There is an apparent tautology in the phrasing of the Divine Master: "If any man will come after me, . . . let him follow me." But there is none in reality, for the words "come after me" and

---

[1] Lk 9: 23. Since this is the decisive text in the moral and spiritual message of Jesus, it will be useful to compare St. Luke's phrasing of it with that which appears in the Gospels of St. Mark and of St. Matthew. St. Mark writes: "And calling the *multitude together with His disciples*, He said to them: 'If any man will follow me, let him deny himself and take up his cross and follow me' " (8: 34). St. Matthew says: "Then Jesus said to His disciples: 'If any man will come after me, let him deny himself, and take up his cross and follow me' " (16: 24).

(*a*) It is to be remarked that these words are addressed to all, not to a few select heroes of asceticism: St. Luke uses the word *all*, and St. Mark, the word *multitude*.

(*b*) St. Luke employs the term *daily*. This denotes that the carrying of the cross is not to be an exceptional thing or even an occasional thing, but a sustained course of action, a regular mode of life.

(*c*) Both St. Mark and St. Matthew connect this saying with the sharp rebuke given to St. Peter, when the latter would not hear of the cross being the lot of his Master or of himself.

"follow me" have not the same sense. The meaning can be paraphrased thus: *The man who wishes to be in my following and share the life experience that is mine* (and Jesus, as has been pointed out, enjoyed continual happiness) *must tread the path that I myself tread. He must brace himself to face the rude experience that is mine.* Those who listened to Jesus had come to Him confidently and hopefully. On His assurance, they had thought happiness within their reach, and when they stretched out their hands to lay hold of it, He offers the Cross to their eager grasp. They looked to Him for the bread of life, and He proffers them the hard, bitter wood of suffering.[2] Was this His solution of the problem of existence? Were they the victims of a cruel mockery?

The words of the Savior are uncompromising. They are undoubtedly a hard saying,[3] but they are no mockery. Jesus loves men with a love worthy of the immeasurable greatness of His heart. Loving them, He yearns for their peace and happiness. He had left heaven to bring it within their reach. If the road He traces for men is hard to gain, He traces it, not because it is hard, but because it is the only one. It is not unfeelingness on the part of the Savior, but the inevitableness of moral necessity, springing from the state of men, that fixes the road that leads to beatitude. And yet, when mankind has disclosed to it the secret of the soul's contentment, it is profoundly disappointed with the revelation.

> *Men quarrel with their Savior, for they look to Him for a salvation that would exempt them from suffering.*

There is, throughout history, a melancholy sameness in the reactions of mankind, sighing for redemption, to the Redeemer who would answer its appeal. "As it is Jesus Christ, yesterday and today and the same forever,"[4] so man, looking for salvation, is yesterday and today and the same forever. The one thing fallen man desires to know is

[2] Lk 9: 23.
[3] *Imitation of Christ*, bk. 2, ch. 12; Jn 6: 60.
[4] Heb 13: 8.

WHY THE CROSS?

how to live his life on earth so as to be happy. This is the very thing that Jesus desires to let him know. And yet, as was prophesied by Simeon, the Redeemer ever remains "a sign to be contradicted."[5] The sick world, like a patient in the delirium of fever, is forever turning on its physician and submitting him to violence and maltreatment.[6] It is because the problem of happiness is so intimately bound up with the problem of pain. There is no purification of soul without suffering. Through purification the soul reaches that close intimacy with God and that vision of Him which makes the soul happy. When men are told that the beatitude they seek is conditioned by suffering, they find the doctrine a hard saying. They will have none of it, and will continue to indulge the hope that they can reach the goal of human desire by another way.

> *The road to happiness is through purification of soul. Purification involves pain. The connection between the two is not arbitrarily established by God: it arises from man's dual birth.*

Jesus was a lofty idealist as regards the destiny toward which He directed the aspirations of His fellows. His ambitions for them knew no limits short of the divine. He would make them sons of God and co-heirs with Himself.[7] Being a lofty idealist, He was at the same time, as is usually the case, an intense realist. He saw that man's true happiness is found in its perfection in what is offered in the life to come. Hence if man is to be happy in the present he must attain to such a participation of the happiness to come as is possible in the conditions of time. The obstacles that impede the soul's vision of the Divine Beauty are the real source of human misery, for they are the one bar to human contentment. The clearing away of these obstacles involves toil and hardship and pain, but this pain prepares the way for peace and joy and contentment.

[5] Lk 2: 34.
[6] Such is perpetually the fate of the Church: *the Mystic Christ.*
[7] Rom 8: 17.

Jesus told Nicodemus that if a man wishes to enter the Kingdom of God, he must undergo a rebirth.[8] The statement implies that man had been already born. In his first birth, man is born of the flesh. By it his vision is circumscribed by the things of earth. He is blind as regards the things of God. Even when he comes to a second birth through water and the Holy Spirit, his vision of divine realities remains to a great extent clouded. The second birth does not do away immediately with the evil effects of the first. Spiritual cataracts, as it were, dim the soul's sight. If it is to see clearly, the surgeon's knife must be called in to take away the impediments to vision. The cross is the instrument employed in this divine surgery. By the cross is not meant, exclusively, the Cross of Jesus, but man's own personal cross taken up daily and borne in union with that of the Divine Master. "Christ's cross does not justify by being looked at, but by being applied; not as merely beheld by faith, but by being actually set up within us, and that not by our act, but by God's invisible grace. . . . As then, the cross in which St. Paul gloried was not the material cross in which Christ suffered, so neither is it simply the Sacrifice on the Cross, but it is that Sacrifice coming in power to him who has faith in it. . . . It is the Cross, realized, present, living in him, sealing him, separating him from the world, sanctifying him, afflicting him."[9]

> *Man becomes happy by becoming like to God. The cross, willingly accepted and borne in union with Christ, effects this likeness.*

Owing to the disorder and conflict that reign in the world (a disorder of which Catholic theology alone gives an adequate explanation), life will, in any event, take the cruciform shape. Men, in spite of all their efforts to escape suffering, must suffer. Suffering of itself does not transform or purify. A crucifixion can be a mere execution.

[8] Jn 3: 5
[9] Newman, *Lecture on Justification.*

WHY THE CROSS?

One died blaspheming on a cross by the side of Christ. To transform the cross from being an instrument of torture into an instrument of salvation, what is required? Man must bravely accept life as a cross to be borne daily.

Jesus, much as He loves mankind, and indeed, because He loves mankind so much, cannot will any other fate for it than that of the cross. In His desire to enable men to attain the grandiose destiny of divine adoptive sonship,[10] He wills the means that condition the perfecting of the divine adoption. The cross is that means. In the loving designs of the Savior, the cross is not meant to be an accidental or a violent intrusion into life. He deliberately plans existence for us so that it may be the crucifixion or destruction in our souls of what stands between us and God. On the other hand, prompted by our instinctive repugnance to suffering, we are prone to clamor to the Redeemer to remove from our path the irksome, the disagreeable, and the painful. Man is persuaded that were suffering removed from his life, he would be happy. God's view is not this. He knows that, without suffering, our souls cannot be purified of the dross that clings to them in consequence of the original prevarication. Without purification the soul cannot freely enjoy what it is created to enjoy. It cannot be happy by any other way.

This diversity of view is at the heart of the conflict between the redeeming God and redeemable man. Men quarrel with their Savior when He does not, as they do, identify unhappiness with suffering, happiness with the absence of suffering and the presence of the good things of this earth. God is right, and man is wrong. Jesus had experience of the truth of His theory of life. Though constantly tried, He was unvaryingly happy. On Mount Tabor, a ray of the inner glory of His soul piercing the veils of flesh was sufficient to cast His three devoted followers into a delirium of bliss. In the intoxication of his joy, St. Peter babbled incoherently, the experience he had being

---

[10] Jn 1: 12: "As many as received Him, He gave them power to be made the sons of God."

too much for rational thought or speech. St. Luke says of the apostle that he uttered words, "not knowing what he said." [11] It is not without significance that the theme of conversation between Jesus and His heavenly assistants in this scene of glory was His approaching passion. "Behold two men were talking with Him. And they were Moses and Elijah, appearing in majesty. And they spoke of His decease that He should accomplish in Jerusalem." [12]

The great paradox of the gospel is that we must sacrifice life to gain life. The cross gives life through death.

The gospel of Jesus is the message to us that we must die to live. The paradox is based on an inner conflict at the heart of our spiritual existence. For we are, in a spiritual sense, born twice. There are two lives in our soul. One is the enemy of the other, and waxes or wanes at its expense. Born of the flesh, we inherit a vitality that, in the realm of the spirit, exercises a function similar to that of cancer in the realm of the body. The cancer has a life of its own. It develops at the expense of the healthy organism it consumes. If bodily health is to be recovered, this parasitic growth must be destroyed. In a similar way, the supernatural health and vigor of the soul are conditioned by the destruction of the evil vitality of corrupt nature in us, of that vitality which is the sad heritage of Original Sin. The cross is the instrument that serves to mortify, in the literal sense of the word, that unhealthy life in the soul which conflicts with the life of God therein.

The mention of the cross should not cause dismay. It is true that the associations of the term are fearsome. In what is essential, the cross is nothing more than what, in the way of restraint, must be imposed on our unsupernatural tendencies in order to keep them subject to the law of reason and of faith. Man, being a fallen creature, necessarily suffers in every act of renouncement de-

[11] Lk 9: 33. St. Mark notes the same effect of the ecstasy on St. Peter's soul—"For he knew not what he said" (Mk 9: 6).

[12] Lk 9: 30–31.

manded of him, if he is to conform to the demands of the Christian moral code. To act supernaturally costs pain to fallen nature. The enduring of such pain is the carrying of one's cross. "What Christian language calls the cross, by analogy with the suffering and death of Christ, are the daily physical and moral sufferings that come from our relations with the external world and with our fallen fellow-creatures. But above all, the cross means the sufferings more directly sent by God, to create in us a greater resemblance to Jesus Christ. . . . The necessity of the cross has two principal reasons. The first is that we bear in ourselves the roots of an evil that strikes deeper into us than we think. The second is that a closer intimacy be established through it, between us and our great models, Jesus and Mary." [13]

The cross, then, can have its degrees. God, by what He directly wills for us, or permits to happen to us, can give it a more intense form, in view of effecting in our souls a deeper purification and, in consequence, a closer contact with Himself. The more thorough the crucifixion that is willingly borne, the greater the degree of happiness, because the more perfectly will God be revealed to the soul. Jesus said to His Apostles on the eve of His Passion: "He that loveth me, shall be loved by my Father, and I will love him, and will *manifest myself* to him." [14] This manifestation will follow the progress of our purification. Our life will be in exact ratio with our death. "For whosoever," said the Savior, "will save his life [and therefore not consent to the death of the evil life in him] shall lose it [that is, real life], and whosoever shall lose his life for my sake and the gospel shall save it." [15]

> *To enjoy union with God, the soul must be purified. This purification has to be accomplished here or hereafter. It costs much less in this world than in the world to come.*

[13] Garrigou-Lagrange, *La Croix de Jésus*, p. 460.
[14] Jn 14: 21.
[15] Mk 8: 35; Lk 9: 24; Mt 16: 25.

In this text, the words "for my sake and the gospel" are to be noted. It is clear that the gospel is the gradual revelation of the cross as the key to the riddle of existence. The cross, not stoically submitted to as an instrument of torture, but bravely accepted as an instrument of healing, destroys the obstacles that lie between man and his happiness. Salvation, in its finality, consists in the destruction of these obstacles. To be happy is to see God. To see God is, as St. John insinuates, conditioned by becoming like to Him. "Dearly beloved, we are now the Sons of God: and it hath not yet appeared what we shall be. We know that when He shall appear, we shall be like to Him: because we shall see Him as He is." [16] Our happiness is attained when the undivine in us, that which in us is unlike God and alien to Him, is purged away from our souls. This purgation, if not done in this life, is wrought out with extreme agony in the life to come. Purgatory is a loving invention of God, which pursues man, for his own good, even beyond the gates of death. [17]

Multitudes, failing to profit on this earth by all that Christianity provides for them to effect the divinization of their souls, quit the world, the task not completed. Were there no purgatory, souls that leave this earth unpurified, though not entirely estranged from God, could never enjoy the beatific vision. Nothing defiled can enter heaven, enjoy intimate union with God, and share His beatific life. Faith, laying hold of sufferings and uniting them with the Cross of Christ, enables man to accomplish, during the time of pilgrimage, what otherwise has to be accomplished at incalculably greater cost, when the time of trial is past. [18]

---

[16] 1 Jn 3: 2. These words refer to the state of Facial Vision; they are applicable, in due proportion, to the state of faith, for faith is inchoate vision.

[17] See St. Catherine of Genoa, *Treatise on Purgatory*, ch. 7–8, where these ideas are developed fully.

[18] St. Catherine writes: "No tongue can confess, no mind can conceive what is the pain of purgatory. The pain experienced there is, in its intensity, like the pain of hell itself."

WHY THE CROSS?

So bitter is the process of purification in the world to come, as compared with the same process as wrought out on earth, that God, in His love, gives largely of the Cross to His friends in order to save them from the fate of quitting the world unpurified and, consequently, immediately inapt for the beatific vision.

It is bitter for man to learn that the main obstacles to his happiness are to be found in himself rather than in his circumstances. They reject Christ, because of His Cross.

Christ's revelation to man was that the obstacle to his happiness was in himself, not in his circumstances. The way to achieve it was first to destroy the secret disorder that reigned in himself, before flinging himself against the manifest disorder that was to be found in things. Mankind found this teaching hard and unpalatable. Christ's views ran counter to the rooted prejudices of the Jews and to the human reasonings of the Gentiles.

"For the word of the Cross, to them indeed that perish, is foolishness." [19] In solving the concrete mystery of life, in deciding this question of such moment for men—namely, how can this life, which is actually one of trial and affliction, be made a happiness-giving experience?—who is likely to be right, God or man? It is folly for the creature to match his puny wisdom against the infinite wisdom of his Creator. "For the foolishness of God is wiser than men." [20]

God, through His divine Son, revealed to men the secret of happiness. He knew what would be the tragic issue of that revelation. He knew the opposition, the hatred, the anger, that would be roused up in men when there should be revealed to them the conditions of their happiness. Yet God did not, for all that, refrain from His merciful purpose. "Therefore having yet one Son most dear to him, he also sent him unto them the last of all, saying: they will reverence my son." [21] There must have been a

[19] 1 Cor 1: 18.
[20] 1 Cor 1: 25.
[21] Lk 20: 9–18; Mk 12: 6; Mt 21: 33–41.

deep emotion in our Lord's words as He, prophetically, set before His hearers this supreme effort on the part of God to persuade men to their own good. In colossal ingratitude and in even more colossal folly, men turned on the One Who would alleviate their hard lot. "But the husbandmen said one to another, this is the heir: come, let us kill him, and the inheritance shall be ours. And laying hold on him, they killed him and cast him out of the vineyard."[22] Men once killed the heir and thought that, by stifling his voice, the inheritance of the earth would be theirs. In all ages the same crime is repeated, instigated by the same idle expectations. Men, again and again, seek to slay Christ, living in His Church, and indulge the hope that once they have silenced Him they will be left in tranquil enjoyment of the earth and the fullness thereof. They persist in regarding Christ—and Christ because of His Cross—as the great barrier to their happiness and well-being. Men would willingly enough give ear to the preaching of the Church if the preaching of the Church were a Christ Who was not a Christ crucified. "But," says St. Paul, "we preach Christ crucified; unto the *Jews*, indeed, a stumbling block, and to the *Gentiles*, foolishness."[23]

"Behold," says the author of the *Imitation of Christ*, "the Cross is all, and *in dying* to thyself all consists: and there is no other way to *life* and to true eternal peace, but by way of the holy Cross and daily mortification."[24] A religion that would hold that Christ's sufferings in His Passion dispensed all His followers from the necessity of suffering, a religion that would see in Christ's Cross the elimination of all other personal crosses, such a religion would find a ready acceptance among men. But to regard life as having no meaning unless it means a purification, to judge life shapeless unless it assumes a cruciform shape, every instinct in fallen man is up in arms against such a theory of

[22] Mk 12: 7–8.
[23] 1 Cor 1: 23.
[24] *Imitation of Christ*, bk. 2, ch. 12.

existence. And yet this was the gist of the good news that Christ brought to men. They received the good tidings as being very ill tidings indeed, and were stirred to wrath and hatred against the Messenger. Error was more palatable to men than the truth. "And this is the judgment, because light is come into the world and men loved darkness rather than the light, for their works were evil." [25] This was the fate of the "good tidings" in the lifetime of Christ. It continues to be its fate down along the ages.[26]

By the few are the good tidings received with joy; by the vast majority the message is received with rage or incredulity. By some, the words of Christ are combated with violence and hate. This is the case in almost all the civilized countries of the day. By others, and these even the professed adherents of Christ, the words of Christ suffer mutilation and distortion, and, if they are admitted, it is with many qualifications and reservations. For the persuasion of the few, the Savior gave a practical demonstration of His theory by taking up the Cross Himself and dying on it. He had taught without succeeding in bringing conviction to the minds of His hearers. His life and works had not succeeded in persuading men to the truth; where His life had failed, His death would succeed. The object lesson of Calvary was to prove the most convincing of His arguments. "And I, if I be lifted up from the earth, shall draw all things to myself." [27]

[25] Jn 3: 19.

[26] The fate of the gospel in Judea is its fate, in miniature, throughout the whole world and during all time. It meets with opposition from the mass, composed of all kinds and conditions of men, religious and irreligious (typified by Pharisee and Sadducee), believer and unbeliever (typified by Jew and Gentile), learned and unlearned (represented by the doctors of the Law and the common crowd). There is always opposition from the vast bulk of men, acceptance on the part of the comparatively few.

[27] Jn 12: 32. In this chapter the Cross has been envisaged solely under its ascetical and mystical aspect. In a subsequent chapter, the Cross as an expiatory and redemptive sacrifice will be considered.

The Cross of Christ is a veritable theory of life.

If the passionate resentment of mankind against the Cross were analyzed to its depths, it would be found to have its origin in a deep-seated conviction that, after all, the Crucifixion is not only a historical event, but also a theory of life. There is bitter hostility to the Cross because it forces on man's attention a truth to which he would gladly blind himself; but which some primeval spiritual instinct in him reveals as inescapable. Not only in an obscure way is it felt that what the Cross symbolizes is the law of religion (for all men, from the beginning, sacrifice is essentially linked up with religion), it is also felt to be a law of life. The egoist, the man who in all things seeks himself and strives to divert all things to himself, inevitably loses himself, and the world as well. He finds, at the end, a shrunken miserable personality and a pitiful isolation. The man who flings away his life in sacrifice, recovers it, enhanced, in the gratitude of generations and in enlargement of personality. It is a law of things that men and women achieve themselves by devoting themselves. Individualism has to be abandoned to attain individuality. Egoism has to be renounced in order to acquire personality.

The Cross is the only solution of the problem of life.[28] Man has to be executed on it or annealed and purified through it. Hence it was that St. Paul insisted, saying: "I judge not myself to know anything among you but Jesus Christ and Him crucified." [29] One has the full meaning of Christianity when all the import of this text has been

---

[28] "The Cross has put its due value upon everything which we see, upon all fortunes, all advantages, all ranks, all dignitaries, all pleasures. . . . It has given a meaning to the various, shifting course, the trials, the temptations, the sufferings of man's earthly state. It has taught us how to live, how to use the world, what to expect, what to desire, what to hope. It is the tone into which all the strains of this world's music are ultimately to be resolved" (Newman, *Parochial and Plain Sermons*, vol. 6, sermon 7, "The Cross of Christ, the Measure of the World").

[29] 1 Cor 2: 2.

grasped. The whole meaning is not conveyed in the formula "Christ crucified for us" but in the words "Christ crucified for and in us." Crucifixion is a hard word, but, in spite of its hardness, we cannot escape the conclusion that Christ inculcated it and that Christianity demands it. What is the reason of this hard law? It is necessary to go back to the very origin of things to find the explanation.

Happiness for men is found in the vision of God; in the vision face to face, hereafter, and in the vision of faith, here and now. Men's happiness on earth is proportioned to the degree of perfection to which the vision of faith attains. The Cross of Christ has won for fallen mankind initiation into the faith. The same Cross, taken willingly into a man's life and impregnating with its virtue his own personal cross, is the instrument that cleanses the soul's vision and gives it an ever clearer perception of divine realities. The soul's vision of God is proportioned to the soul's likeness to God. The cross of life, accepted and embraced and united with the Cross of Christ, purifies the soul of the undivine in it and assimilates it ever more to God. The soul thus loses its own evil life to find its true life. The Cross, being the instrument of life, is the key to happiness. This is the paradox of the gospel. The paradox has its origin in the historical event with which the story of man opens.

CHAPTER SIX

And He said: Let us make man to our image and likeness.
—GENESIS 1: 26

To understand the meaning and purpose of human activity, we must study it from the point of view of God, and not of man.

TO GRASP THE SIGNIFICANCE of the spiritual experiences that, through the whole course of history, mark the life of man, considered as a moral and religious being, it is necessary to have an insight into the ideas that presided at his creation. As the product of a divine idea, he must have been made after a certain plan and destined to fulfill a definite purpose. To have a thorough understanding of anything that comes from the inventive faculty of an intelligent being, one has to see it through (and in) the idea that gave it birth. Man is a complex structure. Some inadequate notion of what he is, and what he is for, and how he ought to function might be gleaned from a study of him in action. But the phenomena of the moral and religious life of man, considered individually or in society as revealed by history, manifest strange contradictions. There is seen such loftiness of aspiration allied with such meanness in achievement, such a warm approval of what is noble coupled with a disgraceful surrender to what is base, such lofty flights into the pure, the heroic, the serenely spiritual followed by a bewildering descent into the false, the perverse, and the sordidly sensual, that the contemplation of man in action is likely to shed but a deceptive light on the problems of human existence. On the other hand, man and his destiny can be seen in due perspective if one can grasp the idea that God had in creating this mysterious being, namely, that man is a composite of spirit and matter.[1]

> *What is meant by saying that man is created to know, love, and serve God here on earth?*

It might seem an easy thing for one instructed in the faith to have a clear and accurate idea of the end for which man is created. It is stated in simple terms in that textbook from which every duly taught Catholic child derives the first knowledge of his religion. The catechism says: "Man is created to know, love, and serve God here on earth and to see and enjoy Him hereafter in heaven." Nothing, apparently, could be more lucid. Yet the statement is not so self-explanatory as it might easily appear to be. Do the first notions that children form of knowledge, love, and service illuminate for them the terms in which man's destiny is expressed?

What does knowing God mean? *Knowing*, as applied to the usual tasks that face the learner, signifies "acquiring knowledge of." Is one "knowing God" by applying oneself assiduously to a study of books that discuss God and divine things and by following attentively instructions on these matters? Is this study a fulfillment, in part, of the purpose of creation? Is it one and the same thing to know God and to know a great deal about God—His nature, His attributes, and His works?

How does a person love God? Children know what the term means as applied to the relations between their parents and themselves. Does loving God mean feeling toward God as one does towards one's father and mother? Must one "feel" toward God like that, under the alternative of not being able to realize the purpose for which one is created? Love, as experienced by the child, is not a thing that can be commanded. The child loves his parents

---

[1] It is only he who makes a thing that has, in the full sense of the term, an idea of it. God having made man, has alone the idea of man and man's life (*John of St. Thomas*, vol. 3, q. 15, *de ideis*).

instinctively and "feels" that they naturally and without effort have affection for their little one. How could love be commanded? Does not there seem to be an impossibility implied in the very command to love a person?

What does service of God imply? Those who, not being of the family, execute the household tasks are said to be rendering service. For it, at due times, they receive a recompense. The members of the family employ servants because they find it inconvenient or difficult or impossible to carry out the household duties themselves. They need the help of others. To dispense with such services would mean the disorganization of their regular life; hence they are quite willing to reward those on whom they are dependent and from whose labors they profit. Is service of God anything like this? Has God a need of man and man's labors? Is God dependent in some way on His own creatures? Does He profit by their toil? Is it something that He cannot dispense with, without grave inconvenience to Himself? Once these questions are asked, it becomes clear that the usual meaning attached to the term *service* scarcely applies when it refers to the duties of the creature to the Creator.

The good Christian child, of pure heart and limpid mind, very likely rightly interprets—not, of course, by a process of reasoning, but practically—the injunction of the catechism relative to knowing, loving, and serving God. But the adult, with a more analytic knowledge of the meaning of the terms *knowledge, love,* and *service,* will find it hard to explain how life, as he lives it, comes to be a process of knowing, loving, and serving God. It is difficult to see how the life of the average, fairly good, but worldly Christian squares with the exigencies of the catechism. Do the deliberate activities of each day verify the notions of knowing, loving, and serving God? Have they anything approaching to this significance? If knowing God, for instance, means not knowing things about Him, but knowing Him as a man knows his friend, the fulfillment of the end of creation would imply this growth in understanding, effected through the daily doings and endurings. Does the living of his life, by the average Christian, give him a better understanding of God? If not, it would seem that he is not, through his life's activities, fulfilling the purpose of creation. It would mean that his life was being vainly lived.

If these thoughts begin to torture the mind of a person of religious instincts but of average conduct, he will strive to dismiss them with the persuasion that, provided he is living a fairly "decent" life, avoiding excess, doing no great wrong, and attending (with a certain fidelity) to the official duties of his religion, he is somehow or other "knowing," "loving," and "serving" God. In the mind of such a person there gradually takes shape the notion that a life not stained with habitual wrongdoing is somehow or other capable of being explained as a service of God. And by another act of implicit reasoning, service is understood to be, by some hidden process of assimilation, equivalent to "knowing" and "loving" God.

Now, to come to know God is not merely to grow in knowledge of His attributes; it is to become intimate with Him, to become conversant with His ways, and to enter into His views. To know Him is to have such an understanding of Him as will issue in interest in, and love of, Him. And many an adult Christian will have to confess that, as a child, he knew God better, in this sense, than he does as a man.[2] He will have to confess that God was a more real and personal being for him in the days of his childish ignorance than He is in the days of his manhood's knowledge. Yet life is a failure unless advancing years and experience bring God more into a man's mind

---

[2] Compare this fine sentence from John Ruskin's *Modern Painters*, 1:90: "Childhood often holds a truth with its feeble fingers, which the grasp of manhood cannot retain—which it is the pride of utmost age to recover." What an apt commentary on our Lord's quiet condemnation of adult complacency and self-sufficiency: "Unless you be converted and become as little children, you shall not enter the kingdom of heaven."

and heart. Real service is impossible without knowledge and love. Without faith, it is impossible to please God or to serve Him; without love, the service is not acceptable. Hence the one thing that is important for a man to know is how to use life's activities and life's experiences in such a way as to make them yield this knowledge and this love of God. For it is only in this way that a man's acts can be invested with an abiding worth.

To give a significance that is enduring and not merely transient to life's deliberate activities, a man must have a clear vision of the issues that life, as a whole, is meant to have. A man cannot know how he is to act unless he knows what he is to become. This knowledge is not attainable if the "knowing," "loving," and "serving" of the catechism is not submitted to a more searching analysis than is given to it by the average adult Christian. As has been pointed out, these terms do not reveal their meaning as readily as one might expect. They are far less simple than they appear. A historical survey and a critical examination of the theories of moral and spiritual values held by the successive generations of men will throw little light on life's ultimate purpose. To understand man rightly, it is necessary to understand God's views with regard to him.

God's purpose in creation was a purely disinterested one. His purpose was to give and not to receive: He had all to give.

What was God's idea in creating man? In calling rational creatures from nothingness he must have acted with a purpose, since He is an intelligent being. The Creator could not have acted with a view to acquiring something for Himself, for, since He is all-sufficient to Himself, there is nothing that He can acquire. Men and angels can render God glory, but they cannot supply a need. The creature is said to serve God, but nothing can accrue to God from such service. God cannot be in a condition of dependence vis-à-vis His creatures. He cannot *want* anything from them. Whatever positive benefit comes from creation, that benefit falls to the lot of the creatures. The motive in creating is wholly disinterested. God created in view of communicating something to, and not in view of receiving something from, the work of His hands.[3] God is generous in the highest degree and in a unique manner because in acting He never seeks His own advantage. He always acts out of sheer goodness.[4] St. Thomas says: "The goodness, in virtue of which God bestows His gifts on His creatures, is as great as the divine essence. It is, therefore, infinite. Hence one may *hope* to receive from God nothing less than Himself. Wherefore the good that we ought to look for at His hands is, rightly, and above all else, that infinite good which it is within His power to enable us to gain, by His aid. It belongs to a power of infinite resource to lead to an infinite good. Such a good is eternal life, which consists in the enjoyment of God Himself."[5] "The Creator," writes the Venerable Libermann in his turn, "made man in order to communicate to Him the riches of His own inner life and being, in this world, through grace, and in the world to come, in glory, where the imperfect possession of God, which belongs to the time of pilgrimage, shall give place to the perfect. It is for this union that God is said to have created man to His own image and likeness."[6]

The words of St. Thomas, in which he says that God, being infinitely kind, must give with infinite generosity and, therefore, must bestow on His creature nothing less than Himself, need some explanation. God could, had He so willed, have created man for a much less exalted

---

[3] See *Summa theologiae*, I, q. 44, a. 4, c. Some things in exercising causality are, at the same time, the recipients of an effect. These are imperfect causes, and hence, they, when acting, aim at acquiring something by their action. But this is not the case when there is question of the First Cause, God. He must be exclusively a Cause. He cannot act for the purpose of acquiring some good for Himself. He acts only to communicate His perfection, that is, His own excellence or worth.

[4] Ibid., ad 4.

[5] *Summa theologiae*, II-II, q. 17, a. 2, c.

[6] Ven. Libermann, *Écrits spirituels.*

destiny and to achieve a perfection of a purely finite nature. But when He, by imparting to the soul the infused divine virtue of hope, thereby emboldened His creature to extend its ambitions beyond all that the realm of nature could offer, and when, at the same time, He assures it that His infinite power is ever at its disposal to enable it to achieve its lofty ambition, then it must be nothing less than the divine that is proposed to the creature as the goal of endeavour.

God might, in creating man, have given him no gifts or powers other than those that strictly belong to the constitution of human nature.

A rational soul is a thing of marvelous beauty and power. In its faculties it traces the image of God.[7] By the intellect the soul has the power of acquiring a knowledge that is bounded only by the limits of the created material universe. By thought, it can master and thus, in a certain sense, possess all things, though in their ideal form only. Aristotle says that the soul can become, in a certain sense, all things.[8] In this it bears a striking resemblance to God, in Whom all reality exists in the way of form or idea.[9] And when, under the wide sweep of the created intelligence, there should stand revealed all the beauty of the Creator that is imaged forth in His works, man could experience intense happiness in surrendering his power of love and admiration to the appeal of that beauty. The ecstasy that seizes the really great artist, in presence of the masterpieces of nature or art, is a feeble image of that which would lay hold of the soul of man when that soul should be brought to its highest natural perfection, by the complete conquest, in thought and will, of the whole material universe. God could bring man to this high destiny by aiding him to give to his natural powers their fullest evolu-

[7] *Summa theologiae*, I, q. 93, a. 4, c.

[8] Aristotle, *De anima*, 3.8.

[9] The divine ideas, of course, are the cause of things. They are not derived, as are man's ideas, from things.

　　　　　　　　　　　　　WHY THE CROSS?

tion. Through this vision of nature there would be revealed in a very lofty manner the attributes of the Creator that find their exercise in creation. From this would arise in man's will a great love and admiration for the supreme source of all the beauty, power, and majesty shown forth in the material universe.

It is not only in the field of knowledge that man would resemble God; he would also bear a resemblance to Him in the field of action. God is sovereignly self-determining in His creative works. By his free will, man is empowered to decide his own actions, choose between relative good things, and determine his own destiny. This freedom—always supposing that God had determined to create him for a purely natural end—would be fully enjoyed within the ample boundaries traced by God's order, identical with the limits traced by man's own rational nature. These limits impose no restriction, but simply mark the scope and range of human freedom.[10] Man might have been called into being by God in order to enjoy this glorious, if necessarily limited, existence, but the beatitude consequent on this natural life raised to its highest perfection would be separated by an infinite distance from the bliss enjoyed by God Himself. The happiness enjoyed by man if created in the natural order would be finite; that of God is infinite. The human soul, though finite, is capable of being gratified with more than its nature and the creative universe can supply. But, of its own powers, it could not burst through the limits set to its natural capacities.

God wishes His creatures not only to exhaust all the possibilities of natural happiness but, rising beyond all that, to experience a happiness that of its nature is divine.

God was not content that His rational creatures should be limited to that happiness which the full evolution of their

[10] "To impose laws on liberty is not to destroy it. To prevent it from going astray on one side or the other is not to impede it. It is but to direct it more surely along the path it ought to take" (Bossuet, *Sermons*, ed. Lebarq, 5:10).

natural powers would yield; He would have them taste the very beatitude that He Himself enjoys. He willed that they should have, not merely a human, but a divine experience. He was not content with creating; He would re-create. He determined to infuse a vitality into the essence of the soul, and energies into its faculties, which would enable it to live a life similar to His own. He willed His creature, endowed with reason, to contemplate what He Himself contemplated and to love what He Himself loved. He threw open to its gaze the boundless realm of the uncreated and offered to its embrace not pale, created reflections of the Divine Beauty, but that infinite, everlasting, ever ancient, ever new beauty itself. God breathed on the already living soul a breath of His own living being, and by that breath the tide of divine life flowed through the realms of the created Spirit. By this act of re-creation there penetrated into the substance of the soul divine grace and into the faculties of will and intellect the infused divine virtues of faith, hope, and charity. Man's rational powers were further strengthened by the infused supernatural moral virtues of prudence and justice. Man's sensitive nature was rectified by the infused moral virtues of temperance and fortitude.

The soul, by divine grace, was fashioned to a likeness with God. It reflected the features of the Creator and became apt to live His life. Happiness is the result of a full life. The infinite happiness of God springs from His infinitely perfect life. Man, vivified by the re-creative breath of God, is enabled to exercise vital activities like to those of God and thus participate in God's happiness. That beatitude was not, of course, to be enjoyed straightaway in full measure. A period of growth and imperfection, measured by the time of earth's pilgrimage, was to be followed by an eternity of maturity and perfection. But happiness was to be man's lot in both periods of his existence—a happiness strictly proportioned to the perfection with which he should live God's life in each: God, incompletely and dimly seen in this world, would be contemplated face to face in the world to come. The shadows and vicissitudes that attend the love of God in time would pass and yield place to a perfect and constant love in eternity. In its everlasting home, the soul is destined to possess in finite measure that same treasure which God possesses infinitely. Sharing in the divine life, it is privileged to participate in that boundless joy which God derives from the experience of infinite life.

The soul tastes divine happiness by entering into intimate and vital union with God dwelling within it.

The privilege of entering into God's life and consequent happiness, though granted in its perfect form in heaven, is not denied to earth, though in a form less perfect. For the soul, by the divine energy with which it is endowed through sanctifying grace, is enabled to react upon God dwelling within it and to enter into ever fuller and more perfect possession of Him. God is present in all things, giving to each the existence proper to it. He is more intimate to each being than that being is to itself. Yet, in the whole universe, it is only of the rational being that it can be said that it holds or possesses God. The rest are upheld by, but do not lay hold of, God. If the soul were without grace, it would be similarly circumstanced. God would be in it, but would not be possessed by it. Through Him and from Him it would derive its natural existence and nothing more. It would lie insensible and unresponsive to the touch of God. It is otherwise when sanctifying grace flows through it. By this element of divine life it is dowered with an energy greater than natural, by which it can react to the presence of God and enter into vital, intimate, and personal relations with Him.

These new relations between God and the soul are vital with the vitality of a divine life. Thus, when over and above its natural existence God gives the created spirit a participation of His own life and being, there is brought about in the relations between Creator and creature a condition that differs widely—it might be said, infinitely—from that which marks these relations when the bond between them is merely that of natural existence. God dwells lovingly and as a person loved in the soul in grace. He is at home there. He becomes an object of the soul's contemplation and its love. The created intellect strengthened by the divine virtue of faith fixes its gaze on the Blessed Trinity dwelling within the soul and wrapped in the veils of created images. The will, fortified by the divine virtue of charity, chooses God in person as the object of its affection. Through the virtue of hope, the soul is encouraged to aspire to intimate friendship with its Creator and is rendered unshaken in its confidence that faith and charity will be ultimately rewarded by an ever clearer vision and an ever fuller possession of the infinite good. By these virtues the soul establishes living contact between itself and God. By them it attaches itself to the Divinity, and from that union it derives a divine life and energy. As at the touch of Moses' wand, waters gushed from the rock to slake the thirst of the parched Israelites, so at the action of faith and charity, waters of life gush from God to refresh and vivify the soul. This is the figure chosen by the Savior to describe this mysterious interchange between the Creator and the creature in the supernatural life.[11] In this contact with God and intimacy with Him is found that happiness for which man was created and for which he craves.

The soul finds its life and nourishment in the Divinity and only there. Deprived of this nourishment, it languishes and dies—though, being immortal, it continues to exist.

The created spirit is a living thing and, like all living things, must have something wherewith to nourish itself and which shall minister to its strength and growth. God,

[11] "Jesus stood and cried, saying: 'If any man thirst let him come to me and drink. He that believeth in me, as the Scripture saith, out of his bosom shall flow rivers of living water.'" And earlier He had said: "The water that I shall give him shall become in him a fountain of water springing up into life everlasting" (Jn 7: 37–38; 4: 14).

in His infinite condescension, has deigned to constitute Himself the connatural food of the spirit He has created. The soul must feed on God or die. True, it is immortal and as such must have an unending existence. It cannot suffer dissolution, for, being simple, it has no component parts into which to decompose. But mere existence is not life.[12] The demons and the damned exist forever and yet are said to be lost in eternal death.

God is the life of the soul because God is its food. By its intellect and will, the soul, as it were, lays hold on God and assimilates Him to itself; or rather, is assimilated to Him. For, whereas, in the natural order, the food that is consumed is elevated to the condition of the living organism that nourishes itself by it, in the supernatural order the process is reversed. The soul does not draw its food to a human condition, but by it is itself raised to a divine condition. Feeding on God, it becomes gradually divine.

The body requires nourishment only at intervals. The soul has an incessant need of what ministers to its life. In every act of faith, inspired by charity, it supplies this need. God alone can satisfy the soul. It is not meant to experience a moment of dissatisfaction. "Jesus said: 'Whosoever drinketh of this water, shall thirst again: but he that shall drink of this water that I will give him, shall not thirst for ever. . . .' The woman saith to Him: 'Sir, give me this water, that I may not thirst, nor come hither to draw.' "[13] Hence the acts of the divine virtues are intended by God not to be occasional or intermittent. In His plan, every pulsation of the soul's deliberate life is meant to be one of faith,

[12] The body itself can be said, in a certain sense, to exist perpetually, for the elements of matter of which it is composed are not annihilated after the bodily structure has been broken up. Yet the body is said to be dead when the soul departs. What the soul is to the body, by analogy, God is to the soul.

[13] Jn 4: 13–15. Compare these words of Bossuet: "The soul drinks of a water unsuited to it, when it seeks pleasure in the objects of sense. The wise man teaches that the soul need not quit itself, nor divert streams from some distant mountain, since it has within itself an everlasting and inexhaustible living fountain" (*Sermons*, 5:161).

animated by hope and charity. Every movement of the will that has not this tendency to union with God is lost. It is a casting away of real life.

The soul is a capacity for the infinite. It is, therefore, a capacity for God.

The soul's great reality lies in this, that it is a capacity for the infinite, while being itself a finite thing. The only living being that can physically—that is, in its substantial reality—find entrance to the soul is the God that made it. To everything created, even to angels and demons, the soul is an inviolable sanctuary. The consequence is that the soul cannot find in any created thing what can minister to its true life and enlarge its being. It cannot, by taking thought, or by cleaving to creatures, add one cubit to its stature. It is the reason why all efforts to satisfy itself with creatures end in dissatisfaction. This is the law of our creation. "*Irrequietum est cor nostrum, donec requiescat in te,*" writes St. Augustine, addressing himself to God. Our heart is ever restless until it rests in Thee.

The Venerable Libermann echoes this thought, saying: "God made our souls mere empty things in themselves. It is true that they are possessed of powers and faculties in virtue of which they bear a resemblance to God, but these are mere potentialities of that which as yet is not. Not possessing any reality in itself wherewith to satisfy itself, the soul can and ought to seek in God that happiness of which it feels the want. The soul created to enjoy God is made in consequence to be happy. It receives in its creation an impulse to go outside of itself or rather to enter into itself and there find that which, not being anything of itself, can make it happy. It is not possible for it to have or to find this blessedness in its own substance, otherwise God would not have been true to His wisdom in creating it as He did. The soul, then, being in extreme need of finding wherewith to satisfy itself and quiet its cravings, and not discovering the wherewithal in itself, resembles a man tortured by hunger and by thirst. This is the image employed by Divine Wisdom. This hunger and thirst set in activity those three powers by which it directs itself toward God, in order to nourish itself on the divine food of His grace and His justice. These three powers are faith, hope, and charity. . . . This triple tendency toward God of the faculties of the soul, memory, intellect, and will, operating through the divine[14] virtues of faith, hope, and charity, is called in scriptural language, to hunger and thirst after justice. All those who have the grace to tend in this way toward God receive His communications and so find their happiness. 'Blessed are they that hunger and thirst after justice, for they shall have their fill' (Mt 5: 6)." [15]

God demands that man conform his will to the divine will, for, unless that conformity exists, God's loving purposes in creating cannot be realized.

What does God demand of man in return for the divine benefits conferred on him? Strange as it appears to our calculating instincts, God demands nothing; all that He asks is that man should be content to receive and to set up no barriers against what God is only too anxious to give. Man is required to conform his will to that of his Creator, for without such conformity God's communication to man is impossible. If the human will is set in opposition to the divine, contact between the Creator and the creature is broken and the stream of divine life is cut off from the human soul. A comparison drawn from electrical lighting illustrates this truth. So that the electric bulb and filaments glow with light, the lamp must be connected to electrical energy. If disconnected by the turning off of a switch, the light goes out and darkness results.

[14] These virtues are called divine because they have God Himself for the term of their activity. It is, for instance, God Himself, in Person, Who is loved in the exercise of the virtue of charity. A human virtue is that which would have something of, or belonging to, humanity as its object.

[15] Ven. Libermann, *Écrits spirituels*, p. 17.

God does not demand the subjection of man's will to Him for any satisfaction to be enjoyed because of such subjection. He demands it because it is an indispensable condition for the work of sanctifying the human soul. Man must use his freedom to subject himself willingly to the divine ruling. God will not force his submission. "God who made us without our will," says St. Augustine, "cannot save us without our will." "The life of grace does not consist in this subordination of the human will to the divine. The subordination of, or conformity of, the will of the creature to that of the Creator is but that which conditions the divine life. That divine life is a substantial communication of the life of God to the soul." [16]

God's action in creating man was an action of divine disinterestedness. The purpose of it was to give and not to receive. It was an action of infinite generosity, because what was bestowed on man was nothing less than the Divinity itself. The Creator willed man to participate in the bliss of the divine life and to share in the divine experience. All that was demanded of man, in return, was that he should be willing and ready to receive the gift of God. The gift is the vision of God by faith in this world, to expand into the vision face to face in the world to come. Heavenly beatitude is but the full and final flowering of grace. Man disposes himself for this by using his freedom to keep his will subject to the will of God. Want of subjection ruptures the relation between the creature and the Creator. It breaks contact, and without that contact it is impossible for God to give Himself to man. In the beginning, God so endowed man's nature with exceptional gifts that this conformity of the creature's will to that of the Creator's involved neither hardship nor struggle.

[16] Ibid., p. 71.

CHAPTER SEVEN

Only this have I found—that God made man upright, and he hath sought out many subtleties.
—ECCLESIASTES 7: 29

There are two ways in which the creature's will is made one with that of the Creator: the first way is by direct acts of love of God through the exercise of the infused virtue of charity; the second way is by the practical fulfillment of God's will in executing life's tasks.

MAN WAS CREATED, as was seen in the previous chapter, to enter into relations of personal love with his God. By the infused virtue of charity, he could unite himself with his Creator by the ties of a mutual affection. In the direct act of loving, the creature makes his will one with that of the Creator. The exercise of love unites the wills of those who love. But there is yet another way in which man can effect that oneness. It is by fulfilling the will of his Maker in the conduct of his life.

Though elected to the sublime privilege of enjoying loving intercourse with God, man remains, nevertheless, in his condition of creature and subject, and with a definite task to acquit on earth. In one act of choice, an angel determines his destiny, for good or ill. Not so man. He does not attain the goal of existence in one stride. His life of trial and testing is not worked out in a moment. Normally it is made up of days and months and years. Neither is he alone in running his course. In God's designs he is one of a vast number sharing the same nature and created for the same end as himself. In fulfilling himself through his earthly career, man is brought into a multiplicity of relations with his fellow men as well as with God.

A number of obligations arise from these relations. The duties that devolve upon man spring from the very constitution of his nature. *What he has to do is decided by what he is.* God, having made him what he is, must necessarily exact of him that he act as befits the nature and supernature with which he has been endowed. At the dawn of reason, the child is but a man in the making, or, to use a philosophical expression, he is but a man *potentially*. His life's duty is to evolve that potentiality and to become actually a man. Fullness of bodily stature and maturity of years do not confer this perfection. The development of the virtues that constitute true manliness alone completes and crowns human endeavor.

Being (by definition) a rational animal, man has attained to what is appointed him when the stamp of reason is impressed on his life of thought and of action. "It is of the very essence of human virtue," says St. Thomas, "to incline a man to good. But what is the good for man is that he should be according to reason."[1] But since the child of Adam has been raised to the dignity of adopted child of God, this life of reason must be transfigured by a filial affection for Him Who is at one and the same time Lord and Father.

It is impossible for the wise Creator to fashion a being after a certain idea and to permit that idea to be contradicted by the work of His hand. God could not create man to be a creature of reason and faith, and allow of his conducting himself in flagrant violation of the laws of reason and of faith. Man was made to be man, and he must bear himself as such. If he refuses to do so, if he is false to his own nature, he brings himself into violent conflict with the will of his Creator. The union between the two is ruptured, and man is cut off from the source of divine life.

---

[1] *Summa theologiae*, II-II, q. 141, a. 1, c., and passim.

The service of God for man consists in "doing the truth in charity." [2]

Man serves God by realizing himself as man and doing this out of regard for his Maker. He is the product of a divine idea, and his function in life is, by his own efforts, aided by grace, to actualize that idea. "Man," says St. Thomas, "is fashioned by God as a work of art by the artist." [3] What is strange about this work of art is this: it does not issue in its full perfection from the hands of its Author. By the right use of its free will and by the usage of the power with which it is equipped, it is meant to achieve itself.

Man is not born just. He forms himself to justice. In becoming what he ought to become, he serves and glorifies his Maker. The just man is the glory of God. He is the result of his own efforts and God's cooperation. As a masterpiece of craftsmanship sheds distinction on the artisan, so a creature who, in spite of human frailty, but aided by God, becomes a true man is a triumph of God's grace. Hence God is glorified in His saints, for they realize in their lives His ideal of manhood. *They serve God rather by what they have become than by what they have done.* [4]

God does not need our deeds. He is interested in the way in which we do them. It is a moral suicide for man, who has been made a reasonable being, not to act in all things according to the requirements of reason. This, however, is not the limit of man's obligations. He has been created for a supernatural destiny. His acts must be inspired by a divine virtue, be upborne by a divine force, and tend to a divine object. He has been created not merely to conform to reason, but to love God. But in his elevated condition he still remains man, and must, in his actions, remain true to himself. He must still be reasonable, but his reason must be penetrated with the light of

[2] Eph 4: 15.

[3] *Comp. theol.*, pt. 2, ch. 4.

[4] Thomas says: "Who is there so dull of wit that, seeing the upright life of the faithful, does not glorify the name invoked in such a life?" (ibid., pt. 2, ch. 8).

faith. God looks to man, not only to be *reasonable*, but to be *faithful*.

Man must not only be man: he must be a man who is also a child of God. "Children," says St. Thomas, "ought to imitate their parents; wherefore he who addresses God as father ought to aim at imitating God. His duty is to avoid all those things that effect an unlikeness and give earnest attention to all those things that create a resemblance to Him."[5] God aims at deifying his creature. Manhood[6] is the condition of deification. God cannot deify what is of impulse or of disordered passion, what is unjust or intemperate, what is animal, or what is done for an unworthy end. In a word, *He cannot deify the unmanly.* The supernature with which man is dowered, elevates and, therefore, presupposes nature. It cannot elevate what is not in accord with man's true nature, what is not prudent, just, brave, and temperate.

Good acts, considered in themselves, are not necessarily either the service or the glory of God. Man does not serve God in performing acts of virtue unless he performs them virtuously. "Moral acts," says Aristotle, "can be ranked as just or temperate only when they are of such a nature as the just and temperate man would perform. But the just and temperate man is what he is, not by the mere performance of such and such actions, but by showing the spirit and acting after the manner of one whose character is just and temperate."[7] God cannot be content with our doing just things; He is content only with our acting justly. He is not satisfied with our doing true things, but only with our acting truly. What he desires is that in all our actions we should be true to ourselves. If we are true to ourselves, we are true to Him. His requirements of us are conveyed in the words of St. Paul: ". . . but *doing the truth in charity*, we may, in all things grow up in him, who is the

[5] Ibid., pt. 2, ch. 4.

[6] By *manhood* is meant what is according to the nature of man as such. This is equivalent to what is according to reason.

[7] Aristotle, *Nich. Ethics*, bk. 2, ch. 3.

WHY THE CROSS?

head, even Christ."[8] The significance of these words is now clear. Man serves God, fulfills His will, and realizes His purpose in creating, by "playing the man" in all circumstances and so doing the truth—that is, proving true to himself. But he must, in addition, act thus in charity—that is, in a spirit of filial regard for God, his father, and for that father's honor.

The terms in which the Venerable Libermann sets forth the purpose of man's creation admirably recapitulate the ideas developed in the preceding pages. He writes thus: "God made us that He might unite us with Himself: that He might communicate to us, in virtue of this union and as conditioned by it, the riches of His own being: and, finally, that we, as His creatures, should carry out the life's work He has appointed to us, with devotedness and in the proper spirit."[9]

This statement gives precision to the words of the catechism. To know God is to deepen and intensify one's spirit of faith. This intensification is achieved by acquiring a more profound insight into the mysteries of the true religion: but, above all, faith grows in vitality when a man disciplines himself to a sensitiveness to the intimate contact that God has with his life; and when he develops a vivid realization of his own personal responsibility to his Maker in all the details of his life, in its decisions and in its acts. This awareness of the nearness of God to one's hourly existence provokes the soul to turn with love to the great Being Who, in spite of His transcendence, has such a tender regard and concern for His creature.

This is the way to grow in love of God; it is to exercise constantly the divine infused virtue of charity. Direct affective contact of two wills is the primary characteristic of love. Such contact cannot exist without man's feeling it imperative to conform to God's requirements and to rise to God's standards in the daily conduct of his life. If man

[8] Eph 4: 15.
[9] *Écrits spirituels*, pp. 1–2.

loves God and he understands, as understand he must, that his Creator desires that he should prove himself a true man in his dealings with his fellow men, with circumstances, and with himself, he cannot but strive to respond to God's expectations of him. He will endeavor, out of regard for his Maker, to "play the man" habitually, and thus not bring the Author of his being to shame. The reason why God looks for this perfect conformity of the created will to the divine will is that this conformity is the intrinsically necessary condition for the imparting of the divine life to the human soul. This, as has been said, is God's ultimate object.[10]

Man finds an innate difficulty in effecting an inner harmony in his nature. In him, sense tends to conflict with reason and thus rupture the conformity of his will to that of God.

Unless the human nature in man maintains an inner harmony in itself, and thus satisfies the requirements of reason (as enlightened by faith), God cannot carry out His designs in its regard. It is metaphysically impossible

---

[10] Here there is question of the secondary end of creation. The primary end is the glory of God. It is only for shallow thinkers that this proposition savors of egotism. Were God's life not a self-conscious life, it could not be a happy one. To be conscious of the beauty of the divine reality and to exult in it—this is God's happiness. That consciousness of, and exultant joy in, the Godhead is the intrinsic glory of God. Man, called to grace and glory, is thus called to participate in this conscious life of God. To share God's life is to share God's exultancy. To behold the Divine Beauty, to extol it and to exult in it, is true beatitude. But this exultant apprehension of, appreciation of, and joy in the Godhead revealed, is the extrinsic glory of God. It is obvious it is coincident with the creature's beatitude. The extrinsic glory mirrors the intrinsic glory. God does not create to acquire beatitude, but to impart beatitude. When, then, God is said to have created the world for His own glory, this must not be understood as if God were moved to create in order to secure the admiration, the applause, and the adulation of creatures. The glory that they give is not something extorted from them, but something that arises spontaneously from the perfections with which they have been endowed.

for Him to deify the disorderly.[11] Man finds difficulty in reconciling the conflicting claims of sense and spirit. His sensibility—that is, the inclinations of his feeling and emotional nature—is not necessarily controlled by reason, but is capable of receiving such control. Because man is a reasonable being, the sway of reason must extend over all his free activities. If there is in any part of that kingdom of man a successful revolt, he is found faithless to his true self—to his nature and to the God Who created that nature. He defeats the purpose of his creation. He is, if left to his own resources, ever menaced by this defeat. For, by reason of his sensitive nature, he tends strongly toward those things which promise immediate delight and satisfaction and is prone to sacrifice for them the remote and less tangible satisfactions promised by reason and faith. Ease, comfort, luxury, pleasant tastes, touches, sights, sounds, honors, distinctions, wealth, sentimental affections, flattery, indolence—all this makes a strong appeal to man and tempts him away from the life of reason to indulgence in the life of sense. Only through the possession of the virtue of temperance will he be able to maintain a constant and tranquil domination over the stirrings of his sensibility.[12]

[11] This could not be too much insisted on or repeated too often. The supernatural is not to be likened to a sort of "plating" of precious metal, which can be fixed on to and give a fair appearance to another metal, however base it may be. The supernatural penetrates and sublimates nature. It can do this only when the nature is true. It cannot sublimate the corrupt.

[12] This life of the sensibility in man is often, but incorrectly, termed his "animal life." The expression is to be avoided. Something corresponding to the life that embraces such activities as have their source in the animated organism in man is found in the animals, but the life that man has in common with the animals exists in him in a far superior manner. In him the life of sense, by being brought under the control of reason, can be made reasonable, but, even when not so controlled, it has a range, an amplitude, a virtuality, a force, a variety, a quasi-spirituality, that it has not in the animal. Sense life in man has a wider meaning and embraces all that vitality of the soul which is attended by organic reactions. It is that vast complex of feelings,

The *role* of temperance is to enable a man to observe due measure in according satisfaction to his sensitive being; but a man's difficulties are not ended when he has acquired the habit of observing the golden mean prescribed by reason in the use of pleasures. He is, at times, called upon to face hardships, pain, and danger, and even death, if he is resolved not to swerve, under any threat, from the law of right conduct. If he is to prove steadfast in all crises and never prove faithless to manly virtue, he must, by constant trial and self-discipline, acquire the virtue of fortitude.

Temperance and fortitude maintain order in a man's own inner being: the one renders him proof against the appeal of pleasure, the other renders him strong against the fear of pain. But man is not meant to live an isolated existence. Life brings him into multiple relations with his fellow men. He works out his destiny as a member of the social body. He has contacts with equals, superiors, and subordinates. He must bear himself reasonably toward all. This is not easy, for, under a radical impulse toward expansion, man is tempted to realize aggrandizement at the expense of his neighbors. The thirst for greatness leads to all kinds of injustices. A man frequently finds himself a prey to the suggestion that he can elevate himself by lowering another. It is only by the acquisition of the virtue of justice that the tendency to seek aggrandizement at the expense of a neighbor's property or reputation is mastered.

---

sentiments, emotions, imaginings, passions of joy, fear, love, sadness, anger, indignation, etc., which constitutes a great part of the vital experience of each rational individual. When a man is said to lead "an animal life," this is ordinarily taken to imply that he is given up to the grosser satisfactions of sense; but properly speaking, it is equivalent to living a life according to the senses. This means a life in which the vast bulk of a man's vital sense activity is not under the control of reason, but is little more than a series of responses to external stimuli playing on the sensibility, including the imagination. A sense life is a life of impulse as opposed to a life of deliberate and reasoned choice.

WHY THE CROSS?

Finally, there is need of constant vigilance, quick decision, and unerring judgment if a man is to secure that all his deliberate activities serve to promote his final happiness. Prudence is the virtue whose function it is to enable a person to decide, easily, promptly, and correctly, what he is to do or to avoid doing, in each case calling for decision, in order to tend unswervingly toward the goal of perfect manhood.

The ways in which man can swerve from the law of reason are manifold. They are not exhausted when he has overcome his tendencies toward intemperance, cowardice, injustice, and imprudence. He can sin against his rational nature itself by the perverse use of the highest prerogative that he enjoys, namely, free will. He is exposed to the danger of taking pride in this power he has, of being master of his own destiny. "God made man from the beginning and left him in the hand of his own counsel." [13] He may, forgetting his condition as creature, aspire to make the dictates of his own reason and the inclinations of his own will his ultimate rule of conduct. His pride might suggest to him that it does not become his dignity as a free being that his line of action should be traced for him by a reason higher than his own, and imposed on him by a will other than his own. In this, man would prove himself a traitor to true manhood; for it would be to lay claim to an independence, an autonomy, that is repugnant to the essential dependence of the creature. Man could, by a special privilege of God, be made secure against the assaults of sensuality, imprudence, injustice, and even death; he could not be immunized against the lure of a false independence.

The preternatural gifts of integrity and immortality were God's remedy against the insubordination of the senses and the corruption of the body.

Seeing that God's purpose in creating man was to communicate to the human soul a participation of his own divine

---

[13] Sir 15: 14.

life, and seeing that His intention was that this communication should become richer day by day, the divine plan was in danger of being frustrated by the inherent weakness and instability of human nature. The uninterrupted process of deification is conditioned by the constant adherence of the created will to the will of the Creator. Such adherence requires that man should, in each circumstance, square his conduct with the demands of his rational nature. By an act of sensuality or cowardice, or injustice, or precipitation in judgment, or of pride, relations between God and man could be severed, to man's great loss. The Lord, from the beginning, adopted measures against this danger. He would not take from His creature the power of freely choosing between God and himself and electing the one or the other as his supreme good: but He fortified man against the danger of conflict between sensibility and reason. By the preternatural gift of integrity, man could, without toil or effort, impose the law of reason on his sense tendencies. The gift is called preternatural because it bestows something that does not belong strictly to the constitution of human nature. Normally, the rule of reason over the lower faculties is constitutional and is imposed only after much struggle. The moral virtues of temperance, fortitude, justice, and prudence, according to the ordinary law of things, could be acquired only after years of sustained and unremitting effort. By the gift of integrity, the moral rectitude that is the fruit of the virtues was bestowed in a moment. Without any cost to himself, order was established in man's composite nature. Sense was subject to reason, and reason, in its turn, subjected itself readily to God. It was not tempted from its allegiance to the Most High by the solicitations of sensuality. Undisturbed by passion, the will of man readily conformed itself to the will of God.

God was not content with dispensing man from the laborious pursuit of virtue by establishing, at the outset, perfect harmony between sense and reason; He, as well, furnished him with an antidote against the natural tendency to disintegration, which belongs to all composite things. It is in keeping with the nature of the body, composed as it is of diverse elements, that it should, under the action of external forces, tend to infirmity and dissolution. God gave man a preservative against decay: He made him immortal; He enabled him not to die, though He did not take away radically the natural destination to death. Man was preserved from death by the preternatural gift of immortality. God's benefits did not end here. Man was not only dispensed from the toilsome acquisition of the moral virtues, he was also saved from the slow and painful quest of knowledge. To his intellect, without labor on his part, was given an understanding of human things, surpassing in range and depth anything that the world has since known.[14]

All this preternatural splendor of moral and intellectual beauty was bestowed on man in order that no obstacle might be presented to the progressive divinization of his soul. The rectitude given by the gifts of integrity, science, and immortality made him an apt receptacle for the inflow of the divine life.

There is another important aspect of the divine plan that must not be overlooked. The supernatural and preternatural privileges were conferred on the first parents of the human race, not on an individual title. Divine grace and its attendant perfections were made to be the ornament of human nature itself. It came to the persons through their nature. Hence every child of Adam, in deriving his nature from his parents, was meant to receive it invested with the glory of grace and integrity. As each one would reach the age of responsibility, he would experience no opposition in himself to the free evolution of the divine life in his soul. Each person would, of course, retain the power to prefer himself to God, the power of freely choosing his final end.[15] But if he chose rightly, then his

[14] The knowledge of our Savior and that of the Blessed Virgin are, of course, excepted.

[15] This is on the supposition that human nature would not have been confirmed in grace if our first parents had successfully withstood their trial. There is no good reason to assert this.

life would be a steady progress toward an ever closer assimilation to God. The gifts of grace would remain unequal, but all men would, in their own proper measure, resemble the Blessed Virgin Mary in her uninterrupted ascent to the summits of spiritual perfection.

Sanctifying grace knits mankind into one supernatural organism, forming of all men one Mystical Body.

Even in the supernatural scheme, man was made to tend toward his perfection in the framework of a spiritual society. It is his nature to be a member of society. The elevation by grace respects this radical exigency of the human species.

In the plan of God, men were destined to be bound together, not only by the ties of nature, but by the ties of supernature. As in their veins was to flow the common blood of the human family, so through their souls was to course the common life-giving stream of grace. As all were unified on the plane of nature, so all were meant to be unified in the supernatural plane. Men were meant to form not merely one family, they were planned to function as members of one Mystical Body, all sharing in the same supernatural life. The whole human species was to work its way to its final goal as one man.[16] "In this way," says St. Thomas, "the whole multitude of men, destined to receive human nature from the first parent of the race, is to be considered one group or rather one body of a single individual: in this multitude each man, Adam himself included, can be considered a single person or a member of the multitude, which in its own order of nature is derived from a single individual." [17]

---

[16] Although this body (i.e., the whole Mystical Body of humanity) be composed of a great number of members, still, in the eyes of God, it is but one body. God is the source of unity. Sin is the source of disunion, for it brings separation from God, the source of unity. (See Ven. Libermann, *Écrits spirituels*, p. 61).

[17] *Quaest, disp. de malo*, q. 4, a. 1. Porphyry, quoted by St. Thomas (I-II, q. 81, a. 1), says that "in virtue of their participation in the same species, the multitude of men are as one man." Accordingly, continues

As the life blood flows through all the members of the living body, supplying its suitable nourishment to each part and enabling it to fulfill its appropriate function, so the life blood of the soul, that is, sanctifying grace and divine charity, was to stream through all the members of the vast, mystic, human body, imparting to each a divine vigor and empowering it to exercise its due role in relation to the other members and to the body as a whole. Adam was created to be the head, "from whom the whole body, being compacted and fitly joined together, by what every joint supplieth, according to the operation in the measure of every part, maketh increase of the body unto the edifying of itself in charity." [18] It is in the realm of the spirit and not in the realm of matter that men can be made one. It is the divine nature of charity that will bring about that unification of humanity and universal brotherhood of men, and not soulless materialism, which is the dream of international atheists.

> *All that God required on the part of man for all these benefits was that man should interiorly and exteriorly profess his willing dependence on, and subjection to, his Maker.*

The realization of the divine scheme demanded, as has been said, the conformity of the human will to the divine will. To be deified, man should stand in the truth. He was a creature, and to abide in the truth for him was to show the disposition of "creatureliness" in thought and in act. He should acknowledge in his heart and profess, in some practical manner, that he depended—and depended willingly—on God for all the glory with which he was clothed. God ordained a sign by which this willing and loving subjection of the creature to the Creator should be testified in a constant and practical manner. St. Thomas

---

St. Thomas, "the multitude of human beings descended from Adam are so many members of one unique body of one specific kind."

[18] Eph 4: 16.

writes: "Because the state of justice depended on this, that the human will should subject itself to God, the Lord made certain injunctions by which He forbade man to eat of the tree of knowledge of good and evil. The eating of this was not prohibited as being in itself evil, but in order that in this small matter men should do something for the sole reason that it was commanded by God." [19]

The fruit of the tree of knowledge was for man's use, as well as all the other fruits of the garden. Man's abstaining from personal usage of it was the outward sign of his free subjection to God. It was a kind of sacrifice appropriate to the religion of Eden. No hardship or pain was caused by this deprivation. Sacrifice is a visible sign or symbolic action instituted by God, by which man acknowledges God's supreme dominion over him and his total dependence on God. The expropriation from man's usage of something belonging to man—an expropriation carried out by real or equivalent destruction—is the ordinary form of this symbolic gesture of dependence. In the Garden of Eden, the fruit, which man did not allow himself to consume, was destroyed as far as his usage of it was concerned. As really as if he burned it on an altar, he, by his own act, deprived himself of the power of using it. This non-usage was an eloquent testimony, daily renewed, that not only the fruit, which was thus made sacred to God by being distrained from man's usage, but what that fruit symbolized, namely, man and all that man possessed, wholly belonged to God. To this daily sacrifice on the part of the creature corresponded a constant communication of divine life on the part of the Creator. The whole essence of religion is comprised in sacrifice and communion.

> *"Blessed are the pure of heart, for they shall see God." The beatitude was verified in the days of original justice.*

For a brief space, God's plan was realized on earth. Human nature in Adam and Eve was perfectly docile to God

[19] *Comp. theol.*, pt. 2, ch. 188.

and receptive of His communications. These two persons received continual infusions of divine grace. Their every act was true, blameless, perfect, and done not solely out of regard for the demands of reason but also in accordance with the requirements of filial love. They "did the truth in charity."[20] The Lord, taking human form, came and walked with them at eventide under the trees of Paradise.[21] This contact with God and intimacy with Him flooded with delight the souls of our first parents. The gladness of their souls affected their senses. They were bewilderingly happy in all their being. "In the beginning the soul tended always and in all things toward God and united itself to Him alone. God, in return, communicated Himself to the soul and in an even more perfect manner. This took place in the higher part of the soul, but perfect harmony, reigning between the higher part of the soul and the inferior part, the effects of the divine communications, made their way from the spirit to the senses and filled them with the enjoyment of God."[22]

The heavenly Father created a fair setting for this happy life of His children. He placed them in a paradise of delights, of a clear atmosphere, pleasant temperature, fragrant flowers, and ever fruitful trees. But the essential element in man's happiness was not contributed by pleasant surroundings, but by the close union of his soul with God. If he lacked God's intimacy and friendship, all the rest would quickly pall on him. Adam was supremely happy because he enjoyed a lofty contemplation of God, though such contemplation as yet was through the veils of faith. Faith was, through life's action, to deepen gradually until, at the end of earth's pilgrimage, it should yield place to the intuitive vision of the divine essence.

Though elevated to such sublime heights of spiritual life, our first parents remained essentially creatures. They

[20] Eph 4: 15.

[21] Gen 3: 8. This verse obviously refers to something habitual on the part of God, in His relations with His creatures.

[22] Ven. Libermann, *Écrits spirituels*, pp. 33, 34.

were not God. The happiness that was theirs was possessed in dependence on another. The divine independence was not theirs. In that, they were exposed to temptation. It could be suggested to them that they might emulate the independence of God and owe naught to anyone but themselves. It was on this suggestion that they made shipwreck of their happiness. "You shall be as gods," said the tempter, "knowing good and evil." Satan said to them in equivalent terms: "This excellence, this rich life, this happiness you hold of God, you could have them in yourselves, as inherent to and as being the prerogatives of your own nature."[23] Satan lied. "When he speaketh a lie he speaketh of his own; for he is a liar and the father thereof."[24] Our first parents yielded to his evil suggestion and, yielding, precipitated the great catastrophe of human nature. Aiming, through pride, at an independence that is intrinsically incompatible with creaturehood, they fell, and in their fall they involved all human nature, that is, the whole race of mankind. In this way was committed the Original Sin. The nature of this great transgression and its consequence must be clearly explained if a proper understanding is to be had of the plan of redemption that God, in His mercy, designed for the salvation of the world.

God created man to communicate to him a participation in the divine nature. This communication cannot pursue its course uninterruptedly unless man is reasonable in all his ways, never swerving from the law of righteousness. For God cannot deify the irrational. If man is to remain constantly true to himself—that is, to his own rational nature—he must possess the moral virtues perfectly. The acquisition of these virtues demands time and labor, for they are acquired only by the constant repetition of good acts. To enable man to be perfectly receptive of the

---

[23] Ibid., p. 24.
[24] Jn 8: 44.

divinity from the beginning, God made man's composite nature harmonious and perfect by imparting to him the preternatural gift of integrity. To this gift he added those of science and immortality. In a moment, man was given the moral rectitude that it would normally take years to achieve. Man could not be tempted to what was base; but he could be tempted to aspire to what was above him. Satan suggested to him to aim at the independence proper to the Almighty. He yielded to the suggestion and sinned through pride. All human nature fell in the fall of its fount and origin.

CHAPTER EIGHT

*By one man sin entered into this world, and by sin, death:
and so death passed upon all men, in whom all have
sinned.*

—ROMANS 5: 12

*Man, having revolted against God, felt instantaneously a
revolt in his own being. His sensitive nature rebels against
his reason.*

THE DISASTER that overtook the human race, through
Original Sin, was one of appalling magnitude. The tie that
bound the human will to the divine in loving subjection
being snapped, divine charity was straightaway extinguished. Charity had been the bond of all creation. It had
preserved order in man's own being; it bound him to his
fellows; it linked all with God. Harmony disappeared with
charity. The creation broke up into a welter of warring
elements—for sin works as a force of disintegration.

The rebellion against God had its echo in man's own
interior being. The willing subjection of the sensitive nature to reason abruptly ended. The orders of reason were
first resisted, then flouted. In the state of justice, a stream
of delight had overflowed from the higher faculties on the
lower. This stream was now dried at its source. Pleasure
and delight no longer came from above. The senses clam-
ored in vain to the spirit for the gratification for which
they hungered. "The little ones have asked for bread, and
there was none to break it to them. They that were fed
delicately have died in the streets. They that were brought
up in scarlet have embraced the dung." [1]

---

[1] *Jerem. thren.*, 4, vv. 4–5.

Starved because of the inability of the spiritual faculties to supply their wants, the appetitive tendencies of the sensitive nature, deaf to the remonstrances of reason, sought the satisfaction of their cravings wherever such satisfaction offered itself. Taste, touch, sight, hearing, imagination, memory—each pursued what promised gratification, indifferent to the welfare of the person. What is called the animal nature[2] in man fell from the dignity of "participated reason" it enjoyed in the state of original justice.

What rendered man's state all the more pitiable was that—the natural light of his intelligence not being eclipsed—he could still see and condemn the disorder in himself and yet remain practically powerless to check it.[3] There was found a mocking irony in the false words of Satan. Adam had tasted of the tree of knowledge of good and evil. He knew what was good and was unable to accomplish it. He knew what was evil and was powerless to avoid it.[4] God knows evil without experiencing it in Himself. It is not so with man, who knows it by contact with it, by finding himself enmeshed in its toils. No wonder that the absurd pretensions of the creature earned the divine mockery. And God said, when He had clothed the nakedness of the first man and the first woman: "Behold, Adam is become as one of us, knowing good and evil."[5]

> *Nature itself revolts against man. The earth yields him sustenance only at the cost of severe toil.*

By the prevarication of him who was appointed by God the lord of creation, creatures were violently wrested from the course traced for them by God's providence. Created to proclaim God's glory, they were made to serve man's lusts.

---

[2] See note 12 in chapter 7, above.

[3] In the state of fallen nature, man can conform to reason in some things, but not for long, and not with regard to all the prescriptions of the whole natural law.

[4] See Gen 2: 9, 17; 3: 5.

[5] Gen 3: 22.

They were torn from that mediate, though perfect, orientation toward God which had been theirs, when they ministered to man in the state of innocence. "For the creature was made subject to vanity, not willingly, but by reason of him that made it subject, . . . for we know that every creature groaneth and travaileth in pain until now."[6]

The earth reflects the rebellion of its master. Man's efforts to retain his despotic control over the exterior world met with stubborn resistance. Labor, sustained and toilsome, has to be endured if he is to extract from the unwilling earth what is needed to maintain him in life. Let him relax his efforts for a while, and the fruitful land becomes a howling wilderness. "Cursed is the earth in thy work," said God to Adam, "with labor and toil shalt thou eat thereof all the days of thy life. Thorns and thistles shall it bring forth to thee: And thou shalt eat the herbs of the earth. In the sweat of thy face shalt thou eat bread till thou return to the earth out of which thou wast taken."[7] With the banishment from the Garden of Paradise, where all man's needs were supplied without any painful effort on his part, began that dire struggle for existence, that life of hardship, pain, and danger which has remained man's lot ever since. His time on earth is one long warfare with the forces of nature. Day by day he has to wrestle with them in order to force them to yield what is required to keep body and soul together during the short days of his earthly pilgrimage. This struggle, bitter as it is and will ever remain, is not the severest chastisement of man's folly in revolting from God.

By his fall, man lost his hold on life and became a prey to all the ills of mortality.

In breaking with God, man forfeited, along with integrity, the preternatural gift of immortality. The barriers to the tendency to dissolution, inherent in the body, were removed. The loss of perfect control exercised by the

[6] Rom 8: 20, 22.
[7] Gen 3: 17–19.

spiritual part of man over the corporeal is the origin of death and of all the pains, disease, and infirmity that precede and prepare the way for it. "The life and well-being of the body depend on its being subject to the influence of the soul, as that which is capable of perfection depends on that which perfects it. On the other hand, death and disease and other corporeal defects are caused by the absence of subjection of the body to the soul. Wherefore, just as the resistance of the flesh to the spirit is the chastisement of the sin of the first parents of the human race, so also is it as regards death and all bodily defects."[8] As a chastisement of sin, man's earthly pilgrimage becomes a return to the dust from which his body was formed. God had warned Adam of this on the day He had placed him in the paradise of delights: "Of the tree of knowledge of good and evil, thou shall not eat. For in what day soever thou shalt eat of it, thou shalt die the death."[9]

> *After the Fall, the rebellious passions interfered with the functioning of the intellect, and even natural truths became difficult for man to seize.*

In the state of innocence, Adam enjoyed immense knowledge. He had infused science from the beginning. He added, day by day, to this initial stock of knowledge. His magnificent intelligence, undisturbed by passion, functioned freely and powerfully. Senses and imagination, being in a perfect state, faithfully served the intellect. The exterior world supplied a vast supply of objects for the exercise of thought. The attributes of the Creator were, without effort and with delight, deciphered from the scroll of creation, spread before Adam's mental gaze. "In those days the first man and woman drew from creatures far more satisfaction than does the sinner who greedily pursues them and places his beatitude in them."[10] The

[8] *Summa theologiae*, II-II, q. 164, a. 1.
[9] Gen 2: 17.
[10] Ven. Libermann, *Écrits spirituels*, p. 34.

due order in which external objects stood to sense and imagination, and these faculties, in their turn, to reason, was rudely disturbed by sin. The dark clouds of ignorance began to gather in the hitherto serene heaven of man's mind. The turbulence of the passions interfered with the play of the reason. Man began to find it difficult to contemplate steadily the truths that conflicted with his perverse inclinations. His judgments became uncertain, wavering, and false. The original light gradually faded. Knowledge declined. Error accumulated. The understanding was darkened. An inclination for the false developed. "The good of man," says St. Thomas, "is to be according to reason." [11] Man lost his taste for this good, developing a sympathy for the opposing evil, for error.

The sin of Adam was not one of sensuality, but of pride.
To understand why the consequences of Adam's act were so disastrous, it is necessary to grasp the full significance of that act. It was no mere weak yielding to the attraction of a luscious and forbidden fruit. It was not the fruit itself that was the temptation, but the prospect that Satan held out to him as a consequence of the eating of the fruit. The head of the human race aimed at being as God. He yielded to the ambition of emulating the Almighty as regards the knowledge of good and evil. This meant the proud resolve to determine for himself, by his own native power, what should be good, and what evil for him to do. [12] He wished to be the rule of his own conduct. He would be the ultimate source, the very fount and origin of what was the true and what was the good for man. That should be good for him, that was according to his own will, not what was according to the will of God. That should be true which recommended itself to his reason, not what was according to the divine ideas. "Both Satan and Adam

---

[11] *Summa theologiae*, II-II, q. 141, a. 1, and passim.
[12] Ibid., q. 563, a. 2, c.

willed to be self-dependent to the contempt of the divine ruling: and from this point of view aimed at equality with God." [13]

The first man, in reaching out for the forbidden fruit, yielded to the ambition to be himself the artisan of his own beatitude. He hoped that by the resources of his own nature and of the world subject to his control, he could achieve his happiness without any dependence on a superhuman power. This was the beginning of that strange aberration traceable through the whole course of human history—the aberration that manifests itself in the perverse ambition of man to attain to the " 'absolute' by his own efforts."[14] The Fall, in the motive that inspired it, is ever being renewed down along the ages.

Adam's act was a practical denial of the essential relation of dependence in which the creature stands to the Creator. It was a negation of his "creaturehood." The eating from the tree of knowledge was a gesture of fearful import: it was a solemn declaration of human independence; it was, equivalently, an unfurling of the standard of revolt against God by the head of mankind and on its behalf. The chief of the race was not unaware of the dreadful gravity of his act and of its consequences. The prohibition had been accompanied by solemn warnings and by the menace of dire consequences in case of its violation. The brief, simple, and unrhetorical narrative of Scripture gives us no insight into the tense and tragic struggle of soul that took place in the garden as Adam wrestled with a temptation proportioned to the grandeur of his endowments. It was a crisis on a scale unparalleled in history. On its issue hung the destinies of the whole human family. Adam had force and firmness of will, was endowed with penetration of intelligence, and enjoyed the intimate friendship of God. Alluring in the extreme must have been the colors of the destiny painted for him

[13] Ibid.

[14] This folly is the germ of all the monstrous systems of Monism—pantheism included.

by Satan, seeing that its appeal overcame the resistance of the strongest will and the mightiest intelligence that the world has ever known, with one exception. The temptation in the garden has its parallel and its contrast in the temptation of Christ in the desert.

The fatal decision was taken, and the fair vision conjured up for Adam dissolved as an unsubstantial dream. There is no happiness unless through union with God. Man is doomed to misery when he ceases to depend on his Maker. When he turns his back on goods that are imperishable and divine, he develops a fatal tendency toward such as yield a satisfaction that is transient and ephemeral. Leaving the true good, which he can attain to by the aid of God, he falls a prey to a craving for the phantom good, attainable by human resources.

No injustice was done to human nature, as such, when it was stripped of its preternatural gifts as a chastisement of sin.

It is easy to understand that sanctifying grace should disappear from the souls of our first parents in consequence of their sin. Charity, the characteristic effect of sanctifying grace, means friendship with God. Mortal sin means aversion from God. It is obvious that these two, being incompatible, cannot coexist in the same soul. The preternatural gifts of integrity, immortality, and science were marks of God's friendship for man, but are not in themselves in radical opposition to sin. The good they bestow remains of the created order. True, it is only by a gift in no wise required by the exigencies of his nature that man could have his bodily *life* prolonged uninterruptedly. Still, unending life is not supernatural life or the life of charity. Neither integrity, nor science, nor immortality gives man any participation in the divine. The perfection given by the preternatural gifts is in one sense natural, in that it perfects man along the lines of his own nature. It is not natural in the sense that it does not spring from, nor is it an exigency of, the constituent elements of human nature. In other words, the perfection given by the preternatural gifts is in no wise required by man's nature, and need not be given to it, and can be absent without human nature being itself wanting in anything that is essential to its constitution.

When punished by the withdrawal of integrity, Adam could not complain that God had taken from him anything that was his right as man. The perfect submission of the passions to reason is according to man's nature: but it is according to nature that this submission be secured only after sustained and intense moral effort and struggle. Sense has its own tendencies; reason has its tendencies. The operations of sense enter into play before those of reason. It is natural, then, that the inclinations of sense should anticipate the inclinations of the spirit. The functioning of the faculties of the sensitive nature is more vivid than the functioning of the faculties of reason. The tangible realities affect man more forcibly than the intangible. To subordinate the appeal of the former to the appeal of the latter, *naturally*, demands effort.

When man had deliberately forfeited the favor of God, there was no injustice in his not being dispensed from this moral struggle, which has its necessity in the very constitution of his being. It was but fitting that man, having aspired to create by his own efforts the reign of reason in himself, should be left by God to his own resources. When man fails in his endeavor, he cannot plead that he has been condemned to an unequal struggle by being deprived of the arms with which his nature, by right, should be equipped. The plea cannot be urged, because God has taken from rational nature nothing that belongs to it intrinsically. Man has only himself to blame if he finds himself a prey to the experience to which utterance was given by the pagan poet: "I see what is right and I give it my approval, but I follow the evil course." The same thought was re-echoed many years later by St. Paul, saying: "For the good which I will, I do not; but the evil which I will not, that I do. . . . I am delighted with the law of God according to the inward man, but I see another law in my members fighting against the law of my mind, and captivating me in the law of sin that is in my members."[15] Man's ambition to be as God, knowing good and evil, has been realized with tragic irony.

As there would have been solidarity between Adam and his descendants had he proved faithful, so is there solidarity between him and them in his revolt.

The crowning disaster of the first prevarication was that Adam in sinning did not sin merely as an individual. Through his act sinned and fell the human nature that existed in him as in its source. Adam and his children form a unity that is closer and more intimate than the social unity that exists between members of the same family. It must be assimilated rather to the union that binds together the members of one human body, or such as exists between the parent stock and the branches that spring from it. As mankind, in the supernatural plane, was constituted by God one Mystical Body, so in its fallen state it remains one, with Adam as its head. The first man was, as it were, an incarnation in himself of the totality of human nature.[16] During a space he was, in himself, all humanity. The nature that was in him shared his destiny. It would ever be what it was in its principle. It was to stand or fall by him. It was to be "graced" or "dis-graced" by his decision. The latter proved to be its fate. The stream of humanity was defiled at its source. This defilement passes

[15] Rom 7: 19–23.

[16] St. Thomas writes: Our first parents were not merely two individuals created by God, but were made by Him as the fountain [*principia quaedam*] of all human nature. This human nature was to pass from them to their children clothed with the divine gift" (*Summa theologiae,* II-II, q. 164, a. 1, ad 3). See also Père Prat, S.J., *Théologie de Saint Paul,* 1:282. The sin of Adam is common to him and us, because we with him form one flesh. At a given time, *all flesh* was concentrated in Adam. It is because we trace our descent to him, according to *the flesh,* that there is established between him and us that solidarity, in virtue of which his sin is ours.

from generation to generation in the process by which life is transmitted.

The solidarity of mankind in the Fall is a mystery akin to the mystery of the solidarity in grace that there would have been had the chief of humanity proved faithful in his trial. By his personal act, human nature in him lost its supernatural and preternatural endowments. To his descendants it was only his nature he could transmit. It was passed on in that state to which it had been reduced by Original Sin, that is, stripped of original justice and reduced to its bare essentials. Adam's act did not pass to his children, but his nature, as affected by that act, was transmitted. Every child of the race, as it comes into being by the way of generation, inherits this nature, shorn of grace and integrity. In Adam and Eve, as being the origin of all humanity, there fell both person and nature.

It is the teaching of St. Thomas that all persons throughout the ages stand to Adam in a relation that finds its parallel only in that which exists between the members and the head in the human body. The great theologian, using this analogy, points out that the different individuals of the human race participate in the guilt of the head of the race in a way that is to be compared to that in which the members of the body that execute a criminal act share in the evil that has its origin in the principle of man's activities, namely, the will. "The wicked glance of the eye and the evil deed of the hand express, after their manner, the sinful determination that has been formed in the spiritual faculties. The outward act of the body bears the impress of the disorder that has its origin in the will. So, too, Adam's descendants bear in their nature the impress of the disorder that arose in the will of the head of the race when he fell from justice." [17]

Hence it is that those who came from Adam's stock, by the channel of generation, lack that proper relation to God which existed in the state of original justice. As an

[17] *De malo*, q. 4, a. 1.

individual involves his whole person in his guilt, so the head of the universal human body involved all the members of that body in his sin. All men are born enemies of God, not because of any personal guilt attaching to them, but because of the nature lacking the order of justice, that they inherit. "In the chief of humanity, it was through the disorder of the person that the nature was vitiated: in the members of the race, it is through the disorder of the nature that the person is tainted." [18]

The fault of Adam was an act of disobedience prompted by pride and self-love. This fatal tendency to a perverse egoism clings to fallen human nature and is at the root of all sins. "To attach oneself passionately to the visible and with a wretched hardihood to set at defiance the invisible after having lost the taste for it, such is the hereditary blemish with which the nature of man is affected. At conception each receives a soul that no longer turns with ease toward God, a sensuality that reason finds it difficult to curb, and an organism that tends to dissolution by the interaction of the elements that constitute it. Since Original Sin consists above all in the absence of original justice and in the loss of the primal innocence, it resides chiefly in that higher part of the soul which is its spiritual summit: in its origin it is in that faculty which sets in motion all the others, that is, the will." [19] The aversion from the uncreated good and the preference for the immediate created good, being what is formal in all sin, is characteristic of the sin of nature as well. The darkness of mind and the tendency to sensuality are but the material elements in the sin inherited from the first parents of the human race.

> *In Baptism is buried what is formal in Original Sin: but the material element, that is, the concupiscences, cling to the regenerated soul after it has been cleansed from guilt.*

Adam received grace and charity through the merits of the Redeemer, Who was to come after the lapse of many

[18] *La Vie spirituelle* (March, 1930), p. 217.
[19] Ibid., p. 227.

WHY THE CROSS?

centuries, but his repentance and his reentry into grace affected his person only.[20] In his restoration, human nature itself was not restored. That nature could reconquer grace only piecemeal, as it were; that is, in each individual person that would receive the favor of God. It was not nature itself, but each person having that nature, that was restored to grace by being incorporated in Christ. As the child of Adam emerges from the waters of baptism, he is a person who is once more a child of God, but whose nature retains some of the flaws left in it by Original Sin, the inherited guilt. The person is sanctified, but the nature has not recovered the perfections with which it had been gratuitously endowed in the beginning. Sanctifying grace is given back by the merits of Christ, but not the preternatural gifts. The nature in each man remains wounded, and only by a gradual process is it able, through the healing action of the grace of Christ, to recover something of its pristine vigor and integrity. "Unhappy man," says St. Paul, "who shall deliver me from the body of this death?" He answers his own question, saying: "The grace of God by Jesus Christ our Lord." [21]

Because of his tainted nature, man, though redeemed, finds it difficult to pursue even a rational ideal; he experiences still greater difficulty in pursuing a superhuman ideal.

In the loss of the gift of integrity, which had preserved the sensitive and rational powers in a perfect harmony, is found the solution of the many perplexing problems presented by human conduct. Man, even in the state of grace, finds a great difficulty in resisting the vivacious appeal of sense and in giving ear to the comparatively

[20] St. Thomas writes: "But what is strictly personal, such as personal acts and everything relating to these, is not transmitted from parents to children. For instance, a man skilled in the science of language does not hand on to his son the science he has acquired by his own personal efforts. It is only what pertains to the nature that passes from parents to children" (*Summa theologiae*, I-II, q. 81, a. 2).

[21] Rom 7: 24–25.

colder appeal of reason. He finds a still greater difficulty in rising above the purely rational and in responding to the call of the divine. He can do great, and even heroic, things, for human considerations, but has to overcome a strong resistance in his nature to do even a small thing out of regard for God. In devotion to an earthly cause, men readily face danger and death, and hardships more testing than death itself. For an empty distinction, for a little applause, they can impose considerable privations on themselves. Men can do much for a corruptible crown, but are reluctant to do even a little for an incorruptible one.[22] An early-twentieth-century writer contrasts, with sadness, the zeal and the self-sacrifice shown by the apostles and disciples of Communism, in pursuit of a purely earthly and material ideal, with the aversion from the spirit of renouncement and self-denial manifested by average Christians in the cause of God. Privations imposed by the fashion of the hour will be readily submitted to and cheerfully borne: privations commanded by God and His Church in the interests of the soul invariably encounter, on the part of the majority, pleas for dispensation. Whatever is human and "sub-supernatural" makes an appeal to the instincts of man's tainted nature: whatever is truly reasonable and, more especially, what is divine finds little response in those instincts. If the appeal of reason is resisted, it is understandable that the appeal of faith should meet with still greater opposition. Man may consent to suffer much for a natural end; he rebels instinctively against suffering for a supernatural end. In this lies the explanation of the sullen hostility to the God of revelation and to His Christ that is ever smoldering in the heart of humanity, and that periodically flames up into open revolt. This spirit of revolt is not confined to the avowed enemies of God: it finds an echo in every soul that is but partially subjugated to the grace of Christ.

[22] 1 Cor 9: 25.

Humanity, lost in Adam, is restored in Christ. God, with
divine magnanimity, Himself undertakes the cost of
restoration.

In Christ alone, man finds salvation. Each child of Adam
finds a return to God's friendship only through mystic
incorporation in the Redeemer. Incorporated in Adam,
he was lost; incorporated in Christ, he is restored. The
first head of the race had the fatal power to plunge all
human nature in ruin: he had not the power to rescue it
from the ruin into which it had been plunged. "By one
man sin entered into this world, and by sin death. . . .
Therefore, as by the offense of one, unto all men to
condemnation, so also by the justice of one, unto all men
to justification." [23]

Had God allowed things to follow their fatal course, the
disaster that fell on the race of Adam would have been
irretrievable. There was something of the finality of
Satan's revolt in Adam's evil decision, because of his clear
view of the consequences of his act and the resolution
with which it was willed. But, fortunately for mankind,
there was a difference. The angel's choice is, by nature,
irrevocable. Man can change. God took advantage of this
reversibility of human choice, to effect the salvation of His
creatures. Though Adam had no power of himself, even
when repentant for his evil act, to effect his return to God,
though he had still less power to restore his children to
their divine inheritance, yet a return to God was possible
for all, if God were to intervene and change the course of
destiny started by the Fall. God did intervene.

The Creator had been infinitely generous, in the literal
sense of the words, in the gifts He had bestowed on his
rational creatures at their creation. Man had, in his folly
and pride, at the suggestion of the tempter, flung back
his divine privileges in the face of his beneficent Lord.
The Almighty showed a divine magnanimity in forgiving
the insult and restoring to man the grace that he had

[23] Rom 5: 12, 18.

forfeited. The magnanimity is the more wonderful in this, that the burden of the restoration and its cost were assumed by the only-begotten Son of God.

Adam sinned by aiming at an autonomy that belongs to God alone. He aspired to this position of being able to determine what was his own good. He wished his own reason to be the ultimate source of truth. He sinned as head of the race. The Original Sin, therefore, not only affected his person but his nature as well. But as transmitted to his descendants, it affects directly the nature, not the person. In Adam, nature was stripped of grace and of all the preternatural gifts that had preserved it from disorder, corruption, and ignorance. It was nature thus deprived of grace and integrity that each child of Adam inherited. Hence, in this regard, sin is called the sin of nature. The whole of human nature was vitiated in Adam; each person is restored in Christ by being incorporated in Him mystically.

CHAPTER NINE

*For if, by the offense of one, many died, much more the grace
of God and the gift hath abounded unto many, by the grace
of one man, Jesus Christ.*

—ROMANS 5: 15

*Man, though restored to God's favor, labors under
disabilities from which he was free in the state of innocence.
His nature remains wounded even though it has recovered
grace.*

MAN WAS RESTORED in Christ, but not to the Garden
of Eden. His condition as "re-created" is not the same as
that which he enjoyed when first created. Grace returns,
but unattended by the glittering cortège of privileges that
followed it in the first days. Man's nature remains unchanged essentially, but is gravely wounded. The preternatural supports for its weakness have been withdrawn.
The environment in which recovered grace finds itself is
not so perfectly adapted to its activity as was the environment of old. It cannot put forth its energies with the same
ease in the regenerate soul as in the soul when innocent.
The loss of the preternatural gifts was followed by the
appearance in the soul of the three concupiscences. "For
all that is in the world," says St. John, "is the concupiscence of the flesh, the concupiscence of the eyes, and the
pride of life." [1] Even when the guilt of Original Sin has
been washed away by baptism, these three poisonous roots
of sin remain deeply planted in human nature. Man, even
when he has been readmitted to the divine presence,

---

[1] 1 Jn 2: 16.

retains a fatal tendency to tear himself away from God, his true happiness, and turn toward creatures that lure him by a mirage of bliss. Regenerate nature is wounded, and hence, though it can make its way toward God, its progress is slow and painful.

The theological virtues, faith, hope, and charity, given back with grace, find their activities hampered and their expansion impeded by the virulent activity of the concupiscences. By the divine virtues, the soul can establish contact with the Uncreated: by the concupiscences it is attracted to the created. The fatal tendency to find happiness in things outside of God is the sad heritage of the Original Sin. Regenerate man has two births. He is born of rebellious Adam before he is born of God.[2] The second birth does not cause all traces of the first to disappear. The child of Adam reveals a perverse inclination to assert his independence from God and to gratify sense and imagination in defiance of reason. Insubordination to any suprahuman authority and a tendency toward sensual indulgence are the characteristics of human nature even when the soul has been liberated from what is formal in Original Sin. To understand the errors and crimes of humanity and its recurrent reversions to a barbarism thought extinct, to understand the contradictory phenomena manifested in one's own inner life, is impossible unless a clear notion be formed of the disabilities under which human nature groans since its original revolt from God. Every Christian must remember that the first effect of his baptism has been to efface the guilt of inherited sin. But he ought to know, too, that even after this holy sacrament has planted in his soul a divine seed and all the principles of life of the new man, the old man in him, nevertheless, remains full of vitality and leaves in human nature many a trace of his persistent vitality. Were it not so, nature (i.e., fallen nature) would not show itself so

[2] Jn 3: 3–6. Jesus said: "Unless a man be born again, he cannot see the kingdom of God. . . . That which is born of the flesh is flesh, and that which is born of the spirit is spirit."

WHY THE CROSS?

antagonistic to grace.[3] Self-knowledge is difficult, if not impossible, without an insight into the nature of the concupiscences that are in us, the characteristic energy of the "old man."

> *The concupiscence of the flesh is a hunger for all kinds of bodily pleasures.*

Man, in the beginning, had enjoyed an existence passed in serenity, in the midst of satisfactions for every faculty, sensitive as well as spiritual. The memory of this blissful period has never been wholly obliterated from human consciousness. As it clings to human thought, it inspires vain hopes and dreams of the restoration to earth of the conditions of life that will banish labor and pain, distress and ignorance. It suggests those dreams that the enemies of God are ever vainly hoping to realize, dreams of an earthly paradise to be achieved by vast plans for the reorganization of the world. Man, in his perversity, never abandons the hope of scaling the heavens by force of arm and might of intellect.[4]

Man is in perpetual revolt against pain. He suffers from a nostalgia for Eden. He longs for the comfort, ease, leisure, freedom from painful toil, and enjoyment of every satisfaction that was meant to be his birthright. He rebels against the disabilities that the Fall has brought on him. He resentfully denies the Fall and refuses to recognize the inevitability of suffering. His senses hunger for the gratifications they innocently enjoyed in the days of original justice. Under the promptings of the concupiscence of the flesh, man hopes to still the conflict in himself by yielding to the desires of his clamorous senses. He expects

[3] See *Imitation of Christ*, bk. 3, ch. 54 and 55.
[4] Gen 11: 9. Each age sees a renewal of these blasphemous attempts. Humanism in the sixteenth, Rationalism in the eighteenth, Liberal Economics in the nineteenth, Communism in the twentieth century—each confidently aspires to the conquest of heaven. They aim at bringing heaven within the reach of earth. All these attempts end as the original one did, in a towering confusion.

to find contentment by giving rein to every impulse that holds out promise of a new sensation to be found in the unrestrained play of his animal faculties. "One must live one's life" is the cry of the old Adam in each individual. Pleasure to the instincts of fallen nature is regarded as synonymous with happiness.

Life for men, insofar as they fall under the tyranny of the concupiscence in them, becomes a bitter struggle for the possession of those means which will enable them to gratify without stint the sense of taste and the sense of touch. Man struggles for the opportunities of procuring those pleasures which he enjoys in common with the animals. The tie that united man's faculties in a perfect harmony being snapped, each faculty tends to pursue its own object, in accordance with its own particular inclination and regardless of the rest.[5] Fallen man has no hesitation in exploiting and degrading his fellow creatures to make them minister to his bodily pleasures. The concupiscence of the flesh is insatiable in its demands. It seeks not merely the gratification of lust; it pursues everything that ministers to the love of ease and abhorrence of suffering.

Analysis of the concupiscence of the eyes: It is the inordinate desire of fame. It is a hunger for the glory that comes from creatures, and a contempt for that which comes from God.
Our first parents had known true greatness. They enjoyed the esteem that is extended to true worth. God Himself regarded them with favor. Their distinction marked them out for the envy of Lucifer, superior though he was to them in nature. It is not a base instinct in the soul to aspire and to love excellence. It is so constituted that it

[5] *Summa theologiae*, I-II, q. 82, a. 2, ad 2. The equilibrium of a composite body being destroyed, the composed elements disperse in different directions, each gravitating to its own proper end. So, the harmony set up by original justice being broken, the diverse faculties of the soul tend each to its own object, regardless of the interests of the person as a whole.

WHY THE CROSS?

must seek growth and expansion. The soul is a capacity for infinite reality to be possessed finitely. God satisfied this innate tendency of the soul in the beginning and, giving it Himself, imparted to it true worth.

With the loss of God went the loss of greatness, but not the hunger for greatness. Powerless to achieve true worth, the soul seeks after a worth that is fictitious. When restored to grace, it can ascend again to real eminence by binding itself to God; but it inherits a fatal tendency to satisfy its craving to be "something of worth," elsewhere than in God. This inclination to find glory through creatures is the concupiscence of the eyes. Under its stimulus, the soul hungers for honor, power, affection, esteem, fame—for all that might testify to its excellence and greatness. Glory and honor are an implicit acknowledgment of the presence of excellence in the person honored. Deep in his consciousness, man has an apprehension of his own emptiness and contingence. All the more eagerly does he hunger for tributes from others, to find in these tributes that which would cancel out the evidence of his own inner experience. He turns passionately and in exasperation from the conviction that he is left to himself, "a person nothing worth."

This is the explanation for the temper that, in the very least of men, makes them jealous of their honor and resentful of disesteem or even indifference. Few are they who are unmoved by what is said or thought of them by their fellows. Almost all can be wounded to the quick by a look, a word, a gesture that would imply their being held in little consideration. Though a man may be inwardly aware of his own insufficiency, he will regard it as a gross insult if he is regarded by others as one of whom account need not be taken. A slight, a reprimand, an oversight— any one of these things is sufficient to throw the average soul into a state of bitter resentment, a brooding sense of wrong, and a desire for vengeance.

In the praises of others, man seeks to find the assurance that his inner convictions deny him. He seeks from creatures as empty as himself the sense of greatness he cannot find in himself. To wealth, men readily pay court. Its possession confers a fictitious glory. Hence it is passionately sought after. In their eagerness for money and the privileges it commands, men treat lightly the sanctity of justice and even the sacredness of human life.

The concupiscence of the eyes is the fertile source of deeds of injustice and bloodshed. In its less violent incitations, it generates bitterness, contention, and quarreling among those who should be united by the bonds of mutual charity or mutual interest. Fallen nature hankers after the limelight. It craves to be taken notice of; to be talked about and to be looked up to. Falsity, pretence, and artificiality disfigure human relations because of this pursuit of an utterly unreal greatness. The vision of truth and reality necessarily becomes obscured for those who yield to the lure of earthly glory. When the Savior remarked the eager struggles among the Pharisees for the places of honor at feasts and the first chairs in the meetings of the Synagogue and their keen ambition to receive salutations in the market place and to be hailed as Rabbis, He said: "How can you believe, who receive glory from one another, and the glory which is from God alone you do not seek." [6]

Analysis of the "pride of life": It is the impulse to make an idol of self. By it, self is put in the place of God. It is the principle from which springs the tendency to the deification of man that continually manifests itself in the course of ages.

Man must worship something. The deep-rooted sense of the relativity of his being is at the origin of this instinct of his nature. Having lost original rectitude, he finds in himself a great reluctance to bow in reverent love and humility before the God of faith. He could, though fallen, pay obedience to the God of reason, but the Deity as revealed

[6] Jn 5: 44.

to him by the process of reasoning is too cold, too remote, too abstract, to receive a fervid worship. An object more tangible, more appealing, has to be sought. Man finds that object near at home. From the day he yielded to the suggestion of Satan to emulate God, he retains a violent tendency to refuse to recognize the relativity of his being and to aim at becoming for himself "the absolute." Under the stimulus of this pride, he tends to make of himself, or of something with which he can in some way identify himself, an idol to worship. A consuming egoism is the most pronounced characteristic of nature as tainted by Original Sin. The sacrifice *of* self, so prompt and joyous in the days of innocence, yields place to the sacrifice *to* self. Influenced by the third and strongest of the concupiscences, man places himself at the center of the universe, demands that all things should gravitate in their orbits in relation to him, and lays claim to the impassivity of God.

In this evil concupiscence is rooted the perverse tendency to deify man or something of man that is perpetually manifesting itself. Men have, in their insane pride, claimed divine honors. Human reason has been enthroned in the place of God. The deification of the State succeeded to the deification of the individual.

Fallen man, from having been God-centered, has become self-centered. He rebels against suffering or limitation of any kind. He is impatient of control. He tends to make his own reason the ultimate test of truth. He is unwilling to accept anything that does not recommend itself to his own judgment. His very agnosticism, while appearing to be intellectual humility, is, in reality, a colossal intellectual pride. Fallen nature tends to make itself the measure of all things, to establish its reason as the source of what is true, and its will as the source of what is good.[7] *Fallen man aims at being God and yet remains*

---

[7] *Summa theologiae*, II-II, q. 163, a. 2. St. Thomas writes: "Man sinned primarily in aiming at a resemblance of God (promised him by the serpent) in virtue of which be should be capable of fixing for himself moral good and moral evil."

very modest in his aspirations after godliness. He would usurp the prerogatives and yet manifests no great desire to imitate the virtues of God. It is true that he is not necessitated to this folly. The Fall has not essentially vitiated human reason. Man can still discern the natural law traced in his own being and recognize it as a transcript of the eternal law as relating to himself. But he has a fatal bias to ignore the ultimate foundation of the law of conduct existing in the divine mind, and to consider the findings of his own reason to be the final rule of things. The violence of the passions in revolt obscures the light of reason and prompts man to substitute for its ruling the dictates of animal instincts. The attempts of man to exalt himself above his native condition serve but to precipitate him downward below the human level. Self-indulgence, self-glorification, self-worship—these are the tendencies that are left in human nature as a consequence of Original Sin.

The Son of God, to save man, makes Himself man.
Becoming incarnate, He traces a plan of life which, if
followed by His disciples, will vanquish the concupiscences.
Left to his own resources, fallen man would have been powerless to extricate himself from the miserable condition into which he had fallen by Original Sin. God the Son came to the assistance of man in his helplessness, and, by the humanity He assumed, became the Redeemer of mankind. The Redemption won back for the human race the power to tend toward God through grace and the exercise of the divine virtues of faith, hope, and charity.

But man redeemed is not in the same condition as if he had not fallen. The original rectitude of his nature is not recovered in baptism. What has been cannot cease to be. The Fall is an immutable fact.[8] Adam can be repentant, but not innocent. The divine life of grace, on entering the

[8] St. Thomas notes that even God, though omnipotent, cannot make the past not to have been. The reason is that such a thing would involve contradiction, that is, a non-sense; see *Summa theologiae*, I, q. 25, a. 4.

soul, finds another life in possession. The stream of life from the New Adam encounters an adverse stream having its source in the old Adam. By rebirth in Christ, man is enabled to seek God once more, but he is not deprived of the unhappy power to seek himself. Until this fatal tendency away from God is conquered, grace cannot develop freely and exercise effective control over man's deliberate life.

The soul of the person redeemed may be likened to a battleground fought for by two contending and bitterly opposed forces. On the one side is ranged grace with the divine virtues of faith, hope and charity, the infused moral virtues of prudence, justice, temperance, and fortitude, and the gifts of the Holy Spirit, all ranged under its standard. On the opposite side are drawn up the three concupiscences with the many evil tendencies having their source in them. Each side struggles to secure the control of man's deliberate acts. The battle is fought out day by day. It sways in one direction or in the other according as grace or nature gains the upper hand. The follower of Christ must use all his endeavor to secure the victory for grace.

The Christian enterprise is an aiming at the conquest of that moral position which was lost in the Fall, as far as that position is recoverable in this life. The conquest can never be absolute. Integrity can never be regained. But something like its equivalent must be fought for by a sustained and uncompromising resistance to the pressure of the three concupiscences. These have to be warred down and reduced to impotence; they cannot be exterminated. The soul is not left to itself in this bitter fight. Christ combats with it. The Savior, by the sacrifice of the Passion, won the right to incorporate every human person with Himself, making each person participate in that life which dwells in the Sacred Humanity in its fullness.[9]

[9] Col 2: 9.

*There are two kinds of union with Christ. One may be called
passive, the other active. The second perfects the first. The
human life of the Christian must imitate the life of Christ.*

The Venerable Libermann writes: "Our union with the
Son of God, Incarnate, is twofold. The first kind may be
called passive. To this we but dispose ourselves and are
mere recipients. This is the union given to the soul as it
emerges from the state of sin. It takes place by the reception of the sacraments of the dead. The sacraments of the
living presuppose this union and increase it by augment-
ing the gifts of grace. *The second kind of union is one which
may be called active.* In it and by it, the soul directs itself
toward the Lord Jesus Christ and acts with a view to increasing and fortifying the union that exists between Him
and itself. The first union is but a state, or disposition of
the soul, which is a benefit of God. The second is *the
exercise of the activity* proper to that state, or propensity
toward God. It is an action of the soul. It is still a benefit of
God, for it is He Who impresses on the soul the movement
toward Himself. The soul, for its part, corresponds to this
impulse from God and allows itself to be carried onward.
The more a soul delivers itself to this second (or active)
union, the more it progresses in perfection and the more
its 'oneness' with Jesus increases. The souls who neglect
the second kind of union cannot hope to become more
perfectly one with Jesus by the mere frequentation of the
sacraments, because these latter produce their effects of
progress only when the requisite dispositions exist. The
dispositions consist precisely in an endeavor to practice
active union with Jesus." [10]

These words trace the program of the Christian life.
The soul is not perfectly redeemed the moment it is restored to grace. That is but the beginning. Man, even
when redeemed, carries within him a nature that needs to
be purged of the evil with which it continues to be in-
fected. The restoration to justice follows an order the

[10] Ven. Libermann, *Écrits spirituels*, pp. 64, 65.

reverse of that taken in the Fall. "Through Original Sin, it is human nature that corrupts and brings disaster on the person. In the redemption it is the person that is first restored, and through the person, the nature."[11] The Christian purifies his nature by effecting a harmony between his way of life and that of Christ. He is not perfectly one with Jesus immediately on receiving the first infusion of sanctifying grace. He effects that oneness insofar as he is successful in securing that the nature in him should, in its deliberate activity, vibrate in harmony with the humanity of Christ. The Christian practices active union with Christ when he strives to resemble the Divine Master in all his reactions to life. His function, as a follower of the Savior, is to handle life as Jesus handled life, bringing to bear on life's circumstances the very principles on which the Savior acted. He must regard all life's issues from the same angle of vision as that of the Redeemer. He must be persuaded that he is not, in his conduct, reacting to life as he ought unless his way of dealing with the duties that fall to his lot reflect something of the manner of the God-Man. This is true belief in Jesus. This is practical union with Him. It is by this path that disordered human nature makes its toilsome way back toward the happy equilibrium in which it once existed.

As it makes progress, grace begins to pour more abundantly into the soul from its source in the Sacred Humanity in which the Divinity resides corporally, that is, substantially.[12] According as nature is purified, grace functions more freely. The state of integrity had been bestowed on man in the interests of the unimpeded operations of divine grace. The return to rectitude, through a conquest of the concupiscences, has the same end in view. The practical imitation of Jesus involves the repression of the concupiscences and a resistance to their promptings. This means a continual crucifixion of self-love at the hands of

[11] *Summa theologiae*, III, q. 69, a. 3, ad 3. Compare I-II, q. 81, a. 1; q. 82, a. 1, ad 2.
[12] Col 2: 9.

men and of circumstances. "All those that wish to live godly in Christ Jesus shall suffer persecution."[13] But suffering, borne in union with Jesus Christ, is the most efficacious means of crushing that egoism which is so characteristic of fallen nature and is the chief enemy of grace.

Life is meant to be a process of purification of the fallen nature of each one of us.

The disorder left in the soul by Original Sin is the one enemy of man's happiness. The way to a happy life is found in the rectification of this disorder. The Savior saw, with sympathy, the struggle that confronted redeemed mankind. He gauged its extent, its bitterness, and its hardships. He drafted the scheme of redemption accordingly: His life on earth was drawn up as a brilliant plan of campaign against the three concupiscences that ravage the human soul.

The success of the individual man in forging for himself his personality in the order of grace will depend on the closeness with which he will adhere to that plan.

Jesus, in unfolding to His hearers the theory of life that was to uplift the human race and restore it in a measure to its original happiness, had ever before His eyes the living, concrete, fallen nature of man in all its miseries, its weakness and its needs. He was no abstract theorist out of touch with reality. He understood perfectly the difficulties presented by the human material that he had to forge to a divine form. He took His measures accordingly.

Suffering was an inevitable fact of life that had to be faced. It was brought into existence by man's own act, and yet man passionately refuses to admit its inevitableness. He hungers after the happiness of the earthly paradise— at least after the element of that happiness which consisted in its immunity from hardship, pain, and other ills of mortality. He sighs for the impassibility of Eden,

---

[13] 2 Tim 3: 12.

though not for the intimate union with his Maker that he enjoyed there. He longs for the earthly paradise, but he does not hunger for God.[14]

Now, though God does not do away with suffering, which is an immediate consequence of the loss of the preternatural gifts, He exercises a divine ingenuity in turning this evil thing into a good. He will not eliminate suffering from life, but He will make it serve to purify, perfect, and so restore to the fallen soul something of its pristine beauty and innocence. The soul, unpurified, can never be happy. Hence, suffering, by a strange paradox being made the instrument of purification, is made the means to happiness.

To men, the Savior speaks equivalently in the following terms: "You cannot be happy unless order be restored in your nature and the internal conflict in it ceases. This order cannot be established unless the disease of self-love be expelled from the soul. Suffering, in union with the suffering Christ, is a most potent remedy of this disease. In any event, as things are, it is inevitable. Revolt only intensifies it. Accepted bravely in a Christian spirit, it removes the obstacles to the inflow of the divine life of grace. Even if, with the growth in holiness, there goes an increase in suffering, there is given additional strength to bear it and an increasing appreciation of its spiritual value. The intimacy with God that results from progress in divine grace is more than ample compensation, even in this life, for the pain that has to be borne. *Believe My words, take My yoke upon you.* True, it is a yoke. But you will discover by experience 'that My yoke is sweet and My burden light,' and you will find rest for your souls." [15]

[14] St. Thomas points out that God willed suffering and toil, and the other disabilities of mortality, to remain after Original Sin is taken away in the sacrament of regeneration, in order that man might not be attracted to baptism by the desire of impassibility rather than by the desire of eternal life (*Summa theologiae*, III, q. 69, a. 3).

[15] See Mt 11: 29–30.

These are not the words of a mere visionary out of contact with the hard realities of human experience. They are the words of one who accepts the fait accompli and, taking things as they are, sets to work to create harmony out of confusion, order out of chaos, happiness out of suffering.

The soul of every adult human being must inevitably undergo something of a crucifixion. Passibility is, of itself, a crucifixion of nature. It depends on man himself whether it is to prove to be the torture of a sin-laden and rebellious creature or a healing operation willingly borne as a prelude to resurrection to a healthy spiritual life.

> *Over against the virulent activity of the three concu-*
> *piscences, Christ sets the active principles of His own life.*
> *To the concupiscence of the eyes, He opposes His poverty;*
> *to the concupiscence of the flesh, He opposes His chaste love*
> *of God; and to the pride of life, He opposes a humble*
> *obedience, pushed even to the death of the Cross.*

The opposite of pleasure is pain. The soul, to work out its purification, must resist the bait of pleasure thrown out by the concupiscences. This is what is meant by mortification. Christ has given the supreme example of this throughout His whole life. In opposition to the concupiscence of the eyes, that is, the eager seeking after that unreal excellence which comes from the possession of purely adventitious advantages, such as wealth or noble birth or high station, Christ calls to the real greatness that is found in the possession of the riches of God. He shows that what creatures can give is but dross as compared with what is offered by God to His creatures.

In opposition to the appeal of the concupiscence of the flesh, He points to the delights that come from the love of, and intimate union with, God. His teaching is not a mere negative one, of detachment from creatures. The process of detachment from creatures is a process of attachment to God.

Over against the gross falsehood of the worship of self, He sets the splendid truth of the worship of the true God. He is not an advocate of a degrading subservience. Whole-hearted dependence on God means man's highest and most perfect independence. Man is truly free and has the utmost autonomy that can belong to the rational being when he is emancipated from all slavery to creatures.

Poverty (which means real wealth), chastity (which means pure love), and humility (which means true exaltation)—these were the virtues exercised in a special manner by Christ as man. Practiced by His followers, in imitation of Him, they serve to withdraw the soul from creatures, empty it of what is at variance with the divine life, and dispose it to unite itself to God freely by the three theological virtues of faith, hope, and charity. The man who has a practical belief in Christ is the man who believes that the only true life for the Christian, the only life that is really a good life, is the one that is stamped by the practice of the three moral virtues of which Christ in His life has given such a glowing example. By the exercise of these virtues the soul is adapted to receive God's grace abundantly. Faith, hope, and charity, then, increase steadily, function with ever greater freedom, and extend their influence over an ever widening area of man's conscious life. The habitual domination of these divine virtues over the deliberate activities of the soul is called the spiritual life. It is so called because, by it, the soul is detached from what is earthly and material and attached to what is divine and spiritual. While united with the body, it has to deal with creatures, but it always succeeds in raising itself, through usage of them, to its God. When the spiritual life has developed, the soul is no longer dominated by the things of sense, nor are its actions determined by their influence. It values what is in the world only so far as it may be made a stepping-stone to God. This is called the life of perfection, because it verifies the divine ideal of human life, the same ideal that God, in creating, had before His mind.

Christ's task was not only to redeem men, but also to teach them a true philosophy of life.

Christ's mission on earth was a complex one. He had to expiate sin by pain and death. He had to merit grace for all mankind by His sacrifice. He had to repair the outrage inflicted on God's majesty, through sin, by a satisfaction in which the honor rendered to God should outweigh the dishonor inflicted on Him by the transgressions of all men. His work did not end there. Having restored men to life, He had to teach them a philosophy of living. His philosophy was clear and simple. It propounded that man's highest good on earth was the attainment of the spiritual life, and that what man chiefly shrank from was a most potent aid to the realization of this spiritual life. Recognizing that happiness was the legitimate objective of human endeavor, He taught that the happiness attainable on earth was to be found only in the spiritual life, that is, the life of intimate union with God. This view of earthly existence was formulated succinctly in the opening words of the Sermon on the Mount: "Blessed are the poor in spirit, for theirs is the kingdom of heaven. Blessed are the meek, for they shall possess the land. Blessed are they that mourn, for they shall be comforted. Blessed are they that hunger and thirst after justice, for they shall have their fill. Blessed are the merciful, for they shall obtain mercy. Blessed are the clean of heart, for they shall see God." [16]

This is the Savior's theory of life. For Him the activities characteristic of the nature inherited from Adam are the sole source of unhappiness. The conquest of self with a filial subjection to God is, in His view of things, the one road to happiness, even in this world. To believe in Him means accepting this viewpoint. Man's nature has been dislocated, as it were, by the Fall. This dislocation is the cause of spiritual discomfort. As a fractured bone, settled into a deformity, has to be broken again to be properly set, so human nature, dislocated by Original Sin, needs to

[16] Mt 5: 3–8.

be broken first before it can be restored to rectitude. The operation necessarily involves a great rending and severe pain. This is the price to pay for the possession of a soul in which God's life of grace can develop without hindrance. This is a philosophy of life that is undoubtedly hard and unattractive: it is uncompromising in face of the clamors of all the instincts of the old Adam in the children of men. Hence it was that Christ, in order to win men over to His philosophy of life, was not content in enunciating that philosophy. He proceeded to live it.

E ven when human nature has been restored in Christ it finds within itself a difficulty in tending toward God. The action of grace is gravely hampered by the triple concupiscence remaining in the soul after Original Sin has been purged away in baptism. Fallen man tends to be egocentric, not theocentric. The Christian struggle consists in a constant endeavor to reverse this tendency. It is a warfare against the concupiscences. Christ's life on earth was a plan of campaign meant to show the Christian how success in the spiritual warfare against the evil in himself was to be secured. To the three concupiscences, Jesus opposes the appeal of His poverty, chastity, and humble obedience to God. To believe in Christ is to accept that the practice of these constitutes the good life. Christ's philosophy of existence is that God is the unique source of happiness, being essentially happy. He concludes, therefore, that man can be happy only in the measure in which he captures God's happiness. The way to this, He points out, lies through the conquest of self-indulgence, self-exaltation, and self-worship. Christ's sojourn on earth was a practical exposition of His philosophy of life.

PART TWO

THE TREE OF LIFE

CHAPTER ONE

Where sin abounded, grace did more abound: that as sin hath reigned to death, so also grace might reign by justice unto life everlasting, through Jesus Christ, our Lord.
—ROMANS 5: 20–21

God, in goodness and power, gathered together the scattered elements of humanity, and built them up afresh into one new Mystical Body in Christ.

ACCORDING TO God's design, the whole race of mankind might be likened to an exquisitely modeled and variously ornamented vase, expressly made to be an apt receptacle for the outpourings of the divine life communicated to creatures. Sin shattered this masterpiece of divine artistry into countless fragments. To a designer of finite capacity, the disaster would have been irreparable. Such a one might, from fresh materials, fashion a new thing of beauty, but he could not piece together the scattered fragments and restore them to their former symmetry and loveliness.

God's power does not suffer such limitations. He might have chosen to fling aside the broken fragments of His first creation, and form new beings on whom to bestow His gifts of grace. What He actually did manifests a supreme mastery over the elements of His own creation. His power is infinite, and His omnipotence is always at the service of infinite mercy, as well as of infinite love. He took up again the broken fragments of humanity and of them remade the thing of beauty that had originally proceeded from His creative hands.

God does not repeat Himself in His works.[1] What He does is done once for all. The act of creation must work itself out to its logical issue. There is no return on it, no abandonment of it. The destiny of man must accomplish itself in accordance with the normal play of the laws that spring from the inner constitution of created things. For God, what has been cannot be as if it were not. For Him it is. Before Him the past and the present are invested with a species of necessity.[2] The free will that was an essential property of the human soul had, in its perverse usage, started a train of events in which one thing should follow from another according to the laws of moral causality. God would not withdraw or paralyze free will and so arrest the sequence. He would but adapt His merciful designs to suit its exigencies.

In spite of the way in which man's prevarication had crossed God's plan and thrown the whole realm of created being into disorder, yet, order was restored without a reversal of a single law of nature. After the Fall, things are allowed to pursue their normal course in accordance with the determinations of man's free will. Yet that course of events, as it flowed in the channel traced for it by man's passions, judgments, and decisions, was made by God to subserve His own designs of mercy. The devastating flood of human wickedness would be permitted to pour itself onward, but would be used by Divine Providence to make fertile in deeds of virtue and lives of holiness the very territories it would lay waste.

In God's plan of salvation, all was arranged with due regard to circumstances, to the laws that govern the free activities of his rational creatures, and to the exigencies of his own attributes of justice, mercy, and goodness. He ordained, therefore, that as by man's act man fell, so by man's act should he rise again. Salvation was decreed to come from out of the heart of the race that lay under condemnation. The sin of revolt should be expiated,

[1] Job 33: 14.
[2] *Summa theologiae*, II-II, q. 49, a. 6.

WHY THE CROSS?

and the expiation should be made through the nature that had sinned. God's power is shown, not in replacing, but in reconstituting what has been ruined by the sinful folly of man. In the scheme of redemption a certain splendor of order and a wondrous congruity are observable throughout.

Two of the Evangelists show an exceeding care in establishing the human genealogy of Jesus. The line of His descent traced back to Adam shows that the Savior is truly of our race, a son of earth like ourselves, and molded of that tainted clay of which we are formed. St. Thomas, in the articles that discuss the soul and body of Jesus, stresses the same truth. "Adam," he says, "and all his descendants, as far as and including the Blessed Virgin Mary, have contributed each his share of that material element of which was formed the body of the Christ."[3] Man's restoration was to be effected by a Son of man like to his fellows in all things save sin.[4]

It was through the Immaculate Conception of the Virgin Mary that God prepared this divine tour de force, by which He would draw blessing from a curse, order from disorder, health from disease, and life from death. It was a dramatic moment in the history of the race when the devil, in the full flush of his triumph, heard those words which revealed to him that his success would turn to defeat and that the race he had vanquished would prove his conqueror. "And the Lord God said to the serpent: I will put enmities between thee and the woman and thy seed and her seed: she shall crush thy head and thou shalt lie in wait for her heel."[5] Marvelous is the magnanimity of God. The very moment when the divine majesty was fresh from the outrage inflicted on it by the ingratitude and rebellion of man, that was the moment chosen to reveal the divine plan of redemption that was to cost God Himself so much. To the rebellious creature, the words of

[3] Ibid., III, q. 31, a. 6, ad 1.
[4] Heb 4: 14–15.
[5] Gen 3: 15.

reproach are brief and are immediately succeeded by others that breathe but mercy and kindness and the will to restore the divine birthright that had been forfeited. The ingratitude of the creature, so far from drying at its source the fountain of the divine favors, proved to be the occasion of their being poured forth in greater abundance than before.

The new Eve, the second mother of the human race, would surpass in grace, in dignity, and in her prerogatives the first mother. Eve was a little less than the angels. Mary would occupy a position to which no angel could aspire. Of her flesh would be formed the body of God, and thus she would be truly named Mother of the Most High. And then the Holy Spirit, the Spirit of Union, having, of Mary's blood, formed in Jesus the perfect model of human-divine perfection, would set Himself to the task of repairing the disaster of the Fall. With infinite patience and forbearance, with infinite goodness and solicitude, He would carefully gather up the broken fragments of humanity. Having assembled them He would straightaway, with a divine artistry, piece them together and adjust them to that mold of perfection that is the Sacred Humanity of Jesus; in this way He succeeds in refashioning the soul of man to a beauty of form surpassing that which was his at the dawn of creation. The Christian is something built up around Christ by the Holy Spirit—he is "God's building,"[6] according to St. Paul. The broken fragments of what was originally the Mystical Body and the vessel of divine grace recover unity, consistency, form, and beauty, through being shaped to and on Christ. "For whom He foreknew, He also predestinated to be made conformable to the image of His Son."[7]

The traces of the great ruin that remain even after the restoration has been accomplished do not mar, but rather enhance, the loveliness that has been recovered. It is as when the marks of sorrows borne and trials surmounted

[6] 1 Cor 3: 9; compare Eph 4: 12.
[7] Rom 8: 29.

add distinction and refinement to an already beautiful countenance. The saints, who forge their way to spiritual perfection through suffering and through successful combat against the sinful tendencies in themselves, are resplendent with a brilliancy and a glory and a charm of soul that would not be theirs had they been the heirs of original justice without the experience of human frailty. The risen Savior Himself is all the more glorious because of the wounds of which He retains the marks.

God does not do things by halves, nor even merely adequately. He does all things superabundantly. God permits evil in view of a greater good, and it is for this reason that the Apostle says: "where sin abounded, grace did more abound" (Rom 5: 20). For the same reason the Church sings at the blessing of the Paschal candle, "O happy fault, which called for a Redeemer so great and so good."[8]

Man restored in Christ is a far grander figure than man would have been had he persevered in the primeval innocence. For man re-created through water and the Holy Spirit participates in the splendor that envelops Him Who, in the full and perfect sense of the term, is a Son of God. This glory and dignity would never have belonged to the child of Adam, even if he had been able to trace his origin to an unfallen first parent. The Venerable Libermann writes: "The Word unites Himself to humanity in order to render to God the Father those human duties of service denied to Him by sinful human nature. To these duties He imparted an infinite value. Humanity (as incorporated in Christ), because of this, is in a far more privileged position after its restoration than it enjoyed prior to the Fall. Then it did not have those intimate relations with the Creator that it now has. The nature of man, in the Sacred Humanity of the new Head of the race, enters into hypostatic union with the Word of God. . . . *In Adam we were* servants, and our adoption was of an inferior degree.

[8] *Summa theologiae*, III, q. 1, a. 3, ad 3.

Now we are really and truly children by the Humanity of Christ, who is our elder brother. With Him we form one Mystical Body."[9] God, in restoring fallen humanity to a position more favored than that which had been forfeited, would seem to have yielded rather to the "divine excess" of His loving-kindness than to the exigencies of His rigorous justice. Yet in the boundlessness of His mercy, no violence was done to any one of the divine attributes.

> *In the work of rescuing mankind from perdition, justice and peace have joined hands.*

The reconciliation of mercy and justice in the task of restoring mankind to the divine favor presented an apparently insoluble problem. On the one hand, the equipoise of the divine attributes demanded that the guilty race itself should, by its own acts, purge away its guilt, atone for its sin, repair the dishonor it had inflicted on the divine majesty, and win back, by meriting it, the supernatural life forfeited in the revolt. On the other hand, the human family, by reason of the guilty state in which it stood, could elicit no act that could duly honor God, expiate sin, or merit divine grace. Right order demanded that man should undo the wrong he had done. But the sinful state of man rendered him powerless to cleanse himself of his guilt. The way out of the impasse was discovered by Divine Wisdom pressed into the service of the divine kindness. God arranged that from the polluted mass of humanity there should emerge One Who, while bearing all the traces of His mortal, earthly origin, should, nevertheless, be utterly free from sin. He planned the rise, from the very guilty race of Adam, of a Person, in nature divine as well as human, completely pure and innocent: "Whereby he is able also to save for ever them that come to God by him, . . . for it was fitting that we should have such a high priest, holy, innocent, undefiled, separated from sinners,

---

[9] *Écrits spirituels*, p. 51.

". . . who needeth not daily to offer sacrifices first for his own sins." [10]

God the Son, becoming man, sanctified the flesh and blood of Adam, by bringing it into personal union with Himself. Human nature, thus sanctified, was in a position to effect the work of redemption and make the seemingly impossible, possible. In the Immaculate Conception of Mary was prepared the way for the entrance into the world of the unsullied humanity of the Savior. It was emi-nently fitting that the stream of graces to issue from their source in the Redeemer should, primarily and in a unique manner, exercise their purifying virtue on her who was chosen to be His Mother. The divine strategy manifested in the plan of salvation fills the thoughtful soul with won-der and admiration. Nothing was overlooked, either in the rights of God or in the demerits of man. Satan, in his defeat, could not plead that God had achieved his success by proving traitor to one or other of his attributes. He could not allege that the supernatural life was given back to man, undeserved because unmerited. He could not plead that the guilty race had been pardoned without having paid the penalty of sin. He could not contend that God forgot what was due to His honor and to His dignity in His haste to show mercy. The worship and the glory that, out of the New Adam, was to arise from earth, more than adequately compensated the Almighty for the insult offered to the divine majesty by the crime of the first Adam and the sins of his children.

For reasons known only to the divine intelligence, and which, therefore, human reason, even when enlightened by faith, cannot explore, it was decreed that the redemp-tion of men should be accomplished at the cost of the sacrificial death of the Son of God. In that sacrifice, the demands of the divine attributes were complied with. The inspired words of St. Paul reveal to us the burden of the mysterious dialogue that took place in the Blessed

[10] Heb 7: 25–27.

Trinity when, in the order of the divine ordinances, the salvation of men was decreed. The Son of God is represented to us as saying: "Sacrifice and oblation thou wouldst not; but a body thou hast fitted to me; *burnt offerings for sin did not please thee.* Then said I, behold *I* come." [11] In these phrases is made known the utter powerlessness of the sacrifices of fallen men to please and placate God. Men might, in a frenzy of expiation, immolate not only their flocks, but also themselves; these torrents of the blood of the guilty race would not avail to wash away the least stain of sin. "But without the shedding of blood there is no remission of sin," [12] as some primordial instinct in man assures him. The holocaust of the body, "fitted to the Son of God," would accomplish what the blood of goats and oxen could not effect. The Incarnate God accepted the conditions laid down by the Divine Wisdom. Then said He, behold *I* come—that is, to supply the insufficiency of all other sacrifices offered by man. Why this mode, the Passion and death of Christ, was chosen for the undoing of the Fall is a secret that belongs to the divine insight into things. A single act of worship on the part of the Man-God could avail to give God a due meed of honor and merit, sufficient grace for all mankind, yet this was not accepted as the price of redemption. Though reasons for the divine decision are hidden from us, we can be certain that the mode actually chosen for redeeming man was one that accords perfectly with the wisdom of God and is most expedient for the salvation of man. [13]

> *Christ's task was not merely to give back grace to men; He had, as well, to heal the wounds inflicted on human nature by Original Sin.*

Men are saved by the death of Christ, but it must not be overlooked that His life too, though not out of relation to the sacrifice that ended it, has its part to play in the

[11] Heb 10: 5–6.
[12] Heb 9: 22.
[13] *Summa theologiae*, III, q. 31, a. 1, ad 2.

salvation of mankind. Christ has not only died for his brethren, He has also lived for them. His death sets their footsteps on the path of justice. His life instructs them how they are to walk in that narrow path. The Sacrifice on the Cross reestablished order in the relations between creature and Creator. His life taught the creature how, when restored to grace, he was to reestablish perfect order in his own inner being. "Jesus," says St. Thomas, "took human nature in order to free it from its corruption." [14] Human nature, as has been already stated, was disjointed by the Fall. It was not fitting that grace should be poured into the human soul, unless the soul should, by spiritual effort, adapt itself gradually to be a more perfect receptacle for grace. Christ, by His life, was to show how a harmony was to be established between the motives, principles, and activities of the human soul and the supernatural life infused into it. "If nature has been raised up, its actions must become noble. . . . God desired to act as man, in order that man might learn to act as God." [15] The life of Jesus shows man how to accord his conduct with his state of recovered justice. Sanctifying grace is in danger of flowing away from the soul unless the fissures left in it by Original Sin are attended to and effectively closed up.

The three concupiscences, in their virulent activity, cause those fissures through which grace may easily be lost. The manner and principles of Christ's life, put in operation by man, are the effective remedy for the wounds of fallen nature. Christ's life was not merely an object lesson in conduct. It was a meritorious cause of those graces which enable a man to triumph over his inherited corruption.

> *Man had lost the true sense of human values. One of the Savior's tasks was to dispel this blindness.*

Though human reason was not essentially obscured by the Fall, yet, in the course of time, the understanding of man

[14] Ibid., a. 1.
[15] Bossuet, *Sermons*, 2: 285.

had become clouded with regard to the fundamental truths concerning his destiny and his conduct. This darkness of mind was all the thicker because the original prevarication of the head of the race had been renewed over and over again by his children and in all the ways that could be suggested by human malice. It was one of the tasks of Jesus to dispel this darkness. Bringing to men the light of truth meant not only enlightening them concerning the inner life of the Godhead, but also instructing them as regards the inner meaning of human life itself. He had to reveal God to man: He had, as well, to reveal man to himself: no mean part of His short time on earth was consecrated to this latter task. It would be a mistake to judge that the sole burden of the discourses of Jesus was the world to come. The Synoptic Gospels contradict such a notion. He was very much concerned with the life that was, as well as with the life to be. His penetrating gaze was fixed on the human existence that came under His practical experience. That glance of His indicated a deep, an anxious, and a sympathetic consideration of all the dark issues and perplexing problems of the life of man on earth.

The books of the Old Testament reveal that the best and most religious of men found immense, if not insuperable, difficulties in harmonizing the exigencies of a mortal existence with those of an immortal existence. Good men who, through no fault of their own, have lost or who remain outside of the Christian revelation experience the same difficulty in the present day. Men, a prey to the demands of ephemeral necessities and tormented, at the same time, with immortal yearnings, find it difficult to live as if the present life meant something and yet to live as if it meant nothing. On the one hand, the instinct of nature imperiously bids men to give fully of their energies of mind and body to the task of creating for themselves as full a measure of life as possible, out of the resources ready to their hand, just as if the actual present life were the true good of man. On the other hand, religious instincts and promptings, supported, too, by reason, bid them regard that life to which they feel tempted to give themselves with such zest, as something vain, shadowy, and empty of enduring worth.

The thoughtful among men are ever bewildered by the conflicting and apparently irreconcilable claims of their varied vital experience. They feel that they should live as fully and intensely as if the present life had a final and ultimate significance; and yet voices within them that may not be stilled bid them be indifferent to what must pass like a shadow. Are men, then, to consider death as the most insistent reality and to regard the existence that precedes it to be of little consequence? Or are they, yielding to the attraction and the appeal that belong to the experience of vital energies fully and freely exercised, to close their minds to the fact of death? Into this world of darkness and of doubt came Jesus like a ray of light. He showed how the conflicting claims of life and death can be reconciled. The reconciliation is not effected by the sacrifice of death to the interests of life or of life to the interests of death, but by marking the place of each in a scheme of existence that pieces time and eternity into one harmonious pattern. According to the Savior's understanding of things, we are not to renounce the effort of living because we must die, nor are we to refuse to think of death because we must live. He solves the antinomies of existence by making it possible for men to give an eternal significance to a transient human experience. He makes this possible by wedding the divine to the human and by drawing all men into the economy of this union.[16]

God showed infinite mastery over the elements of creation by piecing together once more into a thing of beauty the broken fragments of the original mystic body. This work was far more wonderful than

[16] Compare: "Time is the very *stuff* out of which our life has to be made, though only the *stuff*. We make a genuine human life out of this stuff in proportion as we transcend it, as a more 'eminent form' is superinduced upon it" (Taylor, *Faith of a Moralist*, p. 159).

would have been a new creation. His power is shown in this, that He enables human nature by its own acts to work out its own expiation and win back the divine condition it had forfeited. The instrument of redemption, the human nature of the Son of God, was formed of the flesh and blood of Adam. By the plan of salvation, man is not only given back the favor of God; as restored in Christ, he occupies a more privileged position than the one he had lost. He becomes a brother of the Son of God and shares the divine Sonship. This was done without doing violence to God's justice. The balm of the graces flowing from Christ to men heals the wounds inflicted on their nature by Original Sin. Christ is the true light coming into the world, banishing the darkness of men's perplexities. He not only reveals God to man, He reveals man to himself. He bridges the abyss between the relative and the absolute, the finite and the infinite.

CHAPTER TWO

And which of you by taking thought, can add to his stature one cubit?

— MATTHEW 6: 27

There is a treasure of infinite value contained in the materials of which man's life is composed. Christ guides men to the unearthing of this treasure.

THE SALVATION brought by Jesus to men did not consist in the negation but in the rectification of human values. Life on earth can be properly understood, rightly lived, and fully profited only by those who unreservedly accept Christ's values. To the men who wholly reject those values it will remain a despairing problem; to the men who only partially admit them it will prove an irritating welter of anomalies. Christianity is not a system of negation. There is a way of presenting the doctrine of the Savior that makes Christianity appear a negation. Such a way does injustice to His teaching; Christianity offers life, and life is a very positive thing.

Everything that is truly human has an interest and a value for One Who loves to speak of Himself as the Son of man. His mission was not to destroy but to save, not to cast aside but to restore. His task was to take up the strands out of which human existence is woven and, unravelling the tangle and disorder created by sin, weave a pattern of everlasting beauty. Respecting the fundamental yearnings and tendencies of human nature and not discountenancing any of them, He labors to mold them to the form they have in His own soul, modifying their direction and correcting their excesses. It cannot be too much insisted on that it is by, and through, human life that each person is to work out his salvation. Although man's final destiny is otherworldly, that destiny is prepared and achieved through the conditions of the present life. Jesus did not teach men that they had to step out of the stream of existence in order to spiritualize themselves. On the contrary, He taught men that they were to use circumstance to achieve themselves spiritually; He showed them how to do so, by the example of His own dealing with persons and things. He revealed clearly that it was possible for every *legitimate* tendency of human nature to find its appropriate satisfaction, without the ultimate good of life (according to God's view of good) being thereby imperiled.

Man is right in pursuing greatness; he is wrong in seeking a greatness that is purely fictitious.

The desire for great worldly possessions is so universal among men that one is justified in suspecting that this craving points to the existence, though the perversion, of some natural instinct in the human soul. The eagerness for wealth affects groups as well as individuals. States are ambitious to increase their territories; private persons long to enlarge their property. Seeing that the possession of riches affords men ample opportunities of gratifying their love of ease, comfort, and pleasure, it might easily be concluded that wealth is prized mostly as a means of enjoyment. But a careful analysis will reveal that the desire for worldly possessions is rooted in something more fundamental than the thirst for pleasure. The appetite for expansion, enlargement, and greatness is a stronger instinct in man than the appetite for the satisfaction of sense, imagination, and intellect. Capable of reaching toward infinity, man chafes instinctively against limitation. He is ever dissatisfied with what he is and has a consuming ambition "to add a cubit to his stature."

Adam's sin ushered in a world of unreality and falsehood. It is characteristic of this unreal world that those who find themselves at home in it should indulge the illusion that they can enlarge their personality by accumulating for themselves more and more material wealth. The thirst for riches is very frequently the natural desire of aggrandizement. This eagerness of man to enlarge himself, this impatience of limits, is not to be condemned in itself. It is wrong only because it seeks to gratify itself in a false manner. "There is nothing," says Bossuet, "more futile than the means man employs to make himself great. He finds himself so limited and contracted in himself, that his pride rebels at finding itself confined to such narrow limits; but as he cannot add anything to his stature or his substance, to use the words of Jesus,[1] he deludes himself with the notion that he can create greatness for himself, by heaping together as many things as possible. He fondly thinks that he incorporates with himself, makes part of his personality, all the riches he acquires. He cheats himself into the belief that he enlarges himself by extending his dwelling, that he achieves distinction by making wider his boundaries, and that he multiplies himself with his titles."[2] The longing for riches has akin to it the longing for positions of eminence and power. Both are rooted in the same instinct. The desire "to be something" can be ingenious, even where there is a dearth of any great natural endowments, in discovering grounds on which to construct a phantom distinction that sets a man above his fellows in some respect or other.

Man cannot himself add a cubit to his stature: the Savior shows how this innate instinct may be legitimately gratified. To correct the false orientation given to life by the indulgence of the concupiscence of the eyes, the Savior of mankind elected for His own lot a career marked by lowliness of worldly station and poverty of circumstance. But the divine Physician, while applying a remedy to cure the disorder of concupiscence of the eyes, aims at

[1] Mt 6: 27.
[2] Bossuet, *Sermons*, vol. 5, discourse on the Nativity.

preserving that in nature which the concupiscence corrupts. Jesus does not discourage, rather, He stimulates man's desire for greatness. He is ever bidding him to the heights. His ambitions for men are far loftier than the ones they cherish themselves in their most highly colored dreams. He mingles with men in order to point out to them where true greatness lies and by what paths it is reached. There is nothing unwholesome, unmanly, sickly, or fainthearted in His attitude toward things. His choice of poverty and obscurity was no inhuman cult of the squalid and the unbeautiful. His teaching is in perfect harmony with the fundamental exigencies of man's nature. His rejection of the world's goods is not to be attributed to a scorn of those goods in themselves: it springs from a scorn for the meretriciousness of the distinction that they were deemed, in common estimation, to confer. In His love of true greatness He turned His back on what could not possibly make men great. He possessed the knowledge of the whereabouts of the pearl of exceeding value,[3] which all men were seeking, but seeking in places where it could never be discovered. He came not to impoverish but to enrich humanity. "For you know," says St. Paul, "the grace of our Lord Jesus Christ, that being rich, He became poor for your sakes, that through his poverty you may be made rich."[4]

The disciple of Christ might appear poor, but he is really rich. The presumed wealthy ones of the earth are apparently rich but really poor. Jesus finds men dealing with counters and thinking them to be real coin. Pitying their childishness, He yearns to substitute what is of real intrinsic value for these vain tokens.

Jesus teaches that human life contains within itself immense resources. He shows men how to exploit these resources.
The Son of man was thoroughly and intensely real and hated, with all the energy of His strong and limpid soul,

[3] Mt 13: 45.
[4] 2 Cor 8: 9.

the false, the conventional, and the unreal. He came into a world where reality was obscured. Life, as understood by fallen man, was one great fiction, a mighty game of make-believe. The Son of God, in becoming man, would be man in the full sense of the term. He would become man with the thoroughness with which God does all things. There would be no fiction in the doings of the Son of God.[5] *He would not merely play the part of man: He would be it.* Hence, whatever there is of true worth in humanity itself and in the life of man would be an object of choice for God Incarnate. He would get out of human life whatever of real value human life is meant to yield. He would exhaust it of all its spiritual possibilities. Christ does not despise the life of man in its earthly stage: on the contrary, He stresses its value and directs attention to its quasi-infinite possibilities. Real wealth and true distinction, He insisted, could be secured even in this world, if only men knew on which side to look for them. Through the wealth He promised, man could purchase an experience that could never be procured by the gold for which men struggled and fought.

He told man that every fleeting moment of time, though seemingly so unsubstantial, was of immense value, because it could be made large with eternity. He multiplied parable on parable, figure on figure, to persuade his hearers that the moments, hours, days, months, and years were a veritable gold mine, which, if worked under his directions, would yield up unimaginable wealth—real wealth, no counterfeit. *The burden of his teaching was that the human could be made to yield up the divine.* Human life, through Christ's assumption of it, becomes a field in which is hidden a treasure of literally infinite value. This treasure is nothing else than the divine life of grace, which Christ makes it possible for men to acquire and, once acquired, to increase, and that through actions strictly circumscribed by time.

[5] Thomas Aquinas, *Summa theologiae*, III, q. 5, a. 1, and q. 39, a. 7.

To secure this wealth—which can really add a cubit to man's stature, because it can vivify the soul with the strong life of God—a man must be prepared to "sell all he hath."[6] He must, that is, renounce his own values and replace them with those of Christ. The Redeemer's values were based on the judgment that, of themselves, material possessions had not substantial human worth because they could not in any way enlarge or ennoble the soul. His unerring insight showed Him that, when used correctly, they could contribute to the growth of personality, yet, in fact, they most frequently proved an occasion of deterioration for the soul. The poverty and lowliness of the life of Jesus, irradiated by the splendor of his human greatness, were meant to teach men clearly, significantly, and vividly that the only true and lasting possessions were those that could be held by the soul. The only ambition that He judged worthy of a rational being was the ambition that should embolden a man to aspire after the riches of the life of God. The speculation that would amply repay a lifetime of anxious thought and untiring energy was, according to the mind of Jesus, the speculation having for its purpose the continual increase of one's initial stock of divine grace.

The wealth of God is not given to the soul all at once. It is to be increased as a reward for the soul's own efforts, sustained by the supernatural aid of the Almighty. Growth in grace is growth in true greatness. To do and endure after the manner of Jesus, steadily refusing to part with the divine treasure, under the menaces of hardship or the allurements of pleasure, is the active way of promoting this growth. The sacraments can produce great effects when the soul is disposed for their action, through this purifying moral struggle. If the Christian is bidden to lose, it is in order that he may find more abundantly; if he is encouraged by his Master to lay out, it is in order that he may recover his spendings at incalculable profit. "Lay up

[6] Mt 13: 46.

to yourselves treasures in heaven, where neither the moth nor rust doth consume, and where thieves do not break through, nor steal."[7] The Savior's great concern is that men should use their life on earth to the best account.

These ideas are developed by Bossuet, with his customary felicity of language, in his sermons on the Nativity. He says: "Jesus Christ has come as the true reformer of the human race. He is the Master who imparts to us the knowledge that enables us to distinguish between what is of worth and what is worthless. He points out to us how we are to remove from our path the obstacles that prevent us from going to God and initiates us into the secret of contenting ourselves with Him alone. This lesson is not given so much by words as by the manner of the life He elected. For it was not incompetence, helplessness, or misfortune that reduced Him to poverty. . . . He chose that condition. For He believed that worldly grandeur, being false and imaginary, was prejudicial to true greatness. From the heights of heaven He saw that men were attracted only by material goods and purely external pomp. . . . Touched with compassion He came in person to disabuse their minds of their false values, so deeply rooted in their habits of thought."[8]

And pursuing the same theme in another discourse he says: "If the pleasure men seek and the greatness that they admire were real, who would have merited them more perfectly than the Man-God? . . . But, as Tertullian says, He judged these things unworthy of Him and His. . . . The Son of God could have been born to wealth and worldly distinction. If He is without either, it is not through necessity but through choice. His choice is necessarily determined by an unerring judgment of relative values. In His birth Jesus Christ has made the important decision that the grandeurs esteemed as such by the world were not for Him and that He should reject them for Himself. What He has rejected has He not condemned?"[9]

[7] Mt 6: 20.
[8] *Sermons*, vol. 5.
[9] Ibid., vol. 2.

There was a divine congruity in all this. It was surely fitting that One to Whom the solid grandeurs of heaven were familiar should disdain the hollow pomp and empty circumstance of earth. Jesus revealed His innate greatness in showing Himself completely independent of all the things that men prize. The very absence of purely meretricious glory, as shadows in a picture, served to throw into greater relief the real splendor of His Personality. The Divine Reality showed undimmed, its radiance not being obscured by an atmosphere charged with earth-born vapors.

"Wherefore in all He did and suffered there are found in a marvelous harmony human weakness and divine power. He is laid in a manger, and a star of heaven proclaims his glory. He is born among the animals, and the angels chant His praises. At His birth He is swathed in the bands of infancy, and the wise men adore Him. He is rejected by earth and warmly received by the purest of human souls. He is tempted by the spirit of darkness, and His wants are seen to by the spirit of light. He lives in want and dependence, but He feeds the hungry, gives sight to the blind, and recalls the dead to life." [10]

The Savior, while taking care that the necessities, miseries, and limitations to which He was subjected should prove beyond all question the reality of His humanity, saw to it that the reality of the divine should not be wholly eclipsed. Even when He appears most perfectly as Son of man, He knows how to manifest Himself as the Son of God.[11] The divine was the reality He came to give to man. "As many as received Him, he gave them power to be the Sons of God" and so to share in His own greatness and distinction. By word and example He sought to teach men that they were to become great by an inner development of the soul, not

[10] See Thomas Aquinas, *De rationibus fidei*, 7; Bossuet, *Sermons,* vol. 5, discourse on the Nativity.

[11] Even though Christ was a man, yet many signs of the Divinity showed through His humanity; see St. Leo the Great, *Sermon on the Ascension.*

by the external accumulation of goods. His own humanity was the bait He threw to them in order to draw them to the Divinity. "I attach myself to Jesus," says Bossuet, "by that which He shares with man, namely, human nature, so that thereby I may gain a participation of what He shares with God, the Father, namely, the divine nature." [12]

The Savior would not have proved a Savior for us were He only man and not God. Life on earth would be for us without hope, unless it held for us something more durable than the purely human. If it pointed to nothing beyond itself, it would close for us in darkness and a bitter loneliness, leaving all the deep aspirations of our being unfulfilled. Though men, we have a craving for that which is beyond men—for what is divine. Jesus puts the divine within our reach. He carries it in His own Person, in its fullness. It is enveloped in a mesh woven of earthly conditions. The outward appearance is rough and unpleasant to the senses and coarse to the touch. The poverty and hardship of the Redeemer's human life is hardly attractive to self-indulgent fallen nature.

Perhaps it is not rash to discern in the Incarnate God's election of suffering and lowliness and poverty another intention of Divine Wisdom over and above that already touched upon. Jesus once likened Himself to a door. "I am," He said, "the door of the sheep." [13] The Sacred Humanity is meant to serve for men as a door opening on a divine world. Were men to find the circumstances with which, by deliberate choice, He invested His human life too appealing for the instincts of their fallen nature, there would be danger of their halting there and not passing on. Satisfied with the human, they would not lift their aspirations to the divine. The human, in the Christian scheme, must be stripped of all that might give it the appearance of being ultimate and of final value in itself.

The trials, discomforts, and disabilities of all kinds that so frequently are the lot of the faithful should not

[12] Bossuet, *Sermons,* vol. 5, discourse on the Nativity
[13] Jn 10: 7.

generate a disbelief in the power of Christianity to bring happiness to its adherents. Radiant happiness enveloped the cradle of Christianity. To those capable of appreciating that happiness, the noonday does not belie the promise of the dawn. To the sensual and the proud, the cave of Bethlehem will always be repellent. To those who see Christianity from the outside, that is, to the practical unbelievers, it has little charm. Those who know but the externals of the true faith never penetrate to the inexhaustible treasures, not only of healing and comfort, but of love and joy, that it conceals. It is only the saints, and those who resemble them in their tastes, who exploit these hidden treasures.

Physically considered, the cave in which God was born was without either charm or mystery. It is only for the senses that it is shallow and unromantic. To the soul spiritually enlightened it offers a mystery of unfathomable depth—a mystery that can be explored for endless ages without being exhausted and that yields up perennial streams of tranquil joy. Divine treasures are to be found in the cave by all who are willing to accept the human values of Jesus and His judgment as to real wealth and real poverty. To one accustomed to deciphering the handwriting of the Lord, the rugged outlines of the cave form themselves into clear characters from which may be spelled the great truth that the man who has all that the world eagerly seeks but does not have God has nothing; and that he who finds God, though he want all else, possesses everything.

There is in all men, by reason of the natural limitations of their being, an urge toward expansion and a desire for distinction. Following the instincts developed in him by Original Sin, man pursues a false road to greatness. Jesus came to give a right direction to this deep-seated instinct in man. He points out that a human person attains greatness not by what he has, but by what he may become. An

WHY THE CROSS?

accumulation of the earth's goods adds nothing to a man's personality. It is by growth of soul, not by acquisition of material goods, that he becomes great. By his own deliberate choice of lowliness and poverty the Savior strove to enforce His teaching. Poor in worldly goods, He was rich in real wealth, for He possessed God fully. He puts this real wealth, with the greatness it procures, within the reach of his brethren. The lesson of His life teaches men how they are to gain the divine treasures He has merited for them.

CHAPTER THREE

And this shall be a sign to you. You shall find an infant wrapped in swaddling clothes and laid in a manger.

—LUKE 2: 12

Life for man is a quest after the hidden God. God, for His part, furnishes man with indications by which he may find what he is seeking.

THE INCARNATION has given human life many of the features of a romantic adventure in search of buried treasure. God Himself is the rich prize that awaits discovery. Those who will to embark on the enterprise are furnished with instructions that, if interpreted rightly and carefully followed, will inevitably bring the undertaking to a happy issue. As is usual in romances of the kind, the directions given are somewhat cryptic. They are not so clear as to dispense with all toilsome and painful effort in deciphering them. They are not so plain as to preclude all possibility of error in interpreting them. Sound judgment and resolute will are called for in this search. It is interesting to note that the mental and moral qualities that used to be characteristic of conventional heroes in tales of adventure are those that are needed for a successful seeking after God through the intellectual and moral vicissitudes of life.

The bourgeois type of mind is very inapt for the perception of spiritual things. Men afflicted with it run grave risk of failure in the search after God.

To find God at the term of the spiritual odyssey, a man must be endowed with that kind of steady and limpid intelligence which makes its way directly into the heart of reality and is able to distinguish clearly between the essential and the accessory. Such a type of mind is the antithesis of that which is always captivated by the apparent rather than the real and finds itself more at home in the world of matter than in the world of spirit.

Life is bound to prove a disappointing adventure for those who, through a weak yielding to their emotional and imaginative impressions, tend to substitute feeling for thought. Such persons develop minds that are but a passive reflection of phenomena. They are unable to transform a fact into an idea. They have no power to synthesize their experience into a judgment. They see only what meets the eye. Their determinations are but an automatic response to external stimuli. Their views are mere emotional reactions to outward circumstances. They are at the mercy of every fashion. Their impressions are without analysis and their reflections without comparison. Their observations are a query and their wisdom a platitude. Their sayings are an echo and their lives a quotation.

Recent times have been prolific in the growth of this type of human being. Their mentality is that which is described as "bourgeois." It is marked by a smug self-satisfaction and is very resistant to spiritual impressions. The deep things of existence always elude this bourgeois mind. Such a mind merely touches but the fringe of reality. It is shallow, without individuality, lacking in noble ideals and unspiritual. The bourgeois type drifts through life without discovering itself or its God or even the world in which it passes its days. The rapid increase of men of this kind has made of the world a spiritual desert. "With desolation is all the land made desolate, because there is no one that considereth in the heart." [1]

God has not to be sought afar off. He may be found hidden in the ordinary things of life.
To bring the treasure hunt in the supernatural sphere to a triumphant issue, one must have the mental and moral

[1] Jer 12: 11.

endowments that enable their possessor to read correctly the signs God Himself has given to mark His hiding place. This power of discernment will be found only in him who is skilled to sift the true from the false, the lasting from the ephemeral, the real from the specious, and the solid from the unsubstantial.[2]

To discover God, it is not necessary to quit one's ordinary occupations and to journey into the unknown and the uncharted. God is not above men or far off from them. He is not confined to heaven and, in consequence, so inaccessible that men can plead against the search for Him, saying: "Which of us can go up to heaven to bring Him to us."[3] God is very nigh to men always.

He lies in the depths of men's souls. He is shrouded in the circumstances that affect their lives. He is present, if invisible, in the actions, the sufferings, and the trials of daily existence. His modes of concealment are infinite in their variety, but they have certain characteristic features in common. If a man is not quick to seize these characteristics, there is a likelihood that God will pass him by unobserved in life's highways. The spiritually minded man will interpret the signs of God's presence; the earthly minded and superficial man will prove too dull to do so. "The sensual man perceiveth not those things that are of the spirit of God, for it is foolishness to him. . . . But the spiritual man judgeth all things."[4]

---

[2] Compare the following passage from Ruskin: "Great art is nothing else than the type of strong and noble life; for as the ignoble person, in his dealings with all that occurs in the world about him, first sees nothing clearly, looks nothing fairly in the face, and then allows himself to be swept away by the trampling torrent, and inescapable force of the things he would not foresee, and could not understand: so the noble person, looking the facts of the world full in the face and fathoming them with deep faculty, then deals with them in unalarmed intelligence and unhurried strength, and becomes with his human intellect and will no unconscious or insignificant agent in consummating their good, and restraining their evil."

[3] See Dt 30: 12–14, where the words used by the sacred writer concerning the law are applicable to God Himself.

[4] 1 Cor 2: 14–15.

God created us expressly to enjoy the thrilling experience of the romantic search for and discovery of Him. Our lives lose direction the moment they cease to be a voyage for the discovery of God. If, after having been launched on this high adventure through the waters of baptism, equipped with all the graces needful for the undertaking, we turn aside from our objective and drop anchor by the apparently enchanting isles that meet us on our way, then our days become empty of meaning and purpose. Our life becomes a mere aimless drifting from one deceptive mirage to another.

It is the condition of our nature, not capriciousness on the part of God, that makes Him a hidden God for us.

The most encouraging aspect of the spiritual enterprise is that it offers such fair prospects of success. The Lord guarantees it if the quest is genuine. "And when thou shalt seek the Lord, thy God, thou shalt find him: yet so, if thou seek Him with all thy heart, and all the affliction of thy soul." [5] What is more, to seek God is already to have found Him, at least to some extent.[6] And yet the undertaking is not without that element of risk and struggle which gives its spice to adventure. The search is attended with pain, with hardship, and, at times, with trying uncertainty. God, in His dealings with His creatures, is enveloped in a certain obscurity. He reveals Himself in darkness. "Verily," says the prophet Isaiah, "Thou art a hidden God, the God of Israel, the Savior." [7] He is often close at hand when the weary searcher thinks Him to be far off, and, again, what has been taken for the Divine Reality itself is discovered in experience to be but a slight token of Him or a vestige of His passage.

The hiddenness of God is not due to perversity or capriciousness on His part. Such a thing is incompatible

[5] Dt 4: 29.

[6] As in the hymn "Jesu, dulcis memoria": "*Quam bonus te quaerentibus*", How satisfying even to those who seek Thee.

[7] Is 45: 15.

with His truth and His goodness. Neither is it a test to try our perseverance or our insight. He would never, in His love for His creatures, unnecessarily expose them to run the risk of losing Him. It would appear to us that all danger of going astray would be eliminated from our life were God to reveal Himself to us, without disguise. For seeing Him thus, it would be impossible for us to seek our satisfaction in anything else. This reasoning is based on an incomprehension of God and of ourselves.

If a course other than that which seems to us to be the obvious one is chosen by God for the object of revealing Himself to His creatures, it must be because it is the wisest, the safest, and the most perfectly adapted to the requirements of our nature. *It is what we are that conditions the mode of revelation.* The human soul in its actual state could not abide the immediate revelation *of the infinitely pure God.* Not able to endure contact with the fires of the Godhead by reason of its inherited impurity, the soul would shrivel up in the fiery radiance of the divine holiness. Faced immediately with the glowing splendor of the divine sanctity, so far from feeling an impulse to fly toward it, the soul would cower in an agony of terror before it.[8] Bossuet says: "Since the curse that was pronounced against us after the fall, there abides in the spirit of man a certain terror as regards things divine, which not only prevents them from approaching God with confidence, but what is more, paralyzes them with fear in face of all that is supernatural. The examples of this are frequent in Scripture. The people in the desert fear to 'draw nigh to God lest they die,'[9] and the parents of Samson say: 'We shall certainly

---

[8] Compare these lines from Newman's *Dream of Gerontius*:
    The eager spirit . . .
    Flies to the dear feet of Emmanuel;
    But, ere it reaches them, the keen Sanctity
    Which with its effluence, like a glory, clothes
    And circles round the Crucified, has seized
    And scorched and shrivelled it.
[9] Ex 20: 19.

die because we have seen God.' [10] What do these testimonies of Scripture mean? They reveal to us the fright which naturally seizes on all men in the presence of God, since sin has made its entry into the world." [11]

Close contact cannot be established between the Creator and the creature, until the latter, through a process of purification, has been, in some considerable measure, transformed to the likeness of God. God can reveal Himself freely only to what is like to Himself. The creature has an instinctive knowledge of this. It recognizes that reaching God involves undergoing a kind of death. It naturally shrinks from this dissolution of what in it is unlike to God but intimately twined to the inmost fibers of unregenerate nature.

A process necessarily gradual, and ordinarily slow, has to be gone through before the treasure sought in the spiritual adventure can flash on the eyes of the seeker. The sudden discovery of God would be blinding and overwhelming. Such a discovery has to correspond with the progressive purification in which, first, the sensitive nature and, next, the spiritual are cleansed of the dross that holds sense and spirit to earth and to self. All that is of base alloy with the supernatural in the soul has to be got rid of if the soul is to mount freely toward God. It is literally true that in the divine adventure one must not only risk one's life, one must lose it. "Whosoever shall lose his life for my sake and the gospel shall save it." [12]

God carefully educated men so as to prepare their minds for the revelation of Himself.

God is discovered in, and through, the Sacred Humanity of the Savior. God educated the minds of men by a wise course of graded instruction for this discovery. All the appearances of the Old Testament, called theophanies,

[10] Jgs 13: 22.
[11] Bossuet, *Sermons*, vol. 5, discourse on the Nativity.
[12] Mk 8: 35.

were meant to be a foreshadowing of the Incarnation.[13] Subdued as was the glory of the Almighty in these representations, the ideas that the Jews entertained of the awfulness of the Divine Majesty were intensified by them. Yet these appearances accustomed the minds of the chosen race to the notion of the closeness of God to their lives and their daily interests. So, too, by these theophanies their imaginations were undergoing a discipline by which they would not be totally unprepared for the form in which the Messiah should present Himself. The people of Jehovah were so educated by the whole economy of the old dispensation that it should be inexcusable were they to find strange or incredible the idea of God mingling with the ordinary concerns of men.

The Incarnation answers the unspoken longings of all human hearts that find voice in the prayers of the Jewish prophets.

For thousands of years the priests and prophets of Israel had been sending up their cries to heaven with an ever-growing earnestness and insistency. "Drop down dew, ye heavens, and let the clouds rain the just."[14] At length, after the weary years of expectancy, the heavens opened to their prayers, and to earth was given "the brightness of God's glory and the figure of His substance."[15]

When the event to which the world had looked forward for so long came to pass, there were, Scripture tells us, shepherds keeping the night watches over their flocks. What were the thoughts that drifted through the minds of these men on that momentous night? The inspired sacred writer as usual confines himself to an objective narration of the events and does not admit us into the inner sanctuary of the thoughts and emotions of the personages he introduces. But a knowledge of the usual supernatural dealings of God with His creatures can give us an insight

[13] *Summa theologiae*, III, q. 30, a. 3, c.
[14] Is 45: 8.
[15] Heb 1: 3.

into what, most likely, was stirring in the depths of these men's souls as they watched over their flocks in the darkness.

God's action on the human spirit is never violent, arbitrary, or abrupt. His intervention on this occasion must not have been an exception to the ordinary laws that govern His intimate dealings with His creatures. He always prepares the soul for His divine communications by a gradual process. There are, as a rule, certain premonitory signs of a coming change in the relations between creature and Creator. A subtle movement, the cause of which is not apparent, begins to take place in the inner world of thought. Views, judgments of value, theories of life hitherto held unquestioningly, lose their surety. What has been regarded as of solid unshakable reality appears to lack consistence and reliability. What was significant ceases to be so. There is a growing dissatisfaction with a world that had been up to then accepted without question. It is the secret workings of grace that causes this growing recognition of the hollowness of what before had been found sufficiently satisfying. This discontent with accepted values is accompanied by an indefinable longing for something on which the soul can rest securely without risk of betrayal or disappointment.

Something of all this was passing in the souls of the Jewish shepherds on that first Christmas night. God's grace had been secretly preparing them for what was about to happen. They would not be taken wholly unawares. The revelation would come like an answer to the obscure and almost formless aspirations of their inmost being. It would not be out of continuity with the process of thought that had for some time past been taking place in their minds.

The romance of a love of God that was to be intimate and personal was about to invade and brighten the drab, colorless existence of these faithful disciples of the Law. The vague disquiet that had begun to trouble the serenity of their simple, open-air, pastoral lives was about to be dispelled. Their disquiet was not a discontent with their laborious lot, with its patient endurance of heat by day and its anxious vigils during the hours of darkness. The poor, as a rule, are more contented with their lot than the rich. The sounds of festivity borne to their ears from Bethlehem by the night wind stirred no envy in their hearts. It was not so much with their condition in life as with themselves that they were out of sorts. What they yearned for they could scarcely analyze. Their yearning could not be satisfied by the pleasures of the city or by the tranquil enjoyment of a peaceful pastoral life. They felt within them that indefinable yearning for the infinite which, at most unexpected moments, with an overpowering vehemence, seizes on the souls of men—a craving for the infinite accompanied by a profound sense of the inadequacy of everything finite.[16]

Their hearts were torn between the sincere desire for God and the practical experience of their powerlessness to realize, in their lives, the holiness traced for them by the Law. This holiness they knew to be the indispensable condition of close companionship with their God. The ideal evaded their best efforts, as the vivid and attractive hues of the rainbow seem to retreat upon approach. They wanted a life that would not be a mere flight of time. They looked beyond a law that would bring nothing to perfection, because it lacked inner virtue, to a Savior who would give passing events a permanent meaning, take away the hollowness of existence, satisfy their cravings for a life of love, and place spiritual perfection within their power and their reach. They were weary of an existence that, while giving all it had, left them with a sense of possessing nothing.

As they were buried in these reflections, suddenly a light from heaven shone around about them, gladdening their bodily eyes and, at the same time, illuminating their

---

[16] Thomas Aquinas notes: "The shepherds were men of sincerity, full of respect for Moses, and following the ancient ways of the Patriarchs" (*Summa theologiae*, III, q. 36, a. 3, ad 4).

inmost souls. For as the angel appeared, the voice of God made itself heard in their hearts, calling them to a new life, a life of emancipation from the hollowness and futility of earth. At first, as is customary for fallen human nature in the first shock of contact with the supernatural, they were struck with fear.

"Behold," said the angel, "I bring you good tidings of great joy, which shall be to all the people, for this day is born to you a Savior, Who is Christ the Lord, in the city of David." [17] Joy followed fear. The angel's words meant more than the announcement of a historical fact, even though a fact of great import for their own people and for the other nations of the earth. The tidings had a personal significance for them. Their inner life was, henceforth, to receive a new orientation. Their helpless gropings after a sure direction and a definite objective for their moral and spiritual strivings were to cease.

The angelic message marked the inauguration of a new era of spirituality. No longer was their submission to God to find expression in the hard restraints of a law laying hold of, and minutely regulating, almost all the activities of their individual and social life. A timorous and awed service of God was to give way to a trustful love and devotedness to Emmanuel. The love of the human heart finding an adequate object for its affection in the Son of Mary, Who was also the Son of God, would render easy of accomplishment that which proved so difficult under the uninspiring regime of the law.

Already, in the glory that enveloped them, the shepherds began to taste the sweetness of the Lord. Sense and imagination were strongly stirred; the soul itself was sweetly intoxicated. It is thus that God comes into lives for the first time as a living, present, concrete reality, after having been up to then as someone afar off, aloof, almost an abstraction. The soul so far rather knew *of* Him than knew Him. Now He is experienced as very close to

[17] Lk 2: 9–11.

the personal life of the favored individual. His relation with such a one is no longer merely through law and sanction but through a vital touch. The creature, after this contact, is not in the position of one who but dutifully fulfills the law; he has become one who loves the law-giver and obeys out of filial regard, rather than in merely a spirit of duty.

In this first experience of God as having a direct personal interest in the soul for its own sake and not as but one of a crowd, there is all sweetness and light. To wean the soul from the attractions of earth, God uses His own charm as a counter attraction. Under the influence of grace, the world and what it offers are made to appear extremely vapid, God and what He offers superlatively attractive.

Eagerness for its own moral purification and the tendency to hunt after all that promises gratification cause the soul to fling itself with avidity on this new form of delight. The ideal of spiritual perfection attracts powerfully, and the soul has no hesitation in setting out in pursuit of the ideal. So far from recognizing the hardships of the road, it presses forward under the impression that its upward movement will be but a growing intensification of the delight in God that it actually enjoys. Such are the experiences that normally mark the transition from the common routine practice of religion to what is definitely a spiritual and interior life.

> *The shepherds had not to set out on their quest for the Absolute without being furnished with indications of the place and circumstances in which it was to be found. Their qualities of heart enabled them to interpret the signs aright.*

God's messenger is not God Himself. The sweetness and the light of His gifts, though so enchanting, are not the sweetness and light of His own personality. The gifts of God, though they are utterly unlike anything that earth can offer, yet have not the substantiality of the Divinity itself. Though there is so much of heaven in the first strong graces that God gives, still they are but an intimation of His nearness. After the strong glad emotions stirred by these favors have subsided, the soul sees that it has yet much ground to cover before it can enjoy God's close embrace. It sets out expectantly. If the light that shows the way to God is so gladdening to the spirit, surely that which envelops His presence must heighten considerably the pleasure already tasted. So the soul judges, mistakenly.

The shepherds were bidden to leave their flocks and to set out in search of Him Who would give them all their hearts craved for.

They were not to make the journey haphazardly. The searchers after the divine treasure were given a map of the route, marking the hiding place of the pearl of great price, that pearl which would be purchased cheaply at the cost of the whole earth and all it offers. True, as is usual in such cases, the instructions given were somewhat enigmatic. The Savior of their nation and of all the peoples of the earth was to be sought in, or near, the humble city of David. There He would be found wrapped in the bands of helpless infancy and lying in the animals' feeding-trough. How should these instructions be interpreted? They pointed to a very poor setting for so splendid a jewel.

The correct interpretation of the angelic directions demanded the possession of certain qualities of mind, which, in their turn, depended on certain qualities of heart. The shepherds had these very qualities. They were neither shallow nor sceptical. Docile in disposition and humble of heart, they were not wont to question the ways or the designs of God. They were not given to citing the Almighty at the bar of their reason. They never had the ignorant hardihood of being querulous at the dispositions of Divine Providence. They led a mortified, disciplined, unartificial life, free from the stultifying effects of dissipation and self-indulgence. They had unclouded minds and upright hearts. Accustomed to wide spaces, the broad expanse of heaven, the soothing tranquility of browsing flocks, to silence and solitude, they were acquainted with long reflection and deep thought. They had strength, if not sharpness, of intelligence. In close contact with the reality of things by the circumstances of their daily life, they would not be swayed by mere appearances. They were, in short, thoroughly prepared in mind and heart to take the Lord at his own word.

While these good Israelites were, with ready acquiescence, striving to adjust their minds to the message that had been given them—an effort involving some difficulty, for they had, of course, inherited the prejudices of their race—there suddenly appeared to them a multitude of heavenly beings, saying: "Glory to God in the highest and on earth peace to men of good will." The good will of God is always extended to those who show themselves willing to accept God's point of view and to forego their own. Great glory is given Him by those who seek their happiness along the path traced for them by their Maker rather than by the one they, with their shallow interpretation of life, select for themselves.

> *In the inner life of the soul, a period of eclipse usually follows strong graces of light.*

As soon as the angels had finished their song of praise, they disappeared, and everything resumed its habitual appearance. The shepherds said to one another: "Let us go over to Bethlehem and let us see the word that is come to pass, which the Lord hath showed us." [18]

That journey through the darkness, along the rough hill path, is typical of a common experience in the mystical life. When the heavenly host appeared and the atmosphere was flooded with light and all the air vibrated with harmonious strains, the actual world and all it stood for must have seemed something very unreal and unsubstantial. On the other hand the spirit world, which had with such compelling evidence burst at one and the same

[18] Lk 2: 15.

time on sense and spirit, must have appeared solid, real, and significant.

So in the first "felt" contact with the Divinity, no matter how brief the experience may be, everything that is not God, or that is out of relation to Him, is regarded by the soul as hollow and unreal. What is more, it inspires loathing and aversion. But then the vivid realization of the spiritual fades and is replaced by an almost overpowering sense of the seeming solidity of the earthly and material.

According to the normal processes of the spiritual life, so things must have seemed to the shepherds. When the glory of the heavens faded and darkness returned to the earth, they must have experienced a certain revulsion of feeling.

Could they have been the victims of a delusion? Was what they had seemingly just witnessed the creation of an overwrought fancy, enkindled by converse among themselves dealing with the ancient glorious prophecies about the Messiah? They knew that the time of His coming was at hand, for the seventy weeks of years spoken of by Daniel [19] had elapsed. This expected coming must have been the constant theme of their conversations with one another. Perhaps they had slumbered, and they had had a dream that took shape from their discussions?

Everything around them looked so normal, ordinary, and unchanged. The sheep slept or browsed undisturbed. They showed no signs of agitation as animals are said to do in the presence of happenings of an "extra-natural" kind. The stars shone down coldly on the earth, as they had done for centuries. No unusual movement was observable in them. The earth bore its customary appearance of stolid, aggressive reality. The ordinary cares and necessities of human existence were as imperious as ever.

As the shepherds stumbled down the hillside through the dim light, the practical nature of the things about them asserted itself challengingly. As they went with haste,

---

[19] See Dan 9: 24.

the obscurity, the roughness of the track, the squat city opposite with its money-making, its political agitation, and its bright distractions—all this was mockingly real, their brief intercourse with another world fantastically unreal.

How often crises of this kind are experienced in the spiritual life! On certain occasions, as at times of conversion, of intense mental prayer, when graces are abundant and strong devotion grips the inner faculties, affecting imagination, will, and intellect, it is easier to doubt one's own existence than to doubt the existence of God's loving presence in the soul. God tastes sweet and what is not of God loses its savor.[20] Then suddenly the vivid realization of God disappears; the affairs and concerns of human life reassert their claims to unique consideration. What has taken place, one is tempted to think, has been but a strong stirring of the emotions, due to accidental causes.

In such doubts as to the reality of a spiritual experience, the soul has nothing to do but press forward in the darkness of faith, holding firmly to the conviction that has been formed at the moment of spiritual illumination— the conviction, namely, that God is calling it in a particular manner. No matter how convincing may be the arguments adduced by the sense of one's nullity as far as spiritual things are concerned; no matter how sane may appear the judgments of the worldly wise, who are prone to be cynical in these matters; it is the wisest course to believe in a special invitation issued by God to the soul.

---

[20] St. Teresa of Avila writes of this state: "The soul begins to rise above its wretchedness; there is accorded to it some taste of the delights of the state of glory. . . . His majesty begins to communicate Himself to it and desires that she feel this communication. On reaching this state the soul loses all desire of the things of the world; it sees clearly that all it contains could not give it a single moment of the happy experience it is now enjoying. God makes the soul understand that He is near it and that it can speak to Him without words. This Divine Master wishes to make the soul clearly understand that He hears it and makes it feel the effects of His presence. . . . He makes the soul see, as it were with His own eyes, the special help He is according it" (*Life*, ch. 45).

The road to Him will always be through darkness, dimly illuminated by the fitful light of faith.

The faith of the shepherds receives confirmation as they enter the cave. Seeing, they understand.

The shepherds, groping their way through the obscurity of night, are drawn by a faint light that shows from an opening on the hillside. Entering this semblance of a cave, they find "Mary and Joseph, and the Infant lying in a manger." [21]

What were their feelings and emotions at this dramatic moment in Jewish history? Of the chosen race (if Mary and Joseph are excepted, and they, in a sense, belong to all mankind), the shepherds were the first whose bodily eyes gazed on the fulfillment of the Messianic prophecies. These predictions had blazed a path of glory through the annals of their race. Were they taken aback by what they saw at the end of a journey that had begun on such visions of glory? Although the angels' words concerning a manger and swaddling clothes might have prepared them to some extent for what awaited them as they crossed the threshold of the cave, were they disconcerted by what met their gaze?

Here there was no flutter of angels' wings; there were only the shuffling sounds of the animals, slightly disturbed at the invasion of their shelter. There was no mysterious radiance filling the cavern: nothing but the dull glimmer from Joseph's lantern struggled with the darkness. The central figure in the scene was a helpless Infant lying uneasily on the coarse straw and swathed in the swaddling bands. No halo shone around His brow, and no royal crest adorned His cradle. No celestial band of worshipers was visible by His manger: two persons of their own condition knelt there, distinguished in nothing except in the wrapt gaze they fixed on the Infant. But this Child was the Christ the Lord Who had been announced to them!

[21] Lk 2: 16.

They had come, full of eager expectancy, to see Him Who was spoken of by Isaiah in the glowing terms of splendid prophecy: "For a child is born to us, and a son is given to us, and the government is upon his shoulder: and his name shall be called Wonderful, Counsellor, God the Mighty, the Father of the world to come, the Prince of Peace." [22] Contemplating Him Who, they had been assured by the angels, was the subject of these glorious titles, "they gazed on a nature like their own, weakness similar to that of their own infants and a poverty such as the poorest among them did not suffer from." [23]

Yet what met their bodily vision proved no obstacle to their faith. "And seeing," we are told, "they understood of the word that had been spoken to them concerning the child." [24] On their minds, through a secret strengthening of the virtue of faith in them, there flashed, from beneath the harsh and miserable covering of rude circumstance, the gleam of the treasure hidden in the Sacred Humanity. They understood the Word, that is, they grasped the significance of the Incarnation. There was revealed to them, at least in broad outline, the whole economy of the long expected salvation. They understood at that moment what the official guides of the nation never came to understand, namely, the character of the messianic kingdom. The illumination that flooded their souls swept away, as in a torrent, all the inherited prejudice of centuries due to false interpretations of the messianic prophecies. They recognized that the revolution to be effected by this Child was not primarily in the political destinies of their people but in the inner dispositions of the souls of all mankind. He was to be a leader, not in the conquest of the world, but in the conquest of self. They knew that the happiness He came to bring was to be found not through the acquisition, but through the rejection, of what fallen nature chiefly prized. Already they were tasting that happiness.

[22] Is 9: 5.
[23] Bossuet, *Sermons*, 2:278, discourse on the Nativity.
[24] Lk 2: 17.

"The shepherds," the Gospel narrative informs us, "returned, glorifying and praising God for all the things they had heard and seen, as it was told to them."[25]

The story of the shepherds is a light to men in their search for God. It teaches them in what circumstances of life they may expect to find Him.

The shepherds were beside themselves with joy because they had discovered what all men seek. They had not allowed the darkness of the cave to dim the brightness, nor its coldness chill the warmth of their faith. Nothing there, apparent to sense or reason, could provoke ecstatic feelings, and yet they were almost ecstatic with happiness. Their experience is instructive for all those who receive the call to quit the routine practice of religion and to enter into relations of close intimacy with God.

Such persons, unversed in the ways of the interior life, are wont to weave out of their own imaginations a picture of the conditions in which the Savior is to be found. This picture, as a rule, bears little resemblance to the cave on the hillside. They expect to find God in a life that is to run a calm, even course, a life in which there are to be found no rude obstacles, no rough experiences. Suffering, of course, there must be, but suffering in self-chosen conditions of dramatic effect. They expect to find the Prince of Peace in the midst of a court where flourish refinement, courtesy, and graceful charity. When the aspirant after God's intimacy encounters, instead of what was fondly imagined, much that is disagreeable to sense, hurtful to fine feelings, and wounding to the quivering nerves of the soul—when the harsh, the unfeeling, the obtuse, and the coarse make themselves painfully felt, there is the temptation to believe that this cannot be a setting for God.[26]

With the Gospel story open to them, Christians would prove themselves naïve were they to expect that the Savior

[25] Lk 2: 20.
[26] Converts to the faith must frequently, in the early days of their conversion, experience shocks of this kind to their sensibility.

would be discovered in the midst of warmth and ease and comfort. In later days, Jesus, speaking of John, his precursor, said to the multitudes that gathered about Him: "But what went you out into the desert to see? A man clothed in soft garments? Behold they that are clothed in soft garments are in the houses of kings." [27] If the herald is not to be found in luxurious circumstances, neither is the king.

There is a deep analogy between the popular fairy tale and the story of the Gospel.

Father Faber has remarked, in his book on Bethlehem, that the entry of the kings on the scene of the Nativity is like a page taken from an Oriental romance. Of the shepherds, it could with equal truth be said that their story reads like a fairy tale. The thoughtful and religious mind will see in those stories, which are the delight of childhood and which dreary and shallow modern educators would rule out as injurious to the child's mind, picturesque and beautifully imaginative presentations of an important truth of Christianity.

In the conventional fairy tale there is promised a destiny of unparalleled splendor on certain, at first inexplicable, conditions. The destiny is gratuitous; the conditions are apparently most arbitrary. Fulfillment of the conditions demands an effort utterly disproportionate to the greatness of the reward. One must do what is appointed, going forward in faith and not trusting to appearances. If faith triumphs, the protégé of the beneficent fairy enters into a condition of undreamed of happiness. Chesterton, writing with his habitual insight into the heart of reality, says in this connection: "In the fairy tale an incomprehensible happiness rests on an incomprehensible condition. A box is opened, and evils fly out. A vow is forgotten, and cities perish. A lamp is lit, and love flies away. A flower is plucked, and human lives are forfeited. An apple is eaten, and the hope of God is gone." And again: "The vision

[27] Mt 11: 7–8.

always hangs upon a veto. All the dizzy and colossal things conceded depend upon one small thing withheld."[28]

Christianity demands believing, against appearances. It demands that we accept that there is a divine reality under our eyes, when those eyes and human reason protest that there is no such thing. It demands that we believe that this tiny Child, a few moments old, is the eternal God. In a word, Christianity is based on an act of faith. Faith, St. Paul says, "is the evidence" (that is, the shining forth) "of things that appear not."[29]

In this life God for us will be always robed in humanity. His voice comes to us in human accents. His direction reaches us through the operation of pain and sorrow. It is our fault if our perceptions stop at the surface of things, at mere appearances, and so fail to penetrate God's disguise.

The moral of the divine fairy tale is this: God was lost by man, being man's great treasure. The goodness of the Lord would not allow the loss to be irretrievable. God united to Himself a humanity, through which He was to be sought and in which He was to be found. The humanity He espoused is enveloped in loneliness, poverty, humility, obscurity, and hardship—in all that is painful for perverse human nature to face. But he who aspires to discover God must be prepared to find Him in these conditions. Happiness is promised to those who have the faith to embrace what appears to be the very negation of happiness.

The saints are the heroes and the heroines of the fairy tale who, scorning appearances, and proof against the allurements of what the world calls "a good time," bravely hold on to what the world regards as a very evil time. They are rewarded by the discovery of God. The seeker and the thing sought must, necessarily, in the finding, effect contact in the same conditions. "And this shall be a sign to you. You shall find an infant wrapped in swaddling clothes and laid in a manger."

[28] G. K. Chesterton, "The Effects of Elfland," *Orthodoxy*, pp. 97–98.
[29] Heb 11: 1.

The effort to effect union with God has in it the elements of an adventure in search of buried treasure. It involves uncertainty, pain, and great loss, but it has great compensations, and a successful issue to the enterprise is certain for those who follow the directions given by the Lord Himself. The Lord sets forth the signs by which He shall be discovered and maps out the route. The story of the shepherds in the Gospel of St. Luke illustrates this theme. The angels said to them: This shall be the sign of the whereabouts of God. "You shall find an infant wrapped in swaddling clothes and laid in a manger." It would be vain to expect to find God amid pleasant human surroundings. The path to Him is always through what is mortifying for the flesh. But to find Him is happiness. What is happiness?

CHAPTER FOUR

Blessed is the man that shall continue in wisdom, and that shall meditate in his justice and in his mind shall think of the all-seeing eye of God.
—SIRACH (ECCLESIASTICUS) 14: 20–21

Sin did not frustrate God's plans for man's happiness.

AS WE HAVE SEEN in a previous chapter, God, in creating, planned an existence of unbroken happiness for man. The beatitude destined for him at the end of life's pilgrimage was to be but the perpetuation, on a loftier plane and in a more perfect form, of that which had been his from the beginning. Though man crossed the divine plan, God would not allow Himself to be thwarted in the prosecution of His original design. The Fall modified the conditions of the fulfillment of God's purpose; it did not defeat that purpose. Man, when redeemed, recovered the power to achieve, even on earth, some measure of the happiness he had originally enjoyed.

This statement seems to contradict the obvious facts of human experience. The world is rightly called a vale of tears. Suffering is the lot of all. Even the Savior of mankind Himself was not exempt from it. The existence of man seems, as a result of sin, to be irrevocably sundered into two periods, differing widely in the experiences they offer. Distress of all kinds, from which it is vain to hope for escape, is his lot in time: beatitude, apparently, can be his only when he reaches eternity.

Did the Redeemer, regarding time to be irretrievably lost for man, as regards its power to procure him happiness, feel Himself forced, as it were, to concentrate all

His efforts on the salvage of eternity? Is the sole significance of earthly life to be considered merely this, namely, that it furnishes an occasion for patient and heroic endurance, for meritorious struggle, and for the faithful discharge of the onerous duties imposed by the law of God? Is life here below to be regarded not as something to be lived, but rather as something to be lived through?

Many statements in Scripture, if taken by themselves, would appear to justify this way of looking at things. The words of St. Paul: "For that which is at present momentary and light of our tribulation worketh for us above measure exceedingly an eternal weight of glory," [1] must, apparently, be interpreted wholly in this sense.

The fleeting and ephemeral nature of the present life is a constant theme for moralizing in the sacred books. As a description of the transitoriness and unsubstantiality of earthly things, the words of the sacred writer in the Book of Wisdom could scarcely be surpassed. "All those things are passed away like a shadow, and like a post that runneth on, and as a ship that passeth through the waves; whereof when it is gone by, the trace cannot be found, nor the path of its keel in the waters. Or as when a bird flieth away through the air, of the passage of which no mark can be found, but only the sound of the wings beating the light air and parting it by the force of her flight: she moved her wings, and hath flown through, and there is no mark found afterward of her way. Or as when an arrow is shot at a mark, the divided air presently cometh together again, so that the passage thereof is not known. So we also being born forthwith ceased to be." [2]

Only one possible conclusion seemingly can be drawn from these and similar passages. It is that man must perforce resign himself to misery here, consoling himself with the reflection that time is short and the bliss of eternity is purchased cheaply at the price of sorrows that

[1] 2 Cor 4: 17. Compare Rom 8: 18.
[2] Wis 5: 9–13. Compare Job 14: 1-2.

do not last. Now this conclusion, though it contain a large element of truth, cannot be a faithful interpretation of the scriptural exhortations taken in their totality and balanced, as well as corrected, one by the other. Time comes from God's creative hands. It cannot be without its own importance. It is impossible that its only recommendation is that it passes quickly away. To hold that even after the restoration of man time is inextricably bound up with unhappiness is to do a singular injustice to the redemptive virtue of Christ. Since the aim of the Redeemer was to restore happiness to man, it would argue a partial failure in his achievement if redeemed man, in a portion of his existence, at least, could not be saved from unhappiness. This is not an admissible view, however much the sacred text would seem to justify it.

The texts of Scripture, however, do seem to hold this view of the redemption wrought by Christ. The inspired writers adopt the line of thought that runs through the texts quoted above because they are directing their remarks toward the correction of an error to which man is prone. Very numerous are those who, having their imaginations subjugated by the apparent stability of the order of things amid which they live, shape their course on earth as if it were to be never ending. Others who, through cowardice, shrink from the sufferings that God's service demands or who, through the lure of pleasure, are ready to barter their eternal destiny for a present satisfaction are warned that the pains and pleasures of this time are but fleeting, and a little sacrifice now merits an utterly disproportionate reward hereafter.

But it is a mistake to think that duration is the only or even the most important aspect of time. Considered under that aspect it is, of course, negligible as compared with eternity. It compares with it as a point to a line.[3] The imagination can be strongly stirred by a comparison

[3] The comparison is only partially applicable. Both point and line belong to the same category of quantity. Time and eternity are not in a common category.

between the two, considered in this way. Through a forceful impression made on his imagination, man can be moved to take practical decisions with regard to the right ordering of his life.

But, in reality, duration has a very different signification as applied to time from what it has as applied to eternity. Eternity is not time drawn out or indefinitely multiplied. Time and eternity do not differ in that eternity is longer than time. They are not in the same category of being. In reality, they do not admit of comparison. They differ in this: that time admits of change and comes to an end, while eternity, not admitting of change, entirely excludes the notion of end.

More important than duration is what endures. Time cannot pass over into eternity and retain something of its identity. A day will come when time shall be no more. But there is something bound up with time that does not necessarily share its fate. Life may be lived in time but need not come to an end with time. Life is a notion that concerns the destiny of man more intimately than mere duration. It is a notion that is so independent of duration that it can be verified in time or in eternity and maintain its identity in both.

In the writings of the New Testament, as contrasted with those of the Old, the emphasis is laid on life rather than on duration. This is especially noticeable in the pages of St. John. The adjective eternal is coupled with life now and then; but even when this is so, it is clear that the stress, according to the mind of the Evangelist, is on the thing that endures and not on the nature of its duration. *Eternal does not describe so much duration as quality.* Eternal life means life of a certain kind, which can be lived in time as well as in eternity. Eternal life is not necessarily reserved for the hereafter. Quotations might be multiplied to show this.

Our Lord, speaking to Nicodemus, said: "God so loved the world as to give His only-begotten Son, that whosoever believeth in Him, may not perish, but may have life everlasting."[4] Addressing Himself to the Jews, He says: "He that heareth My word and believeth Him that sent Me, *hath* life everlasting . . . but is *passed* from death to life."[5] And speaking on the same theme in another place, He uses again the present tense: "He that believeth in Me *hath* everlasting life."[6] In His prayer for His disciples at the end of the Last Supper, the Savior so defines this eternal life, of which He spoke so often, as to leave no doubt that, in His mind, it is something that does not belong exclusively to eternity. He prayed: "Father, glorify Thy Son, that Thy Son may glorify Thee. As Thou hast given Him power over all flesh, that He *may give eternal life* to all whom Thou hast given Him. Now this is eternal life, that they may know Thee, the only true God, and Jesus Christ, Whom Thou hast sent."[7]

There is in all this a response to an ineradicable aspiration of the human heart. Man cannot reconcile himself to the idea that he is made for a happiness deferred. Every striving, every goal he sets before himself is inspired by the hope that present beatitude, in some measure at least, will be the reward of his endeavor.[8] Were man not urged on constantly by this hope, the world would lapse into a state of listlessness and stagnancy.

In spite of all disappointments, in spite of all reasonings to the contrary, man will not be convinced that happiness of some kind or other is an unattainable ideal here below. It is difficult to assent to the view that all men spend their best energies in pursuing a mirage. If the inspiring motive of human action is the belief that a source of happiness is discoverable here on earth, there is a strong likelihood that such a source exists. A universal tendency postulates

[4] Jn 3: 16.
[5] Jn 5: 24.
[6] Jn 6: 47.
[7] Jn 17: 1–3.
[8] See Aquinas, *Summa theologiae*, I-II, q. 3, a. 6, ad 2. Man naturally desires not only perfect happiness but also anything that approximates to it or is an installment of it.

the possibility of the satisfaction of that tendency. Men cannot be universally mistaken. In fact, they are not.

Men's ingratitude and rebellion did not cause God to abandon or even to narrow His original plans for the well-being of His creatures. He created them in the desire for beatitude, not merely future but actual. He meant this desire should receive its gratification, in some measure, from the very beginning. The happiness of the moment, necessarily incomplete, though satisfying, was to be an earnest or, rather, a foretaste of that which was ultimately to be. The Fall brought trouble into this plan but did not change it. Through it a foreign, a bitter, alloy is introduced into men's present experience. A beatitude on earth immune from pain is no longer possible. But suffering cannot of itself make actual happiness an impossibility.

For the essential notes of the happiness lost in Adam are recoverable in Jesus Christ. Through the Redeemer, Eden can be regained in what constituted the substance of the bliss it offered. By the redemption, a beatitude in this world, imperfect, but nevertheless real, is placed within our grasp. The Son of God lived on earth the life of man, in these very conditions in which every child of Adam has to work out his existence. In Him, the Head of the restored human race, was realized in an eminent manner that happiness which it is possible to experience in time, in spite of the adverse conditions created by the Fall.

Not only does He enjoy happiness Himself; He states explicitly that He has power to communicate it to others. "Come to me, all you that labor and are burdened, and I will refresh you."[9] His own experience is offered to all who are willing to unite with Him and accept His philosophy of life. "To as many as received Him, He gave power to be made the sons of God."[10] He has given the assurance that those who are bold enough to make the hazardous

[9] Mt 11: 28.
[10] Jn 1: 12.

experiment of electing His way of life will find that the apparently harsh and galling will turn out to be pleasant and accommodating. "Take up my yoke upon you . . . and you shall find rest to your souls. For my yoke is sweet and my burden light."[11] Men have only themselves to blame, if, utterly disbelieving in Christ, they find the burden of life intolerable; or if, accepting His statements, but with reservations, they find the yoke of such restraints they submit to exceedingly galling and irksome.

Men err in identifying happiness with pleasure and especially with pleasure of sense and imagination.

It seems like uttering a startling paradox to speak of the Savior's life on earth as a happy one. In what sense can the term be applied to those long years of obscure toil, followed by the brief period of disheartening effort ending in heart-rending failure? The word "happy" must seem utterly inapplicable to those years, wholly overshadowed by the prevision of ultimate tragedy, for those who identify happiness with the constant experience of pleasurable sensation and the complete absence of physical and mental discomfort. But it is an error to judge that happiness is synonymous with pleasure, unhappiness with pain. Sense satisfactions and those of the imagination are common to man and to the irrational animals. It is true, of course, that they can be more intensely enjoyed by man. But to whatever degree of intensity they may attain (and that degree will always be a limited one), these pleasures remain but the satisfaction of man's animal nature. As such, they cannot fully satisfy him; they cannot, therefore, bring him contentment, peace of soul, and happiness.

The gratifications derived from intellectual pursuits are of a far more elevated nature than those that come from the indulgence of sense and imagination. They are noble, and they are worthy of man. The satisfaction that comes from the apprehension of the true or from the

---

[11] Mt 11: 29–30.

contemplation of the beautiful would appear to be the highest good that life can offer. If so, it would be equivalent to happiness. It is undoubtedly an excellent thing. Nevertheless, though it is an ingredient of such beatitude as earth offers, it is not the essential element.

If men are prone to err in conceiving the nature of happiness, they will necessarily err in judging of its opposite. They commonly think that a man cannot possibly be happy if he is prey to constant sickness; if he is condemned to experience habitual poverty and to be buried in obscurity; if he fails to take an important part on the world stage; if he is unsuccessful in his enterprises; if he is thwarted in his ambitions; if he is deprived of the opportunities of intellectual or aesthetic development; and, finally, if he fails to gain the applause and the esteem of his fellows. Now, though all these things mean grievous sufferings for men, neither singly nor in combination have they the power to rob him of essential happiness.

Apart from all consideration of the life of the Redeemer, certain undeniable facts of history justify this contention. The saints in all ages have been persons whose lot it was, generally speaking, to undergo greater trials and sufferings than others are called upon to endure. Yet they were habitually happy, buoyant, and joyous human beings. Were they not so, they would never have been canonized saints. St. Paul is not using conventional language when he says: "I am filled with comfort. I exceedingly abound with joy in all our tribulation."[12] These words of the Apostle find an echo in the heart of every true lover of the Savior through the ages.

The ordinary Christian, looking at the suffering lives of those who wholeheartedly take on themselves the yoke of Christ, finds it difficult to reconcile what he sees with their assurances that they are happy. If he accepts their statements as being true, he will probably conclude that happiness means for the saints something far different from

[12] 2 Cor 7: 4.

what it really is. He would, very likely, think that it stands for something of an inhuman nature and therefore for something to which he himself feels no inclination to aspire. These half-formed judgments would be false. The saints were not violently wresting words from their literal meaning when they proclaimed themselves happy. For the happiness they enjoyed was that which is proper to, and satisfying for, man.

Happiness and the ideal life are synonymous terms.
What, then, is happiness? It might appear difficult, if not impossible, to give a satisfactory definition of happiness, such is the divergence of view among men as to its meaning and as to the ways of securing it. The divergence of view is, however, but apparent. If what men imply when they speak of happiness were submitted to a close analysis, it would be found that, fundamentally, they all attach the same sense to the word. However much men may differ as regards the immediate objects of their striving, they seek everything they desire in order to gain through it as perfect a life as possible. Happiness means for all the ideal, or the perfect, human life.

It would be an error to confuse the condition or the setting in which a perfect existence is found with that perfect existence itself. Adam, in the state of innocence, was intensely happy, not because he lived in surroundings ideally pleasant, but because he lived a life that was ideally perfect. The agreeableness of the garden of delights did not constitute the core of his bliss. Hence, when all access to the reposeful activity and the deathless existence of the earthly paradise was barred to him, the possibility of a substantially perfect human life did not disappear. The human life of the Second Adam was flawlessly perfect, in a setting that differed widely from the Garden of Eden.

If to be happy means to live perfectly, and this must be conceded to be the exact definition of happiness, then there can be no question but that Jesus Christ enjoyed the fullest measure of that imperfect beatitude attainable on earth.[13] It is somewhat unusual to contemplate the life of the Son of man under this aspect. Spiritual writers rarely, if ever, consider His life experience in this light. They dwell more complacently on the idea of the Man of Sorrows. It is perhaps inevitable that they should do so. The trials of life fall so heavily, as a rule, on good Christians that they turn instinctively for solace in their pains to Him Who was so intimately acquainted with grief. They find comfort in the thought that they have a High Priest Who can have compassion on their infirmities, having experienced all that they experienced, except sin.

"For it behoved Him in all things to be made like His brethren, that He might become a merciful and faithful high-priest before God. . . . For in that, wherein He Himself hath suffered and been tempted, He is able to succor them also that are tempted." [14] Suffering creates a kinship and a sympathy among those who suffer.

But, as so frequently happens, an excessive stressing of one truth obscures and may even cause a complete forgetfulness of another and more important truth. A continual insistence on the idea of the Man of Sorrows may easily generate the impression that the life of the Savior was not only a life of suffering but a life that was nothing but suffering. From this may issue the conclusion that it was an unhappy life. Such a conclusion would be erroneous.[15] Pain is not the only evil, nor the opposite of it the only good. Suffering tends, of course, in itself to be a contraction or limitation of life. But it can be made the instru-

[13] This is true even apart from the consideration of the beatitude He enjoyed through the intuitive vision of the Divinity.

[14] Heb 2: 17–18.

[15] These lines were written before the appearance of G. K. Chesterton's *Chaucer* (London: Faber, 1932). In that book may be read the following passage: "The insistence on the Man of Sorrows and the Mater Dolorosa, in artistic expression, belongs to a time after the Mediaeval. It was in the 17th century that the two more sombre moods appeared in the two religions. In the Catholic world it became in some sense a worship of sorrow, in the Puritan world a worship of severity and in some cases of savagery" (p. 265).

WHY THE CROSS?

ment of a higher and more intense life. It can be, but is not necessarily, in opposition to that vital soul expression after which all men aspire.

Christianity is not a morbid cult of pain and distress and squalor and misery. Its native spirit is joyous. The Christian scheme is the presentation to us of a plan by which we can realize an ideal life on earth. The attraction of that ideal and what it supplies give force to triumph over the external and internal hardships that attend the efforts to reach an ideal existence.

Christ does not ask us "to lose our life" as if the agony to be endured in that death were put before us as an object desirable in itself. He urges us simply to forfeit life of a certain kind in order to obtain, through that renouncement, "the life that is truly life." [16] It is gain, not loss, that is the theme of His exhortations. His call is to true riches, not sordid poverty; to real strength, not weakness; to glorious triumph, if apparent defeat; to happiness, not misery. The path to success, in the Savior's scheme, will always appear to human reason to be one that leads only to failure.

If the Son of man invites us to share His human lot, it is primarily the joyousness and the happiness of the perfect life that was His that we are asked to share. The suffering is, as the philosophers put it, merely *per accidens*. It is a means, not an ideal. In the imitation of the life of Jesus, suffering is found, but so are freedom and happiness. He invites men, in the interests of their happiness, to a life such as He enjoys; it is not His fault if we have to wade through pain to reach it. He takes no delight in seeing us writhing under pain; He takes an intense delight in seeing us entering into the experience of the full life that is His, because this gives happiness.

His words relative to the taking up of the daily cross are a statement of extreme condensation. Paraphrased, His thought might be expressed somewhat in this fashion: I,

[16] 1 Tim 6: 19.

the Son of God made man, know what happiness is. I actually experience it. You cannot enter into this experience unless your souls are rendered apt for it. This aptitude is acquired at the cost of purifying suffering. My own soul needs no purification. But in order that you might have the strength to bear the pain that purification involves, I have borne the Cross for your encouragement and example.

Life in its essential features can be as perfect now as it was in the days of innocence.
The object of all human strivings is the best possible existence. The ultimate object of men is that it should be well with them—that it should be as well with them as is humanly possible. To seek happiness and to seek this are one and the same thing. To live excellently and to have achieved happiness are identical. Happiness is simply life at its most intense. The more intense the life, the greater the degree of happiness.

To be happy on earth is nothing else than to attain to the most perfect life attainable in this world in the actual, concrete circumstances of the world. If things were other than they are, if there had been no Original Sin, the perfect life would have a far different setting. But in spite of the Fall, there is open to men the possibility of gaining a beatitude here and now, not essentially inferior to that which was his in the state of original justice.

Happiness, then, is life at its best. Now, life is not characterized by inertness and immobility. A man is not judged to be living in an enviable manner when he is unconscious, though in such a state he is alive and free from pain. The absence of suffering, then, does not make a man happy. Life is a positive thing: happiness must therefore be a positive thing as well. Activity is the characteristic expression of life. The higher the activity, the more perfect the life. The supremely perfect life is the one that is marked by the highest activity of which man is capable. Man climbs to the highest of himself by the exercise of the activities that are proper to him as man. To think true things and to love what is truly good—that is man's work. The energies of sense and imagination but minister to this work, subserving it. The most perfect human life will, therefore, be found in the fullest energy of the power of knowing and of the power of loving. Man is wrought to perfection by thought and by love.[17]

That the vitality of the sense life is far inferior to the vitality of the rational life scarcely needs demonstration. A comparison between the vital energy put forth by an athlete in the rapid movement of a race and that exercised by a man of great intellectual power absorbed in the study of some deep problem that fully employs, without overtaxing, his mental ability shows life on two different levels. The activity of the runner and the activity of the thinker are both expressions of life. Each is excellent. But how much more noble and excellent the vigorous exercise of mind than the vigorous exercise of body. The thinker lives more intensely than does the man who puts forth merely physical energy.

The intelligence of man acquires its full power and its greatest maturity by wrestling with external reality and forcing this reality to yield up the secret of its nature, its properties, and its inner harmonies. Man loves to know. He develops as an intelligent being according as he gains in knowledge, subduing ever widening fields of reality to his thought. In this process he gradually assimilates his

[17] Aristotle, in the *Nichomachean Ethics*, bk. 1, ch. 6, and bk. 10, ch. 7, thus defines happiness: "The human perfection of the good man is a conscious exercise of the [higher] faculties in accordance with the law of virtue. If there be many diverse forms of virtue, the activity of the perfect human life will be that which is in accord with the supreme virtue. . . . If happiness be the unfolding of a life in harmony with virtue, the standard must necessarily be the highest virtue, that is, the virtue of the faculty which is highest. Whatever this faculty be, whether intellect or some other which seems to take preeminence and to have an instinctive perception concerning things noble and divine, the activity of this faculty in accordance with its own proper excellence and reaching its own standard, will be perfect absolute happiness."

mind to the Mind that has made all things to be what they are. He develops as a man and lives ever more fully and perfectly if the growth of his will in perfection keeps pace with the perfecting of his intelligence and of his imagination, the instrument of intelligence. For this it is needed that he should love the order and beauty he discovers in things and should rise through that love to a supreme regard for the Source of the order and beauty he contemplates.

In a word, the more perfectly a man knows what is true and loves what is good, the more perfectly he lives. To live thus perfectly is to be happy, for it is exceedingly well with the man who so lives. But if it is not of stray elements of truth that his mind is possessed; if it is not portions of reality that he apprehends and contemplates, but the one great reality, which contains in itself, and is the source of, all else; and if it is the beauty that belongs to that first reality that he loves with the whole strength of heart and will; then is man supremely perfect and therefore supremely happy. It was thus with Jesus Christ, even during His mortal life.

There was not only happiness in the life of Jesus, there was also pleasure. The two notions are akin but by no means synonymous. Pleasure is the exhilaration or satisfying glow of consciousness that attends on the unimpeded and normal exercise of every vital activity. The perfect functioning of sense, of imagination, of the affective faculties, of the intellect, each is attended with its appropriate satisfaction. "Pleasure follows on the wake of every sensation, and of every process of reasoning or play of thought and fancy. The most pleasurable activity is that which is most perfect. As pleasure ensues as a consequence of each state of sensation, the pleasure will be greatest when the sensation is most excellent and the object that occasions it is of a corresponding excellence. As often as the object perceived and the person who is conscious of the sensation are mutually excellent, pleasure invariably ensues. Pleasure is a resultant from normal, vital activity, as a good color results from the possession of good blood and perfect health." [18]

Where life is at its highest, vital activity is at its zenith. The activity of sense, of imagination, of heart, and of intellect was at its highest in the life of the Savior, inasmuch as He lived so intensely and perfectly. Pleasure, then, of the keenest and the purest kind formed an ingredient of His earthly experience.

God planned an unbroken life of happiness for man. The Fall modified but did not prevent the realization of this plan. Suffering, but not unhappiness, becomes the condition of the earthly portion of men's existence. God does not make unhappiness here be the price to pay for happiness hereafter. To be happy, in the minds of all men, is to fare well, that is, to live excellently. Eternal life is the excellent life. The Son of God gave power to all men that received Him to live this eternal life already here on earth. The Savior Himself suffered intensely, but He lived the highest life possible for men. He was, therefore, happy. He assured men that He could share His own blissful experience with them. It may appear paradoxical to associate happiness with the mental image of One Who is called the Man of Sorrows. But an analysis of the nature of happiness will show that it was fully realized in the earthly life of the Savior.

[18] Ibid., bk. 10, ch. 4.

CHAPTER FIVE

Thou hast given him his heart's desire and hast not
withholden from him the request of his lips: he asked life
of Thee: Thou gavest it him, even length of days, for ever
and ever.

—PSALM 20: 3–5[1]

The earthly life of Christ the Savior was substantially a
happy one, in spite of the limitations to that happiness
imposed by adverse circumstances.

THE HUMAN LIFE of Christ was an eminently satisfying experience. He achieved what all men strive for. He lived excellently. The main effort of human beings seems to be to eliminate suffering and material disabilities from their existence. Really this is for them a means, not an end. They regard hardship and discomfort as an obstacle to their "faring well." It is at this they aim. Jesus, Son of Mary, attained the ideal in spite of suffering. If He drank the cup of sorrow to the dregs, He drained as well the cup of life, even to exhausting all its possibilities. Happiness very real, though not without the alloy of pain, was His experience.

Jesus enjoys in His mortal life that contemplation which
constitutes the perfect human life and therefore perfect
happiness.

Owing to the dignity that was His, because His humanity was that of a divine Person, Our Lord enjoyed in His soul, from the very first instant of His temporal life, the vision

---

[1] The translation is according to the Hebrew text.

WHY THE CROSS?

of God face to face. . . . His soul, being the soul of the Son of God, had ever unveiled before it the splendors of the beatific vision. Jesus, speaking to Nicodemus, said: "Amen, amen, I say to thee, that we speak what we know and we testify what we have seen . . . no man hath ascended to heaven, but he that descended from heaven, *the Son of man who is in heaven.*"[2] In these remarkable words the Savior declares to the Jewish doctor that He, the Savior, is in full possession of the heritage of God—in complete enjoyment of that final destiny for which man has been created.

And, indeed, it is eminently fitting that He Whose function it was to reveal to men the secrets of heaven should have those secrets open, unveiled, to His gaze. It is in the order of things that He Who is appointed by God to guide men to ultimate beatitude should Himself possess that beatitude.[3] During every single moment of His earthly existence Jesus was, as theology terms it, in the condition of *comprehensor.* This means that, while being in some respects a wayfarer like the rest of men, He was in what is termed the "fine point of the spirit,"[4] already at the term of the earthly journey. He contemplated God. In that contemplation His soul put forth all the energy of which it was capable. The vision could not admit of growth or increase. The light of glory, by which the Divine Essence without intermediary is disclosed to mortal gaze, attained in Him its utmost splendor in the first instant of His temporal existence. This splendor of the light of glory in those who are supreme among the blessed pales before the flashing refulgence that it has in the soul of Jesus.

In this apprehension of God vouchsafed to the "Son of man," the human intellect in Him, at a bound, reached the utmost energy of action of which it is capable in the

[2] Jn 3: 11, 13. See Mt 12: 27; Lk 10: 22.

[3] Compare Thomas Aquinas, *Summa theologiae,* III, prol., q. 9, a. 2.

[4] That is the summit—the most spiritual part of the soul, called in French "la cime de l'âme" (or "la fine point de l'âme"). St. Teresa distinguishes between the soul and the spirit.

present order of providence. The vitality put forth in this apprehending of the infinite reality, in the degree in which it was granted to the "Son of man" to apprehend it, is surpassed only by the divine vitality itself.

No angel lives as intensely as Jesus lived even while on earth. That energy of existence was life in its most perfect form—it was happiness intense and unimaginable. If the blessed in heaven were interrogated as to the cause of their bliss, they would without exception and unhesitatingly answer that they are happy because they see God. Jesus saw God. He saw God from the beginning of the thirty-three years: He saw God then as clearly and as perfectly and as extensively as He sees Him now. In that sight and in the life it gave He was supremely happy.

Jesus was happy on earth with a happiness such as Adam never enjoyed in the Garden of Paradise. Even in the days of innocence Adam was still a wayfarer and could discern his God but dimly, in vague outline, through the veils of faith.[5] The Second Adam saw His God face to face in undimmed and unclouded vision. Nothing could disturb the boundless joy that flowed from this contemplation of God. No sorrow, no anguish, no suffering came to cast a shadow on the brightness of that beatitude with which the summit of the Savior's soul was irradiated.

Beneath those lofty heights lay the regions of life in which the soul shared the experiences of the mortal body to which it was united and which it animated. While those regions could be wrapped in the dark mists of woe and pain and bitter desolation, the upper regions and the summit of the soul of Jesus were bathed in a brightness unflecked by the shadow of a single cloud.

Theologians labor to explain how intense suffering is not incompatible with intense joy in the same human being. It is not necessary to enter into these explanations. It suffices for us to know that in Jesus was effected the reconcilement of the two states. Our faith teaches us in

[5] In a glass in a dark manner: enigmatically. See 1 Cor 13: 12.

this that suffering is not only not incompatible with happiness but also that it is not even incompatible with joy.

That Jesus, while being *viator*, or wayfarer, on the earth—that is, one making his way toward an as yet unreached goal—was also *comprehensor*—that is, one who is in repose—is significant. It suggests that, as in Christ the life of time and of eternity presented a continuity unbroken in character, so it should be also for the Christian. However difficult it may be to understand how Jesus, already enjoying the repose that crowns effort, could yet be subject to all the painful experiences that belong to those condemned to struggle, the Gospel bears eloquent testimony to the fact that His life on earth held this twofold experience. The sacred history shows us clearly that Jesus, during the thirty-three years of His mortal life, underwent all that we undergo, sin alone excepted.[6]

Thus we read in the life story transmitted to us by the Evangelists that Jesus wondered, that He was filled with admiration, that He rejoiced in the spirit, that He yearned to gather to Himself the wayward and the obstinate, that He had pity on the crowds, that He groaned in anguish for the death of His friend, and that He sorrowed for the sad fate of His country; in all this we are placed in the presence of no mere fictitious human emotions but ones that are eminently real.

Christ's life was happy even considered apart from the happiness that was His through the beatific vision.

Jesus did not play the part of *viator*, for He was *viator* in the full sense of the term. In feeling, in imagination, in understanding, and in will, He was all that we are. His faculties worked exactly as ours do. It is under this aspect that it is helpful for us to study His life.

The happiness He enjoyed in virtue of the beatific vision does not appeal to us who are wrestling with the problems of the present existence. That vision gave a

[6] "Tempted in all things, as we are, sin alone excepted" (Heb 4: 15).

beatitude to which we cannot aspire as long as we are in the flesh. It is not Christ's life as a *comprehensor* but His life as a *viator* that presents us with the ideal toward which we are to direct our efforts. It is in the respect in which He resembles us that He can be our inspiration and our model. Was Christ's life a happy one considered from this point of view, abstracting from it the beatific vision? That is the question that interests us.

Jesus, in stating that He can give peace and rest and repose to others, implicitly asserts that He Himself enjoys repose in an eminent manner.

To anyone who assents to what has been said, namely, that beatitude is the realization of the best form of life and that this form of life consists in the highest operation of the specifically human powers on their supreme objects,[7] it can be conclusively shown that our divine Lord, even in His mortal career, attained the utmost beatitude that can be had in this world.

Even if the consideration of the beatific vision be left aside, He enjoyed what all those who do not follow His way are vainly striving for. Implicitly there is contained in the Gospel an assurance of this. "Come to me all you who labor and are heavy laden, and I will refresh you."[8] Christ does not invite people to come and share misery with Him. He does not summon them to unhappiness. On the contrary, He bids them come to Him in order to relinquish the burden of unhappiness. In a word, He guarantees to make them happy.

Christ's promise does not deal with a remote future but with an immediate present. The Savior says that He can give happiness. What He holds out to His hearers is not a repose of the spirit and of the heart capable of satisfying only the few and the exceptional, those who have tastes and aspirations different from those of common men.

---

[7] See *Summa theologiae*, I, q. 76, a. 1, corp.: "Propria autem operatio. . . ."

[8] Mt 11: 28.

What He promises is something capable of quieting the restless cravings of every human heart without exception, something capable of satisfying men as men: He Who so confidently asserts His power of doing this must possess in an eminent manner that which He can impart. If Jesus can give repose to men, He must Himself be dwelling always in a peace that nothing can disturb. He must, in a word, be happy.

"The dominant note in the character of Jesus is that of a tranquil recollection, always equal to itself and always tending toward the same end in view. He never speaks as one carried away by the force of His visions: the tone of prophetic exaltation is rare in Him. And yet though charged with the most sublime mission, and moving constantly in that silent recollection, He is alive, in all His senses, to the impressions of the life that surrounds Him. . . . The Gospel bears witness to the fact, that in the midst of the greatest interior and exterior tension, He was possessed of an inner peace and a spiritual joy such as no prophet before His time had known. 'He who has not a stone whereon to lay His head' does not, because of that, speak like a man who has severed connection with all things human. He does not speak like a man of frightening asceticism, or like a prophet swayed by prophetic frenzy, but as a man who is acquainted with inner peace and repose and can communicate it to others." [9]

The secret of this peace lies in the perfection of the life of Jesus. Peace belongs only to rest and repose that ends and crowns striving. It implies the cessation of struggle when the goal has been reached: it marks the ending of uncertainty and combat. This state belongs to man when his powers admit of no further development. Jesus was happy because He was perfect. He was perfect because in Him the human faculties attained their utmost expression. Human imagination, intelligence, and will cannot put forth more energy than they did in the Savior. The

[9] De Grandmaison, *Jesus Christ*, 2:206 (my translation).

operation of these faculties, again leaving aside the consideration of the beatific vision, reached in Him a point of perfection that they never gained in unfallen Adam. In these operations of His faculties, Jesus, in spite of the sufferings to which His sensitive nature was a prey, experienced life in its most perfect form. Of Him it can be truly said that He "lived." He lived a life of unimaginable intensity. He knew the joy of living as no man has yet known it or will know it again.

Jesus enjoyed the highest exercise of the artistic faculty.
The attentive reader of the Gospel cannot fail to be struck by the wealth of imagery it contains. The discourses of the Savior are laden with it. It is astonishing how concrete His teaching is, considering the sublime nature of the truths it was His mission to impart. This fact betokens in Him a fancy of exceptional vividness and power. A constructive and creative imagination, the fertile source of all the products of man's artistic talent, had in Jesus an excellence that far surpassed that of the greatest artists known to fame. The energy, brilliancy, and constructive power of all the combined imaginations of poets, painters, architects, and sculptors could not equal the vigor and vitality and rapidity of the Savior's play of fancy.

He was keenly sensitive to the beauties of nature and responsive to her every mood. Nothing in the world about Him escaped the keenness of His observation. No artist in face of the artistry of God has ever experienced the ecstasy that the Savior experienced. What He saw moved Him deeply: its beauty stirred Him to profound admiration. Gazing appreciatively at a flower plucked by the wayside, noting its delicate hues, its graceful form, its exquisite proportions, its complex structure, He expresses the impression it makes on Him in words, in which one senses vibrant all the feeling of a truly aesthetic soul: "Not even Solomon in all his glory was clothed like one of these." [10]

[10] Lk 12: 27; Mt 6: 29.

He responded to the glory of glowing sunsets, to the bright gleam of the sweeping expanse of water, and to the grandeur of the lonely mountaintop. The rich foliage of the trees, the birds that make their homes therein, the waving fields of corn, the clustering grapes—all this was revealed to Him in its wonder and in its beauty. His imagination was thrilled by what He contemplated, all the more because He could clearly trace in all created things the careful and delicate workmanship of the Divine Artist.

It was not merely the peaceful aspects of nature that exercised their charm over Him. He was sensitive, too, to the power of the raging storm, the swishing rain, the lashing winds, and the foaming torrent: nature in the grandeur of its wrath moved Him to wonder and admiration. That love for nature in all its varied manifestations, so pronounced in St. Francis, existed in Jesus to an eminent degree. But in this universal sensitiveness to the charm of natural scenery and nature's varying moods the Savior had His preferences. The lonely solitude of the mountain exercised a spell on Him: He loved to make its heights the theater of His communings with God. He made His regular abode by the broad expanse of the Sea of Galilee, mirroring in its pellucid waters the cloudless skies of Palestine. What was grand and solid in nature made a particular appeal to Him. An edifice built on a rock expressed for Him the idea of enduring structure, proof against the assaults of the hostile elements.

Keenly alive to all the aspects of the material world, He was not less interested in all the phases of the lives of his fellow men. Nothing of what went on about Him escaped His keen and sympathetic observation. All the manifestations and forms of that varied and richly colored life of Palestine are mirrored in His discourses. Every scene stands out for us in His words, in living and vivid colors. The actors come to life again and pass before our imagination, as beings between whom and ourselves time and space have been suppressed.

The busy marketplace, the bargainings of the merchants, the self-sufficiency of the rich, the thrifty, simple existence of the poor, the calm and meditative occupation of the shepherds, the sowing of the crops, the merry harvesting, the homely festivities of the country village, the joyous start in life of the newly married, the earnest game of make-believe of the children at play in the open square, the pathos of human partings—all these features of the life of His day impressed themselves deeply on His imagination and furnished a rich store of images on which He drew readily for the illustration of His thoughts.

We are prone to draw our similes from that aspect or form of life with which we are in touch and in which we are interested. The comparisons of the soldier will be drawn from war; the sailor will clothe his thoughts in imagery borrowed from the sea; the merchant's metaphors will savor of the stock exchange; and the farmer's speech will be rich with allusions to the seasons and to the wonder of growing things.

It will be noticed that though Jesus seems to have loved in a special manner the life of the shepherd (that life furnishes Him with His most charming and touching similes), yet He was not indifferent to, or unobservant of, any of the ordinary occupations of men. His tastes and interests are universal: so, too, is His imagery. He was truly a man, and therefore everything human was of deep interest for Him.

He did not move through the throngs of His fellows, busily occupied and preoccupied as they were with the business of earthly existence, aloof, disdainful, and unsympathetic. He says Himself that He entered wholeheartedly into all their ways and moods to make Himself more thoroughly one with them and so aid them to become more thoroughly one with Him.[11] And this was not a mere matter of conscientious effort on His part, a doing of

[11] Lk 7: 31–34.

violence to Himself in view of an end to gain; it was natural and spontaneous.

He was a man, and nothing that belongs to human life was alien to Him. His imagination glowed in presence of the mystery and the beauty of God's creation in all its forms, animate and inanimate. In Him that faculty of imagination attained a perfection of activity that can never be surpassed. It reached in Him the utmost energy that is humanly possible. And this energy brought with it a pleasure and a satisfaction such as no artist has ever known.

Jesus used His intellect in the ordinary processes of reasoning, to its utmost capacity.

This splendid imagination was at the service of a superb intellect, keen, penetrating, and powerful. And this intellect was put to the fullest exercise in accordance with its normal human functioning. Its *"rendement"* was full and complete. Mention has already been made of the Savior's beatific knowledge. In addition, His intellect was perfected by infused science; this science gave Him a complete comprehension of all created reality—angels, men, and things—down to the minutest detail. But these forms of knowledge, the beatific and the infused, are not natural to man in his present state. Now, the Savior lived a human life in the literal sense of the term. It is to be expected then that He would also think humanly, that is, have that exercise of intelligence which is proper to man living in the normal conditions of human life. Theology assures us that this is so.

Besides beatific and infused knowledge, Jesus also had what is called experimental knowledge. That is, He, like us, derived ideas from experience. As His imagination was put to fullest use, so, too, His intellect was ever actively exercising itself in abstracting concepts from the images graven on His imagination by the everyday experiences of His life.

The specific activity of man as such lies in reasoning. There is an instinctive impulse in him to press his way from the known to the unknown; he is driven by an inward necessity to analyse the impressions that, through contact with the world of men and things, come to him by way of the senses. He experiences a dissatisfaction that is not allayed unless he has grasped the ultimate reasons of things, their nature, their cause, their origin, and their destiny. His intellect, as it were, wrestles with reality until reality has yielded up its inmost secrets, and only then does the intellect enjoy satisfaction and repose. This repose is its most intense form of activity; for it is an active contemplation of all things in the light of the First Cause and is a grasping of the solution of all the problems that existence offers. This is specifically human perfection.

Jesus had this perfection as well as those already mentioned above. He, too, daily submitted His experience to analysis. He turned the light of His intelligence upon the phantasms of His imagination. He abstracted ideas from them. He collated and systematized these ideas and built them up into such a philosophy of life as can be constructed by such intellectual procedure. His processes of thought in this were exactly like ours. He reasoned as we reason.

In His disputes with His adversaries He drew upon the same sources as they did; He disdained to use any weapons except such as were furnished by their armory. There is no possibility on their part of their misunderstanding His replies to their captious difficulties. Their minds were keen, subtle, and deeply versed in the religious lore of their race. It is on this ground—that of religious controversy—that they engage with Him. It is on this ground that He meets them.

Again and again they return to the attack, always hopeful of a victory in these encounters. The difficulties they raise are, to their minds, insurmountable. They always employ the dilemma. Whatever He says, the Savior, apparently, is exposed to putting Himself in opposition to some principle in the Law. His reply is like the flash of a scimitar through the air. The knot is cut in twain and by a statement of bewildering simplicity. The statement is not only simple, but thoroughly human.

Those solutions of Jesus appeal so much to the natural understanding that they have become the universal heritage of human thought and are constantly applied to the solution of human difficulties. "Render to Caesar the things that are Caesar's, and to God the things that are God's."[12] "Let him that is without sin among you cast the first stone."[13] His dialectic is the dialectic of His enemies. When accused of breaking the Sabbath, He quotes the Sabbath law and their own Sabbath practice against them. "Ye hypocrites, doth not every one of you on the Sabbath day loose his ox or his ass from the manger and lead them to water? And ought not this daughter of Abraham, whom Satan hath bound, lo, these eighteen years, be loosed from this bond on the Sabbath day?"[14]

In defense of His disciples, accused by the Pharisees of violating the Sabbath by plucking the ears of corn, He cites the example of David eating the loaves of proposition to satisfy his hunger. His argument is, if David could, in case of need, do what was technically against the law, why may not the disciples of Jesus do the same, when subject to the same necessity? The argument is very telling because He cites a case that is not only parallel but furnishes an a fortiori conclusion. It was a far less serious thing to make use of a few ears of corn, plucked when passing through the fields, than to turn to personal and profane use the loaves that were sacred.[15]

Jesus not only uses counter arguments against His opponents, He does not disdain to employ, in His turn, the dilemma against them. Being asked on what grounds He took on such an authoritative tone and proceeded in so high-handed a manner in dealing with things, He said: You ask me by what authority I do these things? "I will ask you

[12] Mt 22: 21.
[13] Jn 8: 7.
[14] Lk 13: 15–16; 14: 3–5.
[15] Mk 2: 23–28.

one word, which if you shall tell me, I will also tell you by what authority I do these things. The baptism of John, whence was it? From heaven or from men? But they thought within themselves saying: If we shall say from heaven, he will say to us: why then did you not believe him? But if we say from men we are afraid of the multitude: for all men held John as a prophet." [16] They were caught up on the horns of this dilemma: they never caught Him.

At times He takes the offensive. "And the Pharisees being gathered together, Jesus asked them, saying: 'What think you of the Christ: whose son is he?' They say to Him: 'David's.' He saith to them: 'How then doth David in spirit call Him Lord, saying: The Lord said to my Lord, sit on my right hand, until I make thy enemies my footstool? If David then call Him Lord, how is he his son?'" [17] To concede what was implied in this would be to concede that the Messiah was not merely the son of David—in other terms, that he was more than a mere man. This they would not avow. They dared not answer.

The Evangelist tells us that, from that day, no man had the courage to ask Him any more questions. [18] It was no wonder. Again and again those cunning, keen-witted, subtle foes of His had advanced confidently to the attack. Each time they were driven back in rout and discomfiture and sorely wounded. Jesus was always left master of the field of combat.

> *The language and thought and style of Jesus are characteristic of His race and time and yet are for all periods and for all races.*

In all this there was a splendid play of imagination and of reasoning. These two faculties have an exercise exhilarating in the extreme. Anyone who has taken part in or been present at intellectual disputations can testify to the intense interest of such encounters. All the energies of

[16] Mt 21: 23–26.
[17] Mt 22: 41–45.
[18] Mt 22: 46.

WHY THE CROSS?

memory, imagination, fancy, and reason are gathered up, compressed like a spring of immense power, in order to be thereafter released in a flash of destructive argument. Or to use another image, mind clashes with mind in cut or thrust or parry. It is spiritual sword-play of the highest order. The contending parties in those jousts live at these moments with a vitality into which is poured all the vital energies of their being. It is life at its best.

Our Lord lived this human life. He was master in the art of dialectics. In His public career occasions constantly presented themselves for exercise of that art. His intellect was ever tuned to its highest pitch; its energies were always at their tensest. And these energies were put forth exactly in the manner and in the form that belonged to the circle in which He moved. His arguments, illustrations, language were such as might have been employed by His adversaries. His thoughts take their color from His time, His country, and His people. It is this likeness with themselves that emboldened His enemies to contend with Him in words. But what distinguishes Him is this. What was linked with a particular period and a particular set of circumstances becomes in His dealing with it, something that belongs to all periods and all time and to all men.

"His originality lies in the fashion in which those [provincial] elements are transfigured, transmuted, spiritualized, and so universalized. These lessons, so linked with individual conditions, so strictly dated and localized, given to a few thousands of hearers, in a corner of the earth easily recognizable and strongly hostile to ideas and men from outside its borders—these lessons win understanding and conquer minds in all times and under every sky. . . . Those simple gospel discourses, full of familiar details, of clear and sharply-outlined pictures, of luminous words, go forth to enkindle and maintain the spirit of religion in the hearts of believers of every race. No man that is really man finds them above or beneath him." [19]

[19] De Grandmaison, *Jesus Christ*, 2:226 (my translation).

Accompanying this simplicity in the thought of Jesus is an ease that betokens the presence of a giant strength in His intellect. The skill with which He takes the most insignificant incident in nature or in the life of man and makes it the vehicle to convey the most sublime truth to the imagination and, through the imagination, to the mind of His hearers, marks the transcendency of His genius. Chesterton, in a passage of great acumen, writes with just discrimination of this characteristic of the intellect of Jesus. "There is nothing that indicates a subtle and, in the true sense, a superior mind so much as this power of comparing a lower thing with a higher and yet that higher with a higher still: of thinking on three planes at once. . . . These far-flung comparisons are nowhere so common as in the Gospels: and . . . they suggest something very vast. So a thing, solitary and solid, with the added dimension of depth or height, might tower over the flat creatures living only on a plane." [20]

The author had taken as an example the Savior's moralizing on the lilies of the field. He says: Jesus "takes one small flower in His hand and notes its simplicity and even its impotence: then suddenly expands it in flamboyant colors into all the palaces and pavilions full of a great name in national legend and national glory; and then, by yet a third overturn, shrivels it to nothing once more with a gesture as if flinging it away . . . 'and if God so clothes the grass that today is and tomorrow is cast into the oven—how much more.' . . . Merely in a literary sense it would be more of a masterpiece than most of the masterpieces in the libraries, yet it seems to have been uttered almost at random while a man might pluck a flower."

Jesus attained to the summit of philosophical contemplation. In all this there has been question of the life of the intellect in Jesus as exercised in the conveying of His teaching and

[20] G. K. Chesterton, *The Everlasting Man*, pt. 2, ch. 3. The whole paragraph from which this short excerpt is taken repays reading. The brevity of the citation does not do justice to the author's thought.

in combating His adversaries. That intelligence had, as well, that occupation which is common to all men, the occupation of philosophizing. St. Augustine speaks of *fides quaerens intellectum.* Although the faith sheds clear light on many of the problems of human destiny (and even on the constitution of nature to some extent), yet man's intellect is not thereby debarred from confronting reality and explaining it to the utmost extent that is possible under the light of reason. The human mind ranges freely, following its own light, within the limits traced by the dogmas of faith. Though we know by our faith what is right and wrong in conduct, we are not thereby prevented from philosophizing, in accordance with the principles of pure reason, on the laws and the intimate nature of human conduct.

Jesus had not faith. He had vision. He had, as well, infused science. But this did not prevent His mind from approaching human problems and human issues as ours does. He could philosophize from experience exactly like ourselves. He knew thoroughly all that is investigated in the different branches of philosophy, metaphysics, ethics, logic, and the rest. He worked out in His reason all the problems that are agitated in the schools and that clamor to the human reason for solution. His intelligence could lack no perfection of which it was naturally capable. In its usage, therefore, He reached the highest point of philosophic speculation.

This constitutes, according to Aristotle, the *Summum Bonum,* that is, the utmost happiness attainable by man, if he be obliged to work out his perfection from the resources of his own nature. He says: "A proof that *perfect happiness is intellectual activity or a free exercise of thought,* may be seen from the following considerations. . . . The Gods live . . . and in the case of one who lives, if action and still more production be taken out of his range, what is there left except meditation? Among all forms of activity possible for men, that will be most blessed that is nearest akin to the life of the gods. On the part of men, therefore, their life is blessed only insofar as there is abiding in it some faint resemblance to that heavenly contemplation [namely, such as is enjoyed by the gods]. But of all living creatures not one, save man, is happy inasmuch as they have in no sense any part of the 'Vision Divine.' The conclusion, therefore, is this: *wide as is the range of intellectual activity, so wide is the range of happiness:* those to whose lot it falls to have a more uninterrupted vista of *the truth, realize to an equal extent what it is to be happy*—the vision of truth being precious and glorious in itself. In a word, then, happiness is a species of ecstasy, or meditation upon things divine."[21]

This ideal and the happiness it carries with it, dreamed of by the great philosophers, was fully attained by Jesus. To His intellectual gaze, and that, too, by the natural working of the intellectual faculty, stood revealed all that is discoverable by human reason, of nature and nature's Great First Cause.

Jesus is perfect in His social relations.

In Jesus there was a perfect poise of judgment, a clear discernment, a sense of what each situation demanded that was never found at fault. He unites greatness with simplicity in His every act and every attitude. Reason regulates our relations with our fellows. The dealings of Jesus with His fellow men, friends, and enemies were characterized by a union "of sweetness and majesty, of complete devotedness and a conscious ascendency."[22] The golden mean of the Greeks was perfectly realized in Him. He is tender without being sentimental, kind without being indulgent, severe without being forbidding. He weeps and is not unmanly. He endures but is not stoical. He is hurt but is not "wounded."[23] He complains but is not querulous.

---

[21] Aristotle, *Nichomachean Ethics*, bk. 10, ch. 8.

[22] De Grandmaison, *Jesus Christ*, 2:220 (my translation).

[23] "Wounded"—in the sense it bears in phrases like "wounded pride" and "wounded feelings." It implies that feeling in which the soul shrinks into itself in silent bitterness and cold aloofness toward the author of the wrong.

He upbraids, but without bitterness. He pleads with earnestness, indeed, but with due restraint. He menaces and thunders at times, but He does not storm and rage. He stoops to render the lowliest services and yet preserves His dignity. "He condescends without lowering Himself. He devotes Himself without losing His superiority. He gives Himself but does not surrender Himself." [24] He is loaded with ignominies, and yet He does not lose His majesty. Humiliations are heaped upon Him, and yet He is not humiliated. In the horrors of the Passion He towers above both His cowardly friends and His frenzied enemies. No situation finds Him at fault. His keen intelligence shows Him how to be true in each to what He is by nature and by grace. [25]

In Jesus the will had its utmost perfection, for it bestowed its love on the supreme object of the will.

In Jesus the will reached a perfection proportioned to that of the intelligence. He was as loving as He was intelligent. The operation of the will is to attach itself to what is good. Its highest operation is to cleave to what is best—to the Supreme Good. Our greatness is measured by our love. If we give our affections to what is base, we are dragged down to the level of what is base. If we love what is noble and above us, we are raised to its condition. In the act of intelligence we unite things to our mind and give them, in a certain sense, our own limitations. In loving, on the other hand, we go out to the object that attracts us and tend to be assimilated to its perfection.

Now, Jesus saw God's beauty unveiled, and, in consequence, He poured out on His heavenly Father all the wealth of affection contained in His heart. He had said that the great and first commandment of the Law is: "Thou shalt love the Lord thy God with thy whole heart, and with thy whole soul, and with thy whole mind"—and

[24] "Many believed in His name, but Jesus did not trust Himself unto them, for that He knew all men" (Jn 2: 24).

[25] See De Grandmaison, *Jesus Christ*, 2:216.

added that "the second is like unto this. Thou shalt love thy neighbor as thyself. On these two commandments dependeth the whole law and the prophets." [26] He, the Perfect Man, fulfilled these two precepts perfectly. He loved God, and He loved man with all the force with which a human heart can love. The chastity of Christ was not an incapacity for affection. It was simply love of the most intense kind bestowed worthily, that is, on what alone deserves to be loved. He was, to use the bold words of a great poet, truly a "tremendous lover."

Jesus loved God with all His force.

Jesus loved God with all His strength. To love is to find one's greatest good in another. Such a love impels the lover to pursue the interests and the good of the beloved with all eagerness. The happiness of the beloved is the happiness of the lover. The whole energy the body and mind of Christ was thrown without reserve into the task of promoting God's good, that is, God's glory. He did not allow Himself to be distracted from this work by the strongest ties of nature. "Did you not know I must be about my Father's business?" [27]

The thirty years of restraint in obscurity and the three years of unremitting apostolic labor before the public eye were devoted wholly to promoting the cause of God. He never thought of Himself. He was gladdened by the triumphs of God over the stubborn blindness of men as a mother is gladdened by the glory of her child. "In that same hour He rejoiced in the Holy Spirit and said: I confess to thee, O Father, Lord of heaven and earth, because thou hast hidden these things from the wise and prudent and hast revealed them to little ones. Yea, Father, for so it seemed good in thy sight." [28] His joy is caused by the sight of the successful working of grace in souls and at the glory that redounds to God thereby. The first petition

[26] Mt 22: 37–40; Lk 10: 27; Mk 12: 29–31.
[27] Lk 2: 49.
[28] Lk 10: 21; compare Mt 11: 25.

in the prayer dictated by Him reveals what was uppermost in His thoughts and desires: "Our Father who art in heaven, hallowed be thy name."

He conformed Himself in all things to God's will in the carrying out of His life task.

He loved God wholeheartedly. He was always at one with the will of God in carrying out His mission. He not only slaved in God's service, He slaved in the way and on the objects that God willed. He did not seek God's glory in His own way. "I seek not my own will but the will of Him that sent me." [29] He uses a more forcible expression still: "My meat is to do the will of Him that sent me." [30] In each activity of His ministry He followed the promptings of the Spirit of God within Him. What is related of Him in the opening of His public career describes what was His constant way of action from the beginning to the end. "Jesus was led by the Spirit into the desert." [31]

God was the constant object of the thought of Jesus. The Savior ever enjoyed the happiness of knowing that He was perfectly at one with God.

He loved God with all His mind. He knew God as God is known by no other creature. "Neither doth anyone know the Father, but the Son, and he to whom it shall please the Son to reveal Him." [32] Who can measure the depth of the love that springs from that knowledge!

God was ever the object of His thoughts. That object drew His heart like a magnet at all times. The Gospel bears eloquent witness to this fact. It reveals, on many a page, the yearning that ever possessed Jesus to get away from the crowds and to seek a solitude where He could give Himself up uninterruptedly to loving converse with His Father. His prayer is not always the prayer of petition.

[29] Jn 5: 30; 4: 34; 6: 38; Mt 12: 50; Mk 3: 35.
[30] Jn 4: 34.
[31] Mt 4: 1.
[32] Mt 11: 27; Lk 10: 22.

The greater part of those long hours of communion with God were spent in giving free rein to the effusions of filial love that welled up from the depths of His soul, set free at last to give itself up without distraction or without reserve to the delight of loving and being loved in turn. He Himself certainly practiced the prayer of union inculcated on others, the necessity and sublimity of which He stressed so often. "Mary has chosen the better part." [33]

What passed during those long vigils of the night[34] between the God of heaven and that Man Whom God proclaimed to be "His beloved Son, in whom He was well pleased," is far beyond our imaginings. The experiences of the saints in their raptures and ecstasies are, as it were, a tiny gleam revealed to us of the glowing splendors of that world of fire generated by the outpourings of the human love of Jesus for His Father. The burning love of saints and angels is but a feeble flame compared with the love of the human heart of Christ. For the loving converse of Jesus manifests characteristics such as cannot be found in the purest of saints and even in the angels themselves.

Every human creature aiming at immediate union with the Creator experiences a species of dismay at seeing the mighty fathomless chasm that yawns between the spirit wedded to matter and that Spirit which is absolutely pure, which is nothing but actuality and perfection. This dismay is intensified when, to the native imperfection and limitation of the creature, is added the wretchedness that has its source in ingratitude and rebellion. At the sight of this horror with which their native "otherness" from God is encrusted, the saints experience an agonizing desire of purification—of spiritualization. Until this process is undergone, the approach of the divinity fills them with a veritable terror: this terror, it is true, in all cases passes and yields place to peace and contentment. But it invariably exists at the first contact between the created spirit

[33] Lk 10: 42.
[34] Lk 6: 12.

WHY THE CROSS?

and the divinity. St. Teresa says more than once that on these occasions she felt the hair of her head stand on end.[35]

Nothing of all this is observable in the case of the Savior. His relations with His heavenly Father, it is true, are marked by a complete self-effacement and the most profound respect. In His eyes, as man, God alone is good,[36] and the creature that He is is nothing. But His attitude toward God is an exquisite blending of filial reverence and filial love. There is no anxiety or doubt in His mind about the attitude of God toward Himself. There is no evidence of any sense on His part of a need of a process of purification to be undergone through in order to enter into intimate union with God.

On the contrary, He acts at all times as if that union were to be taken for granted. He prays to God, but He knows that He is always heard, even while, as becomes His creature condition, He returns thanks for being heard.[37] He is, so to speak, always sure of God and sure of His place with God. He moves in the atmosphere of the divine as in His own native air. There is no appearance in Him of a felt need of adjustment to a strange condition.

"This man, to whom no human experience is unknown, knows nothing of moral evil, regret, or remorse. When there is question of intercession, of pardon, of sin, and of compunction, it is always with regard to others. He exhorts to penance: He does not repent. He recommends vigilance and warns each one to see to the salvation of his soul: He is secure. He advises others to fear: He loves. He bids them to seek: He has found. . . . This union of perfect confidence with the deepest religious respect; of an inborn and tender familiarity—conscious of utter blamelessness—with the clearest perception of the horror of sin and of the demands of divine justice; of an unshakable security with a full appreciation of what God is and what

[35] Teresa of Avila, *Life*, ch. 39.
[36] Mt 19: 17.
[37] Jn 11: 41–42.

we are; this union is one of the entrance doors to the mystery of Jesus." [38]

It is the mystery of Jesus, but it is the revelation of the source of the boundless tranquility and calm and peace that marked His life on earth. What incomparable happiness for the human soul lies in the certitude that it is perfectly agreeable to God! Jesus perpetually enjoyed this great happiness. Set apart from us by the beatific knowledge and infused science, Jesus is not completely severed from our condition in the love of His human heart for God. Faith and hope are our portion: vision was His. These are different. The former virtues can no longer exist when the Divinity bursts on the soul's gaze. It is not so with charity. It stands the acid test of death, as gold the *aqua fortis.* "Charity never falleth away." [39]

Immense as is the love of Jesus, based on the vision face to face, there can be a certain community between Him and ourselves in the exercise of the love of God, since the charity of earth and heaven is essentially the same. Love follows on knowledge. Jesus knew God according to the beatific vision—and His will answered to that light of the intelligence by beatific love. He also knew God by His infused science, and His heart responded by a movement proportionate to the clarity of this special, preternatural knowledge. But Jesus, as well, traced the beauty of God in creation, and, *in the beauty of the artist's work,* stirred by what He contemplated through the play of His perceptive faculties, He loved the artist in the beauty of the artist's handiwork.

> *There was not only happiness in the life of Jesus, there was pleasure too, pleasure being the gratification that attends on the free and unimpeded and perfect play of a conscious faculty.*

It is not necessary to dwell on the love of Jesus for men. He loved them and was loved and is loved by multitudes in return. This complement of a perfect life was not wanting

[38] De Grandmaison, *Jesus Christ,* pp. 209–10 (my translation).
[39] 1 Cor 13: 8.

to Him. Enough has been said to show how justly the life of Jesus may be considered to have been an eminently happy life. If happiness is, as it has been defined to be, the highest energy of the highest faculties of man exercised on the most perfect objects of those faculties, then it must be agreed that Jesus was happy. In Him imagination, intelligence, and will attained their highest perfection and their most excellent operation.

Happiness means the perfect life, or life in its perfection. It is not identical with pleasure. But even this element of pleasure was not wholly, but only in part, wanting to the life of Christ. Pleasure results from the normal exercise of a faculty in a conscious being, when this exercise is such as to tax, without overtaxing, the capacities of the faculty. As has been said, pleasure is the satisfying conscious glow that accompanies and has its source in healthy vital action. It is defined by Aristotle as "the mode of activity of a mental state that is in harmony with nature and unimpeded."[40]

This experience Jesus had in a supreme degree from the operation of the faculties specifically human. All the pleasure that comes from the free, vital, and unimpeded play of will and intellect was His in the supreme degree attainable on earth. In the exercise of His imagination He had pleasure to some extent, as has been explained. The highest and best pleasures that spring from the exercise of the imagination were His.

But not all the play of imagination with Him was attended by unalloyed pleasure. Owing to the conditions of mortality to which He submitted Himself, His sensitive nature had its free development thwarted by suffering and sorrow, and its activities were attended more by pain than by pleasure. Hence, though His life was not wanting in pleasures of the higher order, it did lack in large measure the lower, namely, those that arise from the vital functioning of the sensitive soul. But this limitation took

---

[40] *Nichomachean Ethics*, bk. 7, ch. 13.

nothing from that substantial happiness which Jesus constantly enjoyed in the consciousness that He was dear to God and loved with all the tenderness that is lavished on an only-begotten Son.

It is this happiness chiefly that He invites us to share with Him, though He promises, as well, the happiness that springs from contemplation. He said: "He that loveth me, shall be loved of my Father: and I will love him and will *manifest* myself to him." [41] This love of God for us, and the loving contemplation that this love stirs up in our soul, will be ours if we consent to walk on earth as Jesus walked. "But as many as received Him, he gave them power to be made the sons of God, to them that believe in his name." [42]

The life of Jesus Christ offers a flat contradiction to the view that happiness is incompatible with suffering. He suffered as no man has suffered; He was happy, on earth, as no man has been, or can be, happy. It is true that suffering, being a limitation of life, is, in some measure, a limitation of happiness. But, however intense it may become, it cannot corrupt the substance of human well-being. Suffering is an attack on life in its initial or lower stages. It cannot take from what is highest in vital human activity. Hence, it was that, though suffering is a thing that need not be, a thing that should not be, and a thing in itself hostile to life, Christ was able to make of it an instrument of life itself at its highest. Suffering is the fruit of man's usurpation of God's sovereignty. Suffering is a negative thing. Hence it is of man's handiwork, because man's independent creative effort must issue in nothingness, that is, in the absence of reality. God Incarnate submitted to what was man's, not His, creation and made it serve a purpose at once divine and human.

[41] Jn 14: 21.
[42] Jn 1: 12.

CHAPTER SIX

Behold My servant . . . My soul delighted in him. . . . He shall not cry out, nor have respect to persons: neither shall his voice be heard abroad.

—ISAIAH 42: 1–2

The problems of existence cannot be solved by theories born of pure reason: they can be solved only practically.

VERY MANY SOULS, and these the most sensitive, find themselves a prey to an exasperation, amounting to a veritable agony of bitterness, in face of the perplexing problems presented by human existence. There is much in the regular course of events that jars on their sense of the fitness of things. Every effort of reason to construct a satisfying theory of the cosmos collapses in face of inescapable facts.

Trials multiply, most frequently, in the path of those who are least deserving of them. There are sorrows, failures, and sufferings that appear to be without meaning or purpose. Error is, oftentimes, punished as severely by circumstances as deliberate malice. In the catastrophes of nature the good are overwhelmed equally with the wicked. The virtuous and the high-minded are, generally speaking, thwarted, ridiculed, and discredited. The cunning and the resourceful and the unscrupulous rarely lack favor and applause.

Nowhere are these outrages on reason so vividly dramatized as they are in the life of Christ. The Savior was utterly blameless in His conduct, and yet no one encountered such lack of appreciation and such positive opposition as He. He was kind, wise, and beneficent, and yet men turned upon Him with more fury than they would vent upon an avowed enemy of mankind. He was eminently fitted to guide men to the goal toward which they are perpetually striving, and yet He found very few to enroll themselves in His following. He was endowed with every quality that makes for success; nevertheless, *humanly speaking*, He was an utter failure. Nothing but good came from Him, and little but evil was meted out to Him. Christ lived among men and conversed with them daily; He worked for them and He worked with them.

The angels themselves—what is more, God Himself—could not, with the most intense scrutiny, detect a flaw in His conduct; in spite of that, He was little appreciated by the men among whom He lived, if exception be made of a few discerning persons. The success of evil and the apparent failure of good forced itself on the attention of Christ, day by day. He constantly and personally experienced the effects of the one and the other. He, like other men, found his deep sense of what ought to be challenged by the problems thus presented. Unlike other men, He was neither dismayed nor baffled by these problems.

Christ solved the riddle of existence by living. It was not as if He first constructed a hypothesis and then tested it by facts. It was not through practical experience that He found that his theory was a working theory. He held the solution to life's problems from the beginning. He knew He possessed it.

An inability to comprehend the meaning of the evil, the pain, and the cruelty of existence and a passionate resentment against the irresistible invasion of life by what is at one and the same time felt to be both unreasonable and intolerable are the enduring causes of man's unhappiness. One can submit to what one understands. One cannot but experience revolt against what does brutal violence to the reason.

Christ's theory of existence is the only one that can banish this incomprehension from life and, with it, the unhappiness that has its source in that incomprehension.

This is the significance that underlay His words when He said: "Learn of Me . . . and you shall find rest for your souls."[1] Rest implies attainment, contentment, peace and consequently happiness.

To learn of Christ is to adopt practically Christ's philosophy of existence. From the moment a man seriously sets about applying to the direction of his own life the principles that governed Christ's life, there takes place an immediate illumination. There begins to be discerned a definite scheme into which can be fitted, and through which can be coordinated and rendered intelligible, all the elements that constitute the human experience of the disciple of Christ. The impression of a fatal and uncontrolled disorder fades away. The purpose behind happenings that hitherto appeared senseless, the fruitful action of suffering that before seemed purely negative and destructive, all this emerges from the obscurity in which it had been shrouded. The threads of the tapestry of life that looked so unsightly and so hopelessly entangled begin to reveal a firm design of order and beauty. The interrelation between circumstances, that to another would look wholly unconnected, becomes apparent.

To adopt Christ's principles practically and to take His yoke on one's shoulders are one and the same thing. Men shrink from the yoke because to the imagination it conjures up visions of intense strain. Vainly has the Savior assured them that His yoke is easy. The fancy is busy at work forming somber pictures of the rough paths along which the yoke is to be borne. Hardships, toil, want, homelessness, opposition, unpopularity, derision, hatred, and even crucifixion, of a moral, if not of a physical, kind—all these defile rapidly before the mental gaze and inspire terror and repulsion. How could all that be light or easy?

And yet, the Savior cannot lie. He is Truth Itself. Imagination in this, as in so many things, plays men false. It is

[1] Mt 11: 29.

not in the actual experiences of His life that Jesus invites us to imitate Him, but in that fundamental spirit which was the wellspring of His actions in, and His reactions to, the world in which He lived. To take up the yoke of the Savior is not necessarily to do or to suffer such things as He did and suffered, but to show oneself such a man as He was in the arena of life.

To express in a few words what kind of man the Savior was is not an easy matter. It could not be done, had not Christ Himself done it for us.

To imitate Christ is to reproduce in oneself the fundamental traits of His human character. To do this it is necessary to know what kind of man Christ was, to know what was the distinctive feature of His moral physiognomy.

Men, in describing their fellows, constantly endeavor to convey an idea of their personality by a few words that will serve to present a true moral portrait. A man under discussion is described, for instance, as being upright, harsh, unfeeling, unaffected, obstinate, self-seeking, and so on. In these adjectives, or in a combination of them, there can be conveyed a fairly accurate notion of what a man is like. The description, if accurate, will enable one to form a shrewd judgment as to what may be expected of the person, of whom there is question, were he placed in such or such circumstances. In social or business relations with such a one, it becomes possible to decide on the suitable line of action to adopt. One course would be advisable in dealing with the opportunist, another would suit in transactions with the conscientious.

It would be interesting to know if even the immediate disciples of the Savior ever endeavored to "hit off" His character in this way to one another, when discussing Him among themselves. How would they truthfully express Him for what He was?

It would not have been an easy thing to do. It would demand insight into character and spiritual acumen of a very high order. If the disciples of Christ ever made such an attempt, it is doubtful it would have been successful. For, in striving to express what Jesus is, one is seemingly confronted with a personality[2] of disconcerting complexity. In Him is discerned a combination of qualities of the most opposite kinds.

The Redeemer shows Himself of incredible condescension toward sinners, while at the same time inexorable toward sin. He points out that loving the neighbor is a reflex of the love of God, and He states that nobody can aspire to be a disciple of His unless he hates father and mother and those most closely knit to him by ties of blood. He pursues moral evil relentlessly into the most secret recesses of thought—He will not allow any earthly loss, however great, to be weighed in the balance against sin: "If thy eye scandalize thee, pluck it out; if thy hand scandalize thee, cut it off."[3] In spite of that, He shows Himself warmly appreciative of the least elements of good will on the part of sinful men. He is grateful for the least that men will offer Him, and yet He is contented with nothing short of the utmost. A cup of cold water given in His name will not go unrewarded; and then, bewilderingly, a complete sacrifice of one's all is taken as a matter of course. He is delighted with the ordinary workaday virtue and the rugged candor of a Nathanael and turns to tell His followers that they have to be "perfect as their heavenly Father is perfect."[4] He is transported with joy by an act of faith on the part of Peter, and a few moments later he stigmatizes him as a Satan, swayed, and attempting to sway others, by considerations of an earthly character.

The erring and inconstant Peter is made the foundation stone of the Church, while the faithful and virginal

---

[2] Personality is taken here in the psychological sense in which it is ordinarily employed. It is not to be understood ontologically, for, in the order of being, Jesus had not a human personality but a divine.

[3] Mk 9: 42–46.

[4] Mt 5: 48.

John is passed over for this office of trust. He remits sin with an ease that scandalizes the "rigidly righteous," and He demands of all without exception the most exacting self-denial and the most flawless sanctity. He so deals with sin and sinners that one would judge that He regarded moral deformity as the normal thing in men. On the other hand, He as calmly demands complete perfection in conduct on the part of all those who listen to His instructions, as if He were utterly blind to human frailty. He manifests infinite tactfulness in treating with the wayward, infinite patience with the dull-witted, and inexhaustible consideration for the willful. And again His words scorch and shrivel like vindictive lightning when He upbraids the hypocritical. He fulfills the lowliest offices toward His intimates and withal demands of them the most unquestioning loyalty as the price of His friendship. He is meek as a lamb led to the slaughter, and, nevertheless, His eyes can flash with the fire of fierce wrath. He is deeply compassionate toward distress of every kind, yet He calmly exposes His followers to a fate in which suffering is their daily portion. He declares blessed the peacemakers and confesses that He Himself is to be a source of division. He says that heaven is the reward of violent effort, but that only those who are as children shall enter therein.

One might go on almost indefinitely multiplying these baffling contrasts. The more they are considered, the more difficult it might seem to trace a unity in this amazing variety. Yet there is a common element to be found in all. In strength or in weakness, in gentleness or in wrath, in justice and in mercy, in exigence and in condescension, Jesus acts in a way that is thoroughly characteristic. "His greatness lies in the perfect equilibrium in Him of qualities opposed to, but not contradictory of, one another." [5]

[5] "Those whose philosophy tends to a simplification *à outrance* forget that true greatness manifests itself in the possession of opposing qualities which balance without contradicting one another" (L. De Grandmaison, *Jesus Christ*).

He attained the just measure in the expression of the different virtues, because humility was the basis of His human character. Jesus is truly described when it is said of Him that He was above all else a humble Man. As a Man He could be spoken of as the personification of humility. It is His own description of Himself. "Learn of me," He said, "that I am meek and humble of heart."

Humility is based on reverence toward God. It consists in knowing one's true position in the scheme of things and in abiding in that position.

A clear idea of the nature of this virtue, which gave its distinctive "cachet" to the human character of Jesus, is not commonly held. An accurate analysis of it is not without its difficulty. Being but badly understood, its practice is rare.

"Everybody," writes the Venerable Libermann, "thinks it a praiseworthy thing to speak continually of humility and scarcely any one possesses it." A little further on in the same context he says: "I have frequently remarked that the word has scarcely any significance on the tongues of the majority of those [he is speaking of the seminarists] that discuss it. . . . It does not consist in a display of words, nor in the exercise of the intelligence, nor in a play of the imagination, . . . neither is it acquired by one's efforts, by natural activity, by a great output of energy, by painful eagerness. Real humility does not consist in outward action, nor in seizing eagerly upon what is outwardly humble nor in appearing before the eyes of others in a position or action that is lowly and humiliating."[6]

What then is it? It is a virtue that is based on a profound and enlightened reverence toward God. Its motive lies in a lowly and unqualified subjection to the Almighty.[7]

[6] Ven. Libermann, *Lettres spirituelles*, 1:60. See also St. Teresa, *Life*, 2:34; Abbot Marmion, *Le Christ: Ideal de Moine*, in the chapter on humility; and Bishop Ullathorne in his admirable work on this subject.

[7] Thomas Aquinas, *Summa theologiae*, II-II, q. 161, a. 1, ad. 5, and a. 2, ad. 3.

Where there is absent a keen recognition of the illimitable claims of the sovereignty of God, humility cannot exist.

Because of this absence, not only was humility not practiced by the pagans, it was not even known to them. The spirit of restraint and measure in action and aspiration inculcated by Aristotle and the other ancient philosophers has some traits of resemblance to the Christian virtue, but the resemblance is only superficial. The "nothing too much" of the pagans, their horror of the bizarre and the disproportionate, springs from a respect for the reason they esteemed in themselves.[8] What they cultivated did not check or neutralize the inordinate love of one's own excellence that is so opposed to humility and is so fundamental a tendency in fallen human nature.

This evil and inveterate tendency makes a man chafe against the necessary limitations inherent in his condition. To his native limitations as a creature are added the disabilities that weigh upon him as a fallen creature. This complexus of contracting and thwarting elements reduces man to a condition against which he is in a constant state of passionate resentment and sullen revolt.

The instincts of the "old man" are perpetually instigating him to dissatisfaction with his position in the plan of Divine Providence. He is spurred on by pride to aspire after an untrammeled position that is not rightfully his. He claims an excellence that does not belong to him, a freedom from limitation that conflicts with his "creatureliness," an immunity from suffering incompatible with his state of mortality, and an independence of thought and will, which is a divine prerogative.

Humility is the virtue whose function it is to combat these evil tendencies of the pride of life. To aim at a moral position other than that assigned to one by the providence of God, to seek while being a mere man not to suffer from human limitations, is implicitly to revolt

[8] See ibid., a. 1, ad. 5.

against the Almighty.[9] One who has a true reverence for God will not suffer himself to yield to these promptings of pride. From reverence is begotten the virtue of humility, which exercises a moderating and restraining influence on the false and disorderly aspirations of the human will and holds man firmly in his proper place in the scheme of reality.[10]

Man's true place is fixed relatively to the Creator and to creatures. To act as he ought, as befits his position, he must have an accurate and clear vision of that position. Hence, though humility is primarily a virtue of the will, it has a background of intelligence.[11] Without intelligence there cannot be humility. The Christian virtue postulates as well a strong will and sound judgment. Intelligence must not in this context be confounded with learning. The learned are often unintelligent and therefore proud.

Jesus had a most penetrating intelligence. He saw His position with the utmost clearness. His will was resolute in commanding action regulated by His position.

Jesus was in mind and will admirably equipped to practice and exemplify the virtue He so recommended. That will was as unbreakable as the most finely tempered steel. His intellect was of unapproachable power and clarity. He saw, as never man did, what God was, what man was, and what He Himself as creature was. He could not err in calculating the position He was to keep and to hold. His deep reverence for God was the motive that held Him in place, regulating the actions of will and intellect. As gravity draws the stone to earth, so regard for His heavenly Father caused Christ to gravitate to His place in creation. Having an overpowering sense of the rights of God and of the

---

[9] This does not mean, of course, that one is not entitled to better one's condition in life, as the phrase goes. The revolt here condemned is the revolt against the inherent and essential limitations that belong to human nature in its fallen state.

[10] *Summa theologiae*, q. 161, a. 2, ad. 3.

[11] Ibid., a. 2, ad. 3, corp. art.

duties of the creature, He was utterly humble. His humility was the very antithesis of the pride of Adam and was the undoing of that pride.

The intelligence of the Savior was penetrated through and through with the sense of those inspired words that, with tender pathos and delicate poetry, speak of the transcendence of God. Every fiber of His sensitive soul responded to the tones of the great Prophet, saying: "All nations are before Him as if they had no being at all, and are accounted to Him as nothing and vanity. Behold the Gentiles are as a drop of a bucket, and are counted as the smallest grain of a balance; behold the islands are as a little dust." [12] Far from shrinking from the consequences of the truth conveyed in these words of Scripture, He embraced it eagerly with His whole soul. He loved to plunge into His own nothingness as a creature in the presence of the "Allness" of God. In the same act, He delighted in the greatness of God and His own littleness as man.

God the Son become Incarnate espoused the lot of fallen humanity. His humility consisted in His abiding firmly in this position and in His willing acquiescence in all its consequences.

In consenting to undertake the salvation of mankind, Jesus consented to identify Himself with the lot of fallen humanity. The redemption as planned by the Almighty demanded that the Son of men should not only mingle *among* men, but that He should become one *of* them, even more, that He should become one *with* them, as their Head and Chief.

By the Incarnation this became Christ's proper, if self-chosen, position in creation. He accepted all the consequences of it with unflinching, undeviating, and unfailing fortitude. His humility did not allow Him to evade any of those consequences, however harsh.

[12] Is 40: 15.

To abide in His position, He had to forego many of His rightful prerogatives. He was God and could claim the rights of God. He made no such claim. He was a man undefiled, wholly innocent, flawlessly just. He could have considered Himself entitled to be dealt with by men and circumstances as such. He did not allow Himself to do so. In order to redeem, He accepted the position of Head of the rebellious and fallen race. In His love for men He accepted their condition and all its disabilities, apart from moral evil. He consented to be treated by events and by the interplay of human passions, like His fellows.

He shared man's lot completely and set Himself before them as an example in not indulging in sullen revolt against the grievous disabilities that weigh upon fallen mankind. Though Himself unfallen, Christ was as humble in submission to Divine Providence in all the details of His earthly career as if He were really a fallen creature. In this He showed Himself as humble as His fellow mortals showed themselves proud.

Though sharing in Adam's fault and guilt, men, in their ignorant and insane pride, claim to be dealt with by circumstances as if they were as innocent and as divine as Christ. They rail against the conditions of their own making as did the unrepentant thief on the cross. Though laboring under the consequences of Original Sin, they aspire to the prerogatives of God, to His independence and His impassibility, though not, as Bossuet ironically remarks after St. Augustine, to His sanctity and His magnanimity.

Jesus was well aware of the kind of world into which He penetrated in His mission of salvation. He knew that His justice would not be esteemed and that His sinlessness would not be revered. He did not need to experience that His unchallenged perfection of character and conduct, so far from securing Him immunity from suffering, would but involve Him in bitter conflict.

The Savior had no illusions about the "indefinite perfectibility of men through reason and science." His penetrating glance plumbed the utmost depths of human malice. "Jesus," St. John tells us, "did not trust Himself unto them, for that He knew all men. And because He needed not that any should give testimony of man, for He knew what was in man." [13] His very goodness could not but provoke aversion and hatred in the soul that breathes the spirit of the original revolt against the Supreme Good. Having placed Himself deliberately in a world where the light of justice was eclipsed and dark passions raged without control, the Savior knew that He would be dealt with unjustly and that in proportion to His justice. That was His freely chosen lot. He did not murmur at, or rebel against, it.

To clamor to be above or outside the essential conditions of one's destiny is an effect of pride. Christ's humility retained Him in the destiny of the defiled. Having, in a spirit of devotedness to man and love for God, flung Himself into the turbulent sea of angry human passions, He did not cry out against the buffetings He received, nor did He rail against the rulings of Divine Providence.

> *There is an uncompromising finality about the intellectual attitude of Jesus. The absolute sovereignty of God was for Him a ruling principle.*

The foregoing considerations show in what aspect the new Head of the human race was like, and in what aspect unlike, His fellows. He shared their mortality. He did not share their convictions. With the modern decay of the sense of the supernatural there is to be observed a growing tendency to dwell almost exclusively on the affective or the will aspect of Christ's character. The intellectual side is but slightly, if at all, touched upon by writers who are without faith in His divinity. Among them there is a pronounced tendency to represent the historic Christ as in no way a dogmatic Christ.

Now, what may be discerned in Jesus, as more characteristic of Him than His gentleness and mercy, is a certain

---

[13] Jn 2: 24–25.

serene intellectuality. There is a quality of crystal clearness, accompanied by an uncompromising finality about
his thought. In the intellectual sphere there is no toler-
ance in Him. For Him it is yea and nay, and one is not
allowed to shade over into the other, in a way beloved of
moderns. At the center of His conceptual universe is fixed
the conviction that God was all and that man of himself
was nothing. It was a cardinal principle with Him that the
highest of creatures could be nothing but the servant of
God, with no rights except those of total service. Far
would it be from His mind to repudiate the words of the
inspired writer concerning the Messiah: "Behold my servant: I have given my spirit upon Him: He shall bring
forth judgment to the Gentiles." [14] Christ was uncompromising in His assertion that all human affairs, personal,
social and political, should have as their regulating principle the mind and the will of God.

This unyielding, adamantine quality of Christ's views of
the relation of human affairs to God exasperated His
contemporaries, as the reiteration of the same views by
His Church continues to exasperate men all through the
ages. Those proud and self-seeking men of affairs who
listened to Him dashed themselves in fury against Christ's
intellectual position and seethed with rage as they found
that they could not, either by flattery or menace, dislodge
Him from it. He could not but hold them wrong if they
preferred, to the declared will of God, their own views
and traditions as the regulative principles of their public
and private life. He said to them: "Why do you also trans-
gress the commandment of God for your tradition? . . .
You have made void the commandment of God for your
tradition." [15]

It was a particular instance that called forth this re-
proof. But, as usual, the words of Christ have a universal
import. This intransigent vindication of the absolute and
all-pervading sovereignty of God in human affairs was at

[14] Is 42: 1.
[15] Mt 15: 3–6.

the very heart of the conflict between Christ and His contemporaries. It is at the very heart of the conflict in which the Church is ever engaged with the temporal powers. Jesus worshiped a God of divine and transcendent proportions: men would worship a God dwarfed to their own miserable conceptions.

In His reproach to the Pharisees, Jesus placed His finger on an inveterate evil tendency in proud human nature, namely, the tendency to reject God unless He can be contracted to fit into man's petty rational preconceptions and his purblind notions of the congruous in things. Someone has remarked with cutting, though appropriate, irony that God in the beginning made men to His own image and that, in process of time, man repaid the compliment by making God to his. The Jews turned against the Savior when He refused to accommodate Himself to their narrow views of the divine purpose in life, a consequence of their unworthy views of the Divinity.

The absolute dependence on, and subjection to, God, which sprang from man's creaturehood, was, for Christ, the essential truth to be presupposed in all interpretations of the economy of men's dealings with God. This truth was, for Him, the foundation stone of the whole edifice of religion. "For this was I born, and for this I came into the world, that I should give testimony to the truth," [16] said Jesus to the Roman Governor. The central and pivotal truth that Christ was appointed to maintain and vindicate was that God is Lord and King over all creatures, and that from His hands, He, the Savior, holds His kingship. [17]

Man's pride tends to whittle down the absoluteness of God's claims. He presumes to define the limits within which the Almighty is to exercise control over human affairs.
The children of the first Adam, in direct opposition to the Second Adam, ever seek to restrict God's right, to put limitations to His overlordship, and to set qualifications to

[16] Jn 18: 37.
[17] Thomas Aquinas, *Comm. in Evang. St. Johnnis*, ch. 18, no. 9 *ad finem*.

their own subjection to Him. They claim to withdraw whole spheres of human activity from His authority. They resent, as an intrusion, His interference beyond limits they prescribe.

To Jesus this was the wrong of wrongs, the supreme falsehood, the flat contradiction of the truths it was His office to champion. Christ's life was the living expression of this great truth, that God is Supreme and Absolute Lord. It was this that drew upon Christ the frenzied hatred of His contemporaries. But, with humility, He stood rooted in the position that He saw to be His and that He saw, too, to be that of all men. Their pride spent itself fruitlessly on the rock of His humility.

He did not quail before the storm that He created, for true humility inspires utter fearlessness. The Christian virtue is not the nerveless, spineless, spiritless thing that it is supposed by those who rail at it as destructive of human dignity. Christ was humble, yet no one could surpass Him in courage and dignity. He was humble, yet He was truly great—not in spite of His humility but because of it. The true greatness and the perfect freedom of men have their source in perfect subordination to God. To be humble is to be true to what one is in thought and to have conduct based upon that thought.

Christ was the personification of Truth. Satan is Satan, or the adversary, because "he stood not in the truth." [18] Pride is the mark of Satan and of all those who, in greater or less measure, swerve from the essential truth preached by Christ.

There could be but one issue to the conflict between Christ and the world, as there was no possibility of compromise.
His humanity was crushed under the weight of opposition.
Standing in the very center of reality, Christ saw all things in proper perspective and in their right proportions. He had an exquisite sense of balance and measure. His

[18] Jn 8: 44.

enemies, viewing everything through the distorting medium of their pride, saw all things out of proportion. To them the interests of men were magnified exceedingly and the interests of God dwarfed correspondingly. The antagonists of the Servant of Jehovah merited the reproach He addressed to them. "If God were your father, you would indeed love me. For from God I proceeded and came. . . . You are of your father the devil, and the desires of your father you will do. . . . If I say the truth, why do you not believe me. He that is of God heareth the words of God. Therefore you hear them not because you are not of God." [19]

For Christ there could be no such thing as compromise with the world ranged against God. "There could be no fellowship between light and darkness." [20] He knew well to what this uncompromising attitude of His committed Him. He saw that it was inevitable that his unyielding humility should call forth the most violent explosions of the intolerance of pride. He was not blind as to the fate to which He was committing His followers during all time when He said to them: "That which I speak to you in the dark, speak ye in the light: and that which you hear in the ear, preach ye upon the housetops. And fear ye not them that kill the body and are not able to kill the soul: but rather fear him that can destroy both body and soul into hell." [21]

He was not as one addressing, from a position of safety, a stirring call to others to face death without fear. He was an exemplar of the fortitude He inculcated, the foremost in facing the fate to which He exhorted His followers. He entered the conflict provoked by His doctrine armed only with His innocence and humility. His enemies opposed Him inflamed with hate and equipped with all the resources of malice. The Almighty withdrew from His Servant the protection of the Divinity.

[19] Jn 8: 42–47.
[20] 2 Cor 6: 14–15.
[21] Mt 10: 27–28.

There could be only one issue to such a struggle. Christ's humanity was crushed to death. He could not yield the position to which He was assigned by His humility. His stand was in the truth, and He was cut down where He stood. It was as Son of man that Jesus suffered. "He humbled Himself; becoming obedient unto death, even unto the death of the Cross." [22]

The Savior Himself declared that humility was the distinguishing feature of His human character. That humility consisted in His holding Himself firmly in the position that was His through His consenting to be Head of the sinful race of mankind. Pride is the radical evil in fallen human nature. It is an unjustifiable aspiration after an excellence that is not one's due. In Satan and in Adam it prompted an attempt to usurp the prerogatives of the Almighty; it inspired no ambition to emulate His holiness. Christ's humility was the very antithesis to their pride. It sprang from a profound reverence toward God. It dictated thought and action consonant with the position of the scheme of things that Jesus made His own. The pride of fallen man was in irreconcilable opposition to the humility of Christ. The shock of the two was inevitable. It resulted in the death of the Son of man.

[22] Phil 2: 8.

CHAPTER SEVEN

Him who knew no sin, on our behalf He hath been made sin for us, that we might be made the justice of God in Him.

— 2 CORINTHIANS 5: 21

The catastrophic ending to the life of the Savior was the result of the operation of no ordinary human forces.

ON THE MORNING of the Sunday in the last week of His mortal life, Jesus entered Jerusalem amid the enthusiastic acclamations of a multitude composed of citizens and strangers. His malignant enemies saw their snarling protests drowned in the tumult of rejoicing. They felt themselves to be like straws tossed helplessly on the swelling tide of popular favor on which the Nazarene was borne triumphantly. "The Pharisees therefore said among themselves: 'Do you see that we prevail nothing? Behold the whole world is gone after him.'"[1] And yet, five days later, Jesus was hurried through the streets of the city of His triumph amid the execrations of the multitude and the silent dismay of His friends.

Such a sudden reversal in the fortunes of the prophet of Nazareth baffles human reason. Some explanation might be furnished by the ordinary laws of mob psychology, but the explanation is far from satisfying and, to a mind approaching the problem without prejudice, appears wholly inadequate. It is impossible to read dispassionately the history of the tragic denouement of the Savior's life without being intimately persuaded that the cause of it is to be assigned to the clash of superhuman forces.

[1] Jn 12: 19.

WHY THE CROSS?

Faith confirms this surmise of reason. The sequence of the Mass of Easter Sunday shows us Calvary as a battleground, where the two supreme realities of life and death stood locked in a decisive struggle. *"Vita et mors duello conflixere mirando"*; Life and death in dreadful combat strove.[2]

Approaching Calvary, we finds ourselves enveloped in a darkness the human understanding is powerless to pierce. All ordinary human values and realities undergo an utter eclipse. In the gloom, events on a plane higher than the natural, events determined by forces preternatural and supernatural, are understood to be taking place. We feel that if the veil that screens the spiritual world from us were drawn aside we should see the terrific and decisive conflict of all the forces of good and evil, the conflict between all that is for God and all that is set in opposition to God.[3] In that thick gloom of Calvary is fought out the battle between "What is" and "What is not," between the awful reality that is God and the awful unreality that is sin.

Although the hostility of the Sanhedrin to the doctrine of the Savior and their hatred of His Person boded ill for His mission, yet the ease with which He had on all occasions defeated their plans, as well as the miraculous powers He possessed, left contemporaries, especially the Master's own immediate followers, utterly unprepared for the actual issue of things. But to us, reading the Gospel in the light of events before and after Calvary, the thirty-three years of the earthly life of Jesus are seen to be a gradual preparation for the mysterious event in which His mortal life ended.

Hatred of all that Jesus stood for manifested itself from the outset. His presence on earth stirred into active antagonism instincts that had their roots deep in the unexplored depths of evil. To that evil, consisting in a sullen revolt against the absolute sovereignty of God, the Son of God, incarnate, could not but show Himself uncompromisingly hostile. "In the head of the book it is written of

[2] Sequence, Mass of Easter Sunday.
[3] See 2 Th 2: 4.

me that I should do thy will: O My God, I have desired it, and thy law is in the midst of my heart. I have declared thy justice in a great church. Lo, I will not restrain my lips. . . . I have declared thy truth and thy salvation." [4]

Nature, angelic as well as human, which had revolted from the beginning, would not admit the illimitable claims of God. A struggle to the death was inevitable between the Defender of God's absolute rights and the forces ranged against those rights.

The origins of this conflict can be traced back to a point in time that preceded, by thousands of years, the first days on earth of the Messiah. These origins coincide with the first revolt. Every act of sin might be considered as but the outcome and the logical expression of Adam's prevarication; just as all the types, figures, and prophecies, beginning with the early promise of salvation, might be considered as constituting one complete messianic redemptive reality, culminating in the death on the Cross. These two opposing streams making their way through the wide spaces of human events, gradually, in the course of history, converge on Calvary as on the point of junction and conflict. The whole of history prior to the Crucifixion might be regarded as a time consecrated to the mobilization of two armies of colossal proportions.

As dark storm clouds, massing themselves in the heavens, at first slowly and, then, more rapidly move up from the opposing points of the compass and finally blot out the skies, so these two forces of good and evil had been gathering themselves steadily during all time for the final struggle. On Calvary they met with a roar and a clash of conflict that shook the world to its base and woke startled echoes in the very depths of the world beyond the tomb. Beneath the heavy trampling of the unseen powers, the earth yawned open, the rocks were sundered, and the graves yielded up their dead. A pall of darkness spread itself over all this horror.

[4] Ps 40: 8–11.

"Now from the sixth hour there was darkness over the whole earth until the ninth hour, and behold the veil of the temple was rent in two from the top even to the bottom: and the earth quaked, and the rocks were rent, and the graves were opened and many bodies of the saints that had slept arose."[5] Such were the awe-inspiring natural phenomena that revealed to man's senses the dreadful character of the definite clash between the power of God and that of sin. Nothing created, if caught between these contending powers, could escape destruction. It was the fate of the Sacred Humanity to be so involved and to find itself, in consequence, crushed as the grapes in the vine press. "He was wounded for our iniquities: He was bruised for our sins. The chastisement of our peace was upon Him: and by his bruises we are healed."[6]

On Calvary there was made adequate reparation for all the offenses of men.

In the Passion of the Son of God the justice of the Almighty found full scope and free expression. The contemplation of God's unerring judgment, which assesses accurately what is due to infinite justice for what infinite majesty has suffered, and will suffer, from all the transgressions of all mankind, from the dawn of history to the end of time, is truly a solemn and awe-inspiring spectacle. The cost of reparation is determined with scrupulous and infallible accuracy. God might, if He chose, have remitted all debts due to Him on an avowal of repentance from erring mankind. For reasons inscrutable to all but the divine mind itself He adopted a different course. It was decreed that adequate reparation should be made for the guilt of human transgressions. What can be said is that there is a wonderful congruity in the course elected by the Divine Wisdom—a course that admirably promotes the interests of man and the glory of God.

But in the event of condign satisfaction being enacted

[5] Mt 27: 45–52.
[6] Is 53: 5.

for sin, nobody but the Son of God Himself, made Man, could acquit that literally crushing debt. It was only through the humanity of One Who is a divine Person that the exigencies of divine justice could be satisfied. The psalmist gives pathetic utterance to this truth, saying: "No brother can redeem, nor shall man redeem: he shall not give to God his ransom nor the price of the redemption of his soul."[7] Neither by voluntary sufferings nor by divine chastisement could mankind, left to itself, effect a balance between the expiation of sin and what sin deserved. God's justice, seeking adequate satisfaction, could shrivel up all creation in its passage and remain unsatisfied.

Justice and mercy found a foothold on the hill of Calvary and there embraced. "Mercy and truth have met each other: justice and peace have kissed. Truth is sprung out of the earth, and justice hath looked down from heaven."[8] The Sacred Humanity of Jesus sprang from the soil of our nature, and divine justice was able to work itself out on this "flower of the root of Jesse."[9] The Sacred Humanity was crushed under the intolerable weight of God's exactions, but from the broken body the precious blood streamed over the whole earth, fertilizing it and making it fruitful in works of virtue.

> *The cruelties inflicted on Jesus were not due to the promptings of ordinary human passions: they were the expression of the utmost efforts of the malignity of all that is anti-God.*

The sufferings of Jesus in the Passion, whether considered in their nature or their intensity, were horrible in the extreme. No created intelligence can plumb the depth of His sufferings. The prophet Jeremiah places on His lips

---

[7] Ps 49: 8–9. The Hebrew text runs: "For the redemption of their soul is earthly and must be let alone for ever." The literal sense of the text is that man is powerless to buy off death. But the literal sense can be *accommodated* to the spiritual.

[8] Ps 85: 11–12.

[9] Is 11: 1.

WHY THE CROSS?

the plaintive words: "All you that pass by the way attend and see if there be any sorrow like unto my sorrow." [10]

His sufferings stood in an order of things apart. They differ from ours not merely in degree. They were quasi-infinite, St. Thomas tells us. Even the cold restrained narrative of the Evangelist discloses scenes of such fiendish cruelty that the least sensitive must shudder at the recital. Even an unbeliever, if unprejudiced, could not help but feel a sense of revolt against Christ being so brutally treated.

His life had been a record of beneficence. "He went about doing good." [11] When Pilate asked what evil hath He done, no evil-doing was alleged. The answer to the pagan's query was but a fierce clamor for the death of his crimeless prisoner. The appearance of that prisoner, at the moment covered with wounds and blood, was such as should move to pity any heart in which human feeling was not utterly extinguished. It but roused to greater fury men gathered together for the worship of God in the most solemn religious festival of the year.

The crowd proved humane to Barabbas the murderer and showed itself utterly inhumane toward Christ, the good. It is clear that one is in presence here of a malignity that is truly abnormal. It is explicable only in the light of God's mysterious and merciful decree bearing on the manner in which man's redemption was to be worked out.

The triumph of Palm Sunday was more apparent than real. The Jews never truly received Christ because their religious ideas remained in radical opposition to His.

The death of Christ must be considered from two points of view, which, while being interwoven in the plan of Divine Providence, must, nevertheless, be carefully distinguished. Regarded from the abstract historical point of view, Christ's death was evidently the outcome of the irreconcilable hostility of the chiefs of Jewry to the religious

[10] Lam 1: 12.
[11] Acts 10: 38.

and political principles of Jesus of Nazareth. They hated Him unto death. That hatred found, in reality, no serious check in the attitude of the multitude.

Much has been made of the supposed devotedness of great numbers of the simple country people to the cause of the Savior. The entry into Jerusalem is pointed to as the occasion on which this enthusiastic devotion overbore all opposition and had a free course. The mood of the populace is supposed to have undergone a complete change in the course of a few days, owing to the machinations and the skillful propaganda of the priests.

It is undeniable that the Nazarene had some sincere and devoted followers, but they must have been comparatively few in number. They did not constitute the great throng that went out at the city gates, on the morning of Sunday, to welcome Him with loud acclamations and the waving of palms.

Looking at events as dictated by the dispositions of human souls, the execrations of Friday were not inconsistent with the acclamations of Sunday. The change in the attitude of the people presents no problem, for there was no change. Those who thronged around the Savior on Sunday do not so much acclaim Him as they acclaim themselves. To be more accurate, they glorified, not the real Jesus of Nazareth, but a creation of their own earthly dreams and ambitions. "Hosanna to the Son of David," [12] they cried, *"Blessed be the kingdom of our father David that cometh."* [13]

They acknowledge Jesus as king, but as invested with a kingship He abhorred and from which He shrank.[14] They honored Him not for what He truly was but for what their

[12] Mt 21: 9.

[13] Mk 11: 10.

[14] A similar instance of Jesus and the enthusiastic crowds being at cross-purposes had already occurred. The incident is related in St. John's Gospel, chapter 6. The multitude would use force to make Jesus king, after their ideal of kingship. A king He was without their making Him so, but not such as they conceived the messianic king to be.

imaginations made Him. Their loyalty was offered not to Him Who had come and Who, at that moment, was riding into their city upon an ass and upon a colt, the foal of an ass, [15] but to One Whom they falsely supposed Him to be and Whom they are yet expecting.

There was a tragic irony in that triumph. The acclamations were in themselves just, and Holy Church has taken them for her own. The Jews uttered truths, in a certain sense, unconsciously, but what their lips extolled was not the Person to Whom their applause was actually directed. They uttered truth and yet judged falsely. And the truth itself was falsehood on their lips.

On that Sunday the Jews were farther than ever from accepting the true messianic kingdom with its constitution based on humility, poverty, and self-denial. The raising of Lazarus, like, on a former occasion the multiplication of the loaves, had raised their hopes to the highest pitch. They believed that they were on the eve of seeing their ambitious dreams realized. They acclaimed *their* kingdom, not *His.*

On Sunday expectant national egoism strewed the roadway with carpets and palm branches. On Friday national egoism, undeceived and baffled, howled for the death of Him Whom, on false presumptions, they had feted on the Sunday. The instructions in the temple in the intervening days had dissipated all misunderstandings. The position of Jesus had become perfectly clear. The words that fell from His lips pointedly condemned their aspirations, and at each successive pronouncement they saw the progressive evaporation of their hopes. Their disappointment was intense and their fury knew no bounds.[16] "Away with Him—crucify Him," they cried. *"We*

---

[15] Zech 9: 9.

[16] "If you prefer the things of sense to the things of the spirit, instead of being pleased with you, God will punish you for having sinned, for having aimed in each thing, not at the love of what is divine, but at what accords with your own personal inclinations. This is borne out by what is related concerning the triumphant entry of Jesus into Jerusalem. In

have no king but Caesar." This last exclamation is significant. When they had proclaimed Christ their king, it was not for what He was but entirely for what He was not.

Christ's theory of life always finds intense opposition in the unregenerate human heart. The extremes to which the opposition may go vary according to times and persons and circumstances. But in all the forms the opposition takes it remains essentially the same. When pushed to its logical issue by any particular set of circumstances, it will go to the excesses of Good Friday. On that day it precipitated a situation bewildering in its reversal of all that was normal in things. The chosen people of God reject the Son of the God they worshiped with a worship almost fanatical in its intensity. Not only do they reject Him, but they show a preference for a robber and a murderer.

The tragic irony reaches a climax when there is seen the pagan, the worshiper of false gods, pleading with the worshipers of the true God to spare the life of Him Whom

---

the midst of this reception, surrounded by cheering crowds and saluted by the waving of palm branches, He weeps. He knows well that the hearts of the majority of these Jews are far from Him, in spite of their joyful demonstrations and the brave outward show. *May one not say of them, with truth, that it was themselves that this people acclaimed—God being only the occasion and the pretext?"* [italics mine] (John of the Cross, *Ascent of Mount Carmel,* bk. 3, ch. 37).

How frequently and vividly this scene has been reenacted in the course of ages! For twenty centuries the Church, the Spouse of Christ, has been dispensing the benefits of civilization to the nations. At times she seems to win success. She is greeted with applause. But on analysis it will be discovered that men invariably, with the exception of her devoted children, approve her for the wrong reason. The applause is periodically succeeded by fierce clamors for her death. Like the Jews, who protested that they would have Caesar, not Christ, for their king, so the peoples show themselves ready to subject themselves to the most brutal forms of tyranny rather than to submit themselves to the beneficent ruling of the Spouse of Christ. When Lenin stated that "Christianity is 'the opium of the people,'" was he unconsciously paraphrasing the words of the Jews when they said concerning Christ, "This is not a good man; on the contrary *He seduceth the people*" (Jn 7: 12)?

they worshiped. And this pleading is urged at the time when the followers of the true God are gathered together for His worship on the most solemn festival of the Jewish calendar.

Nothing so much as this reveals the dreadful perversity wrought in men's nature by Original Sin, a perversity that can coexist with the practice of the true faith. The incident manifests clearly that an assiduous practice of religious observances can cloak a practical insubordination to God, the Author of these observances. To the world, and to themselves, the Jews appeared to be a people devoted to Jehovah. But their loyalty was really to their own traditions. They who honored not the Son could not be truly honoring the Father Who had sent Him.[17] Their antagonism to the Son of God and to what He stood for hardened day by day and could have only one result.

The national passions of the crowd, the malignant hatred of the priests, the treachery of Judas, the cowardly vacillation of Pilate—all played their part in hastening on the final catastrophe. Yet all these causes combined do not offer an adequate explanation of the death of Christ. Time and time again His life had been attempted, and He had foiled all the efforts of His enemies with the utmost ease. Their ultimate success was not due to an increase in their power or to an intensification of their hatred or to an unexpected change in the attitude of the mob (as has been seen there was in reality no change) but to a change in the attitude of Christ to the forces opposed to Him. The death of Jesus is to be attributed not to a change in His conditions, but to a change in His relations to these conditions in which He found Himself.

> *What befell Christ in His Passion finds its adequate explanation in the mysterious words of St. Paul: "Him who knew no sin, on our behalf He hath been made sin, that we might be made the justice of God in Him."* [18]

[17] Jn 5: 23.
[18] 2 Cor 5: 21.

It is in God's decree regarding the redemption of the human race that is to be found the reason for the apparent powerlessness of Christ in face of His enemies during the last hours of His mortal life. Up to the eve of Good Friday He had kept His enemies at bay, while He worked to achieve the task assigned to Him by His heavenly Father. "They sought, therefore, to apprehend Him: and no man laid hands on Him, because His hour was not yet come." [19] This immunity from interference being secured by His divine power, He had prayed and toiled and preached in order to win men to the truth and to a rejection of their wrong attitude toward God. He had wrought miracles; He had expelled evil spirits; He had comforted the poor and the suffering. At His passage, as had been foretold by Isaiah, "The blind received their sight, the lame walked, the lepers were cleaned, the deaf received their hearing, the dead were raised, and the poor had the gospel preached to them." [20] In spite of all His efforts, the kingdom of sin remained unsubdued. God in His wisdom had decreed another way for subjugating the stubborn hearts of men.

God had decided that the Just One should become as one responsible for sin, in order that sinners might be robed in justice.[21] The expiation of sin could be fully worked out when the Just One should take upon Himself the sinfulness of the race. "But now once at the end of ages, He [as Jesus] hath appeared for the destruction of sin, by the sacrifice of Himself." [22]

It is not merely that Christ took upon Himself the chastisement due to our sins. The thought is much more profound. There is question, not of a substitution of

[19] Jn 7: 30; 8: 20.
[20] Mt 11: 5; Is 35: 5.
[21] "Entre le monogène bien-aimé et eux un merveilleux échange s'établit: leurs misères à eux sont consumés en lui, et ses grandeurs à lui s'écoulent dans leurs petitesses" (E. Mersch, S.J., *Le Corps Mystique du Christ*, 1:195).
[22] Heb 9: 26.

WHY THE CROSS?

persons, but of a solidarity of action. It was decreed that there should be a mystic identification between Christ and the sin-laden human race—He as the Head and they as the members of one Mystic Person. When the purification of sin by suffering had been worked out on that Mystic Person, in the Passion and death of its Head, justice, which by nature is the inalienable property of the Head, is, through the same mystic solidarity, extended to all the members. St. Peter writes: "Christ also suffered for us . . . who his own self *bore our sins in his body*, upon the tree." [23] The words of St. Paul dealing with the same mystery are of a terrifying boldness: "Him who knew no sin, He hath made [to be] sin, on our behalf; that we might become the righteousness of God in him." [24]

It is not that the sins of men are transferred to Christ, but the condition they merit is extended from men to Christ as Head and Representative of the human race. Christ, though guiltless, is responsible, in virtue of His acceptance of the divine decree of mystic solidarity between Him and the race, for the guilt of mankind. Similarly, the justice of Christ is not transferred from Him to men but extends from Him to them when they consent to be one with Him by faith and charity.

"St. Paul in this context deliberately chooses the abstract terms, justice and sin, in preference to the concrete 'just' and 'sinner,' in order to express the notion of collectivity. Jesus Christ, as chief of the human race, whose cause He represents and whose interests He espouses, becomes a sacrifice for sin. He 'is made sin for us.' This means, not in our place, but to our advantage. For in espousing our lot, He shares our destiny. Becoming thus sin for us, He makes us become the justice of God in Him. Jesus is neither sin nor sinner Himself personally, but assumes responsibility for the guilt of mankind as member of a sinful race with which He has consented to identify Himself." [25]

[23] 1 Pet 2: 21–24.
[24] 2 Cor 5: 21.
[25] P. Prat, S.J., *Théologie de S. Paul*, 3d ed., 2:244–245.

God the Father, in His tender compassion for fallen mankind, surrendered His only-begotten Son to this hard fate. "God so loved the world as to give His only-begotten Son, that whosoever believeth in Him may not perish, but may have life everlasting."[26] In the interest of our welfare God surrendered Jesus to the forces of evil that these might treat Him as they willed. He decreed that, at a certain moment in the life of the Savior, "it should be the hour of these forces and the power of darkness."[27]

Up to the appointed moment the Divinity, like a sluice gate holding back the seething waters, stood securely shielding the Sacred Humanity from the deluge of evils that threatened it. Kindness, exhortation, wisdom, and miracles had not availed to vanquish sin. The wisdom of God had decided that sin should be overcome by the complete sacrifice of the Sacred Humanity. Christ recognized the wisdom of God's appointment and humbly submitted to His self-chosen lot, foreseeing its ultimate fruits. "And I," He said, "if I be lifted up from the earth shall draw all things to myself."[28]

On the night of Holy Thursday the destined hour arrived. The protection of the Divinity was withdrawn, and, as at the lifting of the sluice gate the waters rush violently through, so the full tide of human and diabolic malignity rushed on the Sacred Humanity, caught it up in its swirling turbid waters, and hurled it to death. "Waters have flowed over my head. I said: I am cut off."[29] And all this happened because "all we like sheep have gone astray, and everyone hath turned aside into his own way, and the Lord hath laid upon Him the iniquity of us all. . . . Surely he hath borne our infirmities and carried our sorrows."[30]

"It is, therefore, true that, historically speaking, the sufferings of Jesus Christ can be explained by the normal

[26] Jn 3: 16.
[27] Lk 22: 53.
[28] Jn 12: 32.
[29] Lam 3: 54.
[30] Is 53: 6, 4.

play of secondary causes." [31] What He was brought Him into violent conflict with the powers of this world, secular and religious. They did not hesitate to plot against His life, and they finally succeeded in compassing His death. But the utmost efforts of force and hate and cunning would have hurled themselves in vain against the Sacred Humanity did Christ will to throw in front of it, perpetually, the shield of the Divinity. They could succeed only if He allowed it. Men, as far as in them lay, posited the causes of His death: these causes would not have their effect unless He willed it.

"He was offered because it was His own will, and He opened not His mouth," said Isaiah in prophetic vision.[32] These words were corroborated by Jesus Himself; saying: "I lay down my life . . . no one taketh it away from me, but I lay it down of myself." [33] Sin was to be expiated on the condition of Jesus offering Himself as a Victim for sin. This was the condition of man's redemption laid down in the everlasting decrees.

Jesus, in His immense love for God and His consequent zeal to promote God's glory and fulfill the divine good pleasure, did not hesitate to accept this mysterious condition of man's salvation. Rising from the Last Supper, He said: "But that the world may know that I love the Father, and as the Father hath given me commandment, so do I. Arise, let us go hence." [34] With these words He strode straight to His death, offering His Sacred Humanity as a defenseless prey to the fury of His enemies.

By the Incarnation there was established a mystic solidarity between Christ and the human race. This solidarity was divinely planned in view of the adequate expiation of sin and the reestablishment of the human race in justice. The sins of men, not as to

[31] Rivière, *Le Dogme de la Rédemption*, p. 252.
[32] Is 53: 7.
[33] Jn 10: 18.
[34] Jn 14: 31.

their guilt, but as to their chastisement, were extended from all the members of the human race to the just Christ, Who consented, in the Incarnation, to accept the position of Head of mankind, that is, Source, from which the regenerate race should take its rise. In His death, sin was expiated and destroyed.

The barrier of sin being swept away, the native justice of Christ streamed on all members of the race willing to enter into vital union with Him. This was God's plan for the restoration of mankind. Why He does not remit sin directly, without exacting more from man than repentance, is His secret. All that we can know is that the plan adopted was dictated by divine mercy and love for men, therefore, most efficacious in achieving the purpose for which it was framed.

Christ's teachings and miracles did not subjugate the human heart, did not overthrow the kingdom of sin. His triumph on Palm Sunday was more apparent than real. The forces of evil combined to compass His death. He could have defeated them had He allowed to His humanity the protection of the Divinity. In obedience to the divine plan, He withheld that protection. Evil might then do as it willed with Him. Historically, it brought about His Crucifixion. But it could not have done so if He had not permitted it. He was sacrificed because He Himself so willed it. He willed it for the destruction of our sins and our consequent restoration to divine favor.

CHAPTER EIGHT

*But he was wounded for our iniquities, he was bruised for
our sins. The chastisement of our peace was upon him, and
by his bruises we are healed.*

—ISAIAH 53: 5

*Jesus, in His Passion, takes care to manifest clearly that His
victimhood is a matter of deliberate choice.*

ISAIAH, IN PROPHETIC VISION contemplating the
Savior, says of Him: "He shall be led as a sheep to the
slaughter and shall be dumb as a lamb before his shearer,
and he shall not open his mouth."[1] No words could so
eloquently express the utter victimhood of Christ, a
victimhood that can be conceived to have had its formal
inauguration at the Last Supper. In instituting this New
Testament, the Redeemer speaks of His body as being
actually broken and His blood as being actually shed.[2] A
victim, as such, is passive and helpless, completely in the
power of the forces that are to accomplish its immolation.
The consecration of the bread and the wine was the
Lord's formal act of surrender to the career of immolation and consequent powerlessness that, at that instant,
opened out before Him. He wished that the voluntariness
of that surrender should be unmistakable.

It has been said with justice that the Savior in His trials
never reveals that self-consciousness which moves noble
men whose actions are regarded with suspicion, or whose

[1] Is 53: 7.
[2] Lk 22: 19–20. The Greek text uses the present participle, so that
the words run: This is my body which is being broken, my blood which
is being shed.

motives are questioned, or whose fortitude is doubted to protest their sincerity of purpose, their purity of motive, or their resolution of spirit. Yet, in two incidents of these last hours may be traced something of this appealingly human characteristic.

When the supper drew to a close, the Master, knowing what His disciples should have to witness before the shades of night should have again fallen on Jerusalem, took the occasion to assert that the Passion was not to be regarded as a condemnation of Him or His doctrine, but as a solemn attestation before the whole world of His loyalty to God. Rising from the Last Supper to direct His steps toward the garden of the Agony, He said: "That the world may know that I love the Father, and as the Father hath given Me commandment, so do I, arise let us go hence." [3]

Again, when at the garden gate, His enemies were about to lay their murderous hands on Him, at the very instant in which circumstances would appear to point to His being completely helpless in the power of forces too strong for Him, He wills to reveal Himself in a most conclusive manner, as master of the situation. As though He, and not Judas, were the leader, He directs the departure of His followers and dictates the moment of the arrest.

The Agony in the Garden shows Jesus crushed under the intolerable weight of the responsibility He had taken on Himself.

The delicate consideration the Savior has for His followers in the soul-shaking crisis that the Passion would prove for them is manifested through all the events crowded into these last tragic hours. In His greatness of soul, He would, and did, have thought for them in the midst of His own agonies of body and of mind. Carefully as He had prepared them for what was to come, He well knew that

[3] Jn 14: 31.

much must be spared them if their faith were not to reel under the shock to which it would be submitted. Hence it was that in Gethsemane, when about to enter on His mysterious Agony, He withdrew Himself apart from them a stone's throw.[4]

The whole nature and causes of the dreadful mental sufferings that Jesus endured alone, during the long hours of the night-watches, no created intelligence can fully explore. During the days of His pilgrimage, He was wont to speak of His Passion with a species of exaltation. "I have a baptism," He had said, "wherewith I am to be baptized, and how am I straitened until it be accomplished."[5]

But when the moment which He had called "His hour" had come, it finds Him plunged in trembling fear and anguish. "Now is My soul troubled," He falters, "And what shall I say?" [Is it], "Father, save me from this hour." [But how can I utter this prayer, seeing that it is] "for this cause I came unto this hour."[6] As He drew near to the place where He was to wrestle alone with the dreadful forebodings that pressed on Him, He began "to fear and to be heavy"[7] "and to grow sorrowful and to be sad."[8]

"Fear shakes the soul to its very depths by conjuring up vivid images of the manifold forms of overpowering evil that menace it. Sorrow crushes the vitality out of the soul."[9] The sorrow of Jesus was so bitter and heavy that it draws from Him the avowal: "My soul is sorrowful unto death."[10] These words, falling from the lips of One Who always shows such a divine restraint in language, reveal a shuddering abyss of black desolation.

He who had been so steadfast in all trials and dangers falls tottering to the earth under the crushing weight of His anguish. How great must have been the horror of this

[4] Lk 22: 41.
[5] Lk 12: 50.
[6] Jn 12: 27.
[7] Mk 14: 33.
[8] Mt 26: 37.
[9] Bossuet, *Sermons*, vol. 3, discourse on the Passion.
[10] Mt 26: 38.

menacing evil that so tested the almost limitless fearlessness of the Prophet of Nazareth! Being human, He naturally quailed in the face of the vision of the Passion revealed to Him in all its hideous and revolting details.

But this was not the only, nor was it the chief, cause of the agony He experienced. Tradition is unanimous in asserting that what the Savior endured was intimately connected with the sins of mankind. In some mysterious manner, the Almighty allowed His Son to experience in the depths of His Being a realization of the consequences for Himself of His taking on His shoulders the responsibility for the crimes of humanity. He was made to feel what it was to be the Head and Representative of the sinful human race. In spite of His personal innocence, the sins of the members were laid upon Him, the Head. The vast sea of human iniquity rising before Him from the past, from the present, from the future, and from the Passion itself accumulated into one vast tidal wave of black defilement and broke over His defenseless head.

"The sorrows of death surrounded me, and the torrents of iniquity have overwhelmed me with dread." [11] In the dark depths of this deluge He saw the quasi-infinite foulness of all that is in irreconcilable opposition to God. There loomed up before His mental gaze all the sins of all men, in the foulness of their kinds, in their hideous varieties, and in the manifold forms of their uncleanness. He saw all the acts of faithlessness and base betrayals; all the acts of lust and adultery; all the acts of impiety and sacrilege; all the imprecations and blasphemies; all the acts of violence and murder; all the acts of cruelty and injustice; all the falsehoods and apostasies that stain human records.

Because of the mysterious identification wrought by the Incarnation between Him and man and in consequence of His free acceptance of the mode of Redemption determined by divine decree, Jesus sees Himself involved in the

[11] Ps 18: 5.

penal consequences of man's wickedness. The Venerable Libermann writes: "This flesh, holy in itself, is filled, penetrated, covered, clothed as it were within and without, with all the loathsomeness of our sins, with a mass of wickedness which floods it like a deluge and overwhelms it."[12] "The Lord laid upon Him the iniquity of us all."[13] It was His bitter chalice to accept this destiny.

Faced with this appalling fate and made to contemplate it steadily in all its phases and all its consequences; faced too with the task of fully expiating all that evil by sufferings bearing a certain proportion to the fault, it is not surprising that the Savior prostrated Himself in agonizing prayer before God. For three long hours He lay prone on the earth repeating the same words: "My Father, if it be possible, let this chalice pass from me."[14]

There is scarcely any incident in the whole life of the Savior that so reveals the perfect parallel that exists between the movements of His human nature and ours, as this prayer in the garden. He had from the beginning accepted the Passion. He knew the Passion was God's absolute will; He Himself is perfectly resigned to that will; and yet He yields to the perfectly human impulse to plead with God, knowing all the time what God wills and being prepared to accept it.

So God's servants sometimes treat with God, begging Him, if it be His will, not to allow some threatening cross to be laid upon their shoulders. Deep in their hearts they know the cross to be inevitable, and yet they find comfort and strength in their pleadings. It was thus that Jesus prayed; His prayer was conditional. There is a deep pathos in this pleading of the humanity of Christ against the fixity of the divine decree.

And though the prayer could not, and Jesus did not wish that it should, alter the absolute determination of God, the prayer was not without its answer. It won Him

[12] Ven. Libermann, *Écrits spirituels*, 2:157.
[13] Is 53: 6.
[14] Mt 26: 39.

comfort and strength. God was not deaf to the appeal of Jesus, nor unsympathetic. "There appeared an angel from heaven, strengthening Him." [15]

We should need Christ's comprehension of the dreadful malice of sin and what divine justice exacts for its expiation, to have an understanding of the agony that shook the Sacred Humanity in the Garden of Gethsemane. What Christ saw and understood caused His shuddering frame to contract with agony and panic fear. Under this physical contraction of nerves and fibers and arteries, the blood-drops oozed through the pores of the skin and, mingling together, flowed in red streamlets to the ground.

Christ was to redeem us from the curse that weighed on us "by Himself being made a curse for us." [16] As He writhed in agony on the earth before the majesty of God, the saying of the psalmist was fulfilled in Him: "He clothed Himself with malediction as with a garment, and it entered like water into his entrails and like oil into all his bones." [17] Oil has a peculiarly penetrating force. The image expresses the mysteriously intimate identification between Christ as Victim for sin and that wicked humanity whose sins He undertook the task of expiating.

> *All the forces of evil are, by the permission of God and the acceptance of the Sacred Humanity, allowed free play in dealing with Jesus as Victim for sin.*

Up to the time of entering on the Passion, Jesus acted as the accredited envoy of God and had at His disposal the divine omnipotence to vindicate His claims. He could operate miracles at will. He taught with power. His desires were, as are those of a dearly loved child, a law of action for His heavenly Father. "He was [always] heard for his reverence." [18] But now, as He stood before the rabble that, under the guidance of Judas, came with swords and clubs

[15] Lk 22: 43.
[16] Gal 3: 13.
[17] Ps 109: 18.
[18] Heb 5: 7.

WHY THE CROSS?

to arrest Him, He had to face His enemies equipped solely with the endurance of His human nature, sustained by grace. The defense of the Divinity was withdrawn. He now was but a victim for sin.

One last act of dominant power was permitted Him to secure the safety of His followers. But when "the disciples all leaving Him fled,"[19] then Christ passed over into the power of the forces of evil. The flight of the disciples was like a signal that unloosed the malignant powers of earth and hell on the unprotected humanity of the Redeemer. They rushed on Him like dogs let slip from the leash. "A multitude of dogs surround me, and a band of evil doers encompasses me."[20]

Piteous in the extreme was the case in which Jesus now found Himself. He was caught between two forces. On the one hand the divine decree, exacting satisfaction for sin, pressed on Him. On the other hand, sin, because of His individual purity, innocence, and perfect filial love of God, raged against Him with all its might. All the evil generated in mankind by the Fall rose up in implacable hostility against the unique just One. Sin felt in Him an uncompromising enemy. "Let us, therefore, lie in wait for the just, because he is not for our turn, and he is contrary to our doings, and upbraideth us with transgressions of the law, and divulgeth against us the sins of our way of life. He boasteth that he hath the knowledge of God and calleth himself the Son of God. He is become a censurer of our thoughts. He is grievous unto us even to behold."[21]

Nature as tainted by Original Sin looked upon God Incarnate as its sworn foe. He, the true champion of mankind, is regarded as the enemy of the race. His life is thought to imperil that race. He had to be done away with if the people were to be saved. To the Jewish mind the good of the world was bound up with their national good. If all were well with them, ultimately all would be well with

[19] Mt 26: 56.
[20] Ps 22: 17.
[21] Wis 2: 12–15.

the world. Caiaphas was the echo of these thoughts when he said: "You know nothing; neither do you consider that it is expedient for you that one man should die for the people and that the whole nation perish not." [22]

Here as ever the protagonists of the world's good find the world's salvation in warring to death the Savior of the world. "Let us," so planned the powers of this world, "put wood in his bread and cut him off from the land of the living, and let his name be remembered no more." [23] The Passion was the dreadful sequel to these councils. It was the final onslaught of the kingdom of sin and Satan on God. It seemed, as it always seems, to meet with success. The forces of sin tore the Sacred Humanity to shreds. It compassed the death of God, insofar as God could die. He was vulnerable and mortal in the humanity He assumed. That Sacred Humanity was done to death.

Yet this apparent triumph of sin proves its very ruin and its decisive overthrow. God remained master of the field of combat. He dominates even while He allows free career to the forces of evil. He holds them firmly in hand and makes them subserve the divine purposes. God regulates the darkness as well as the light. The hour of the forces of darkness was God's hour too. He used all the efforts of evil against Jesus to work out the satisfaction for, and the expiation of sin: that is, He made the supreme efforts of sin serve for the destruction of sin itself.

As Head of the sinful race, Jesus did not plead His innocence before His judges.

As chief of rebellious mankind the Savior was dragged from one tribunal to another. Witnesses were suborned to testify against Him. Their evidence was lying, inconsistent, and a deliberate misconstruing of His statements. He listened to all that was alleged to prove His guilt, and He was silent. Neither before the high priest nor before Pilate did He urge a single plea that would save Him from condem-

[22] Jn 11: 50.
[23] Jer 11: 19.

nation. "He shall be led as a sheep to the slaughter and shall be dumb as a lamb before his shearer, and he shall not open his mouth."[24] He made no effort to rebut the charges of His accusers.

For His eyes, which looked on the countenance of the high priest and on that of Pilate, saw beyond them the face of another Judge and the sitting of another court of justice. To His vision stood revealed the awful tribunal of the just God. In that presence and before that court He, invested with the iniquity of mankind, stood arraigned and condemned. As Head of sinners, He could not complain of injustice.

Strangely enough, He could have been, and in fact was, declared innocent by His earthly judge. Pilate, after having weighed the evidence, said to the chief priests and to the multitudes: "I find no cause in this man."[25] Not once only in the course of the trial was this assertion made by the judge, for we are told by the Evangelist that Pilate said to the enemies of Jesus *the third time:* "Why, what hath this man done? I find no cause of death in Him: I will . . . let Him go."[26] The Redeemer heard these words but did not acquiesce in them. He knew that His sentence should not be one of acquittal. He knew that before God the whole human race stood condemned and that He, as its Head, was involved in that condemnation. In His heart He murmured in the words of the psalmist: *"Longe a salute mea verba delictorum meorum"*; that is, "In spite of my heart-rending cries, deliverance is far from me."[27]

[24] Is 53: 7.

[25] Lk 23: 4.

[26] Lk 23: 22; see Jn 19: 6.

[27] Ps 22: 2. This is the tense of the text according to the Hebrew. There is a similarity between the Hebrew word for Latin *clamorum* and the Hebrew word for *delictorum*—hence in the translation, the term "sins" has been erroneously substituted for *clamorum*. If the Vulgate version were accepted, the paraphrase would admirably support the ideas in the context. It would run: "This whole affair of my sins makes rescue remote—that is, the sins of the world, which I have taken upon myself, cry out against me and put deliverance beyond my reach."

Jesus recognized that, false and unjust as were the statements of the perjured witnesses, they fell utterly short of expressing the guilt that pressed upon Him. He was silent because He knew that "being made sin for our sakes," He incurred the sentence of condemnation pronounced upon Him by the invisible tribunal of God. Of that sentence the Jews were all unwittingly only the executors. Men imputed to Him crimes He had not committed, "but God put on Him the iniquities of us all." [28] Laden with this guilt, He was to die a death that should proceed to moral annihilation. "He was to become a worm and no man, the reproach of men and the outcast of the people." [29]

Creatures violently wrested from their end through man's perverse use of them avenge their wrongs on the new Head of sinful mankind.

"The chastisement of our peace was forthwith laid upon Him. He was wounded for our iniquities; He was bruised for our sins." [30] In his sin, man had torn creatures from their allegiance to their Maker. Made to serve God's glory, they had been forced to serve man's lusts. Man had imposed on them a slavery under which they chafed. "For the creature," says St. Paul, "was made subject to vanity, not willingly, but by reason of him that made it subject." [31] The hour of their vengeance had sounded. In the Book of Wisdom it is written: "And He [God] will sharpen His severe wrath for a spear, and the whole world shall fight with Him against the unwise . . . shafts of lightning shall go directly from the clouds . . . thick hail shall be cast upon them . . . the water of the sea shall rage against them . . . and the rivers shall run together in a terrible manner." [32] So in the Passion creatures turned on the race that

[28] Is 53: 6.
[29] Ps 22: 7.
[30] Is 53: 5.
[31] Rom 8: 20.
[32] Wis 5: 19–22.

WHY THE CROSS?

had wronged them, avenging themselves on the race through its Head.

The rough stones over which the New Adam was dragged, bruised and tore His delicate limbs. The icy water chilled Him to the bone. The leathern thongs reduced His flesh to shreds and bespattered the Praetorium with His blood. The cords that bound Him hampered His movements. He could not cleanse the spittle from brow and eyes. To hunger, cold, thirst, exhaustion, fear, dejection, dismay, physical and mental anguish—to creatures of all kinds He was surrendered a helpless prey. He does not resist them nor does He protest. A traitor betrays Him with a kiss. He does not withhold His lips. He is seized and bound. He offers His hands to the manacles unresistingly. A servile courtier strikes Him in the face. He does not evade the blow.

All had been foretold by Isaiah: "I have given my body to the strikers and my cheeks to them that plucked them. I have not turned away my face from them that rebuked me and spit upon me." [33] The iron of the nails forces its way with agonizing pain through the torn fibers and muscles of hands and feet; the wood of the groves makes an uneasy couch for the mangled body. Yet He submits to all without a murmur. "He shall be led as a sheep to the slaughter and shall be dumb as a lamb before the shearer, and He shall not open His mouth." [34] The Savior does not resist, because He reads in the fury of creatures against Him the divine decree of His heavenly Father. [35] So creatures work their will on Him, until "from the sole of His foot even unto the head there is no soundness in Him, but wounds and bruises and festering sores which are neither closed nor bound up nor nullified with oil." [36]

[33] Is 50: 6.
[34] Is 53: 7.
[35] See Bossuet, *Sermons*, 5:208.
[36] Is 1: 6.

In the mock crowning and the derisive purple and the futile
scepter is punished man's proud usurpation of God's
sovereignty.

There is a close link between the drama of the Passion
and the scene of the first transgression. In the Passion,
the Fall is being undone, and the great revolt, with all its
evil consequences, is being duly expiated. The earth was
cursed in men's transgressions, and, instead of pleasant
fruits, it yielded for him but thorns. And God said to
Adam: "cursed is the earth in thy work: with labor and
toil shalt thou eat thereof and thorns and thistles shall it
bring forth." [37] Now of these thorns is fashioned a diadem, but a diadem of mockery and torture. The marshes
furnish the strong cane-reed to serve as a derisive scepter.
This symbol of royalty is used by the soldiers to beat the
crown down on the Savior's head, until the thorn points
are blunted against the bone. In his pride, man had
aimed at usurping the sovereignty of God. He aspired to
rule creatures independently of his Creator. It was no
accident that the cruelty of the soldiers took the form it
actually assumed.

A law of retribution runs through all the sufferings of
the Passion. Man in sinning had won for himself a sorry
kind of kingship. God had spoken of it mockingly: "Behold Adam *is become as one of us,* knowing good and evil." [38]
Man's usurpation had issued for him in the very mockery
of sovereignty. He became the slave of the creatures he
thought to rule. For "whosoever committeth sin, is the
servant of sins." [39] The reed and the circlet of thorns were
apt symbols of men's royalty. They expressed with bitter
irony the absurdity of his pretensions. And as Jesus beheld
the wretched pageant of mock worshippers defile before
Him and listened to their derisive salutations; as He heard
the taunts and jeers; as He endured the blows and suffered the blindfolding; He felt in His inmost soul the

[37] Gen 3: 17–18.
[38] Gen 3: 22.
[39] Jn 8: 34.

WHY THE CROSS?

justice of it all. He saw in it the appropriate punishment of man's unholy attempt to seat himself on the throne of the Most High.

Annas, Caiaphas, Pilate, and even Judas are but the unconscious, though culpable, executors of God's chastisement of sin. It was not merely the sordid greed of the traitor or the avarice of the Sanhedrin that causes the price of the betrayal of Jesus to be assessed at thirty pieces of silver. It was the money value of a slave. "And they took the thirty pieces of silver, the price of Him that was prized of the children of Israel." [40] Man in his fall forfeited the liberty that belonged to the child of God and became the slave of sin and Satan.

All sin has its root in pride. Sufferings, therefore, which should be a direct expiation of pride, might be expected to be an outstanding element in the Passion. And so it fell out. Ignominy, degradation, and shame mark every stage of the passage from Gethsemane to Golgotha. Christ was made to drink to the dregs the cup of humiliations. Taunts and jeers, mockery and derision accompany Him at every step. "He was," according to the terrible metaphor of Jeremiah, "surfeited with humiliations." [41] His enemies were not satisfied with exhausting on Him all the inventions of their fiendish cruelty. They made Him the butt of ridicule. Their mocking laughter added a peculiar bitterness to the physical pain He had to endure.

Men before and since His time have been condemned by unjust sentences, and yet the carrying out of these sentences is, in all normal times, invested with the majestic forms of the law. A certain dignity is flung around the last moments of even the worst criminals. But, apart from the superhuman patience with which Jesus endured His sufferings, the Passion, to the outward eye, was lacking in every element of dignity and solemnity.

As, blinded with blood and exhausted with pain, the Son of man stumbled through the rough and dusty streets

[40] Mt 27: 9; compare Zech 11: 12.
[41] Lam 3: 20.

toward the gate of Ephraim, there was no respectful parting of the crowds to let Him pass. There were no long lines of silent, sympathetic, reverential spectators along the way of sorrows. Forcing a passage through the crowds that had come up to Jerusalem for the Passover presented some difficulty. Men jostled against and pushed one another, curious to see the discredited prophet on His way to execution. Reading the jeering legend on the title-board that hung around His neck, they raised shouts of laughter. The contrast between the former high pretensions of the prophet and His present plight stirred their mirth.

The sensuous and the delicate, coming on the spectacle, turned from it in loathing but not in pity. "There is no beauty in Him nor comeliness: and we have seen Him, and there was no sightliness, that we should be desirous of Him: despised and the most abject of men, a man of sorrows and acquainted with infirmity: and His look was, as it were, hidden and despised. Wherefore, we esteemed Him not." [42]

The indifferent merely glanced at Him and hurried on their way, preoccupied by their own concerns. Those whom He had healed of their ills of body and soul and who had, for a time, been inspired with enthusiasm in His cause, were now furious at what they would consider their passing lapse of judgment. They thrust their way to His side to scream curses at Him. The envious, the hostile, and the cruel found a savage satisfaction in His sufferings and rejoiced in the pass to which He had come. And, as the crowds swayed to and fro in the Savior's passage, they continually knocked against the cross, causing the bearer to stumble and to fall. The Nazarene had become the sport of a populace gathered together for a festival.

The mockery, jeering, and contempt reach a climax on the summit of Calvary. The condemned criminals at His side, the priests, the soldiers, and the rabble, all take

[42] Is 53: 2–3.

actual part in it and vie with one another in cruel and biting sarcasm.

"This," they cried, "is the great prophet who could raise the dead to life: let us see now whether He can save Himself from dying. He saved others, now let Him save Himself. One who pretended to be able to move mountains ought not to find it difficult to draw out the nails from hands and feet and step down from the cross." There was no stir, no movement, no reply from the figure on the gibbet. What had become of His vaunted power? Did He not say that He could destroy the glorious temple and rebuild it in three days? Should it not then be a comparatively easy thing to detach Himself from the gibbet of infamy? He had boasted of His friendship with God. He had said that He was the Son of the Most High: "Surely then," they sneered, "we may look to see God Himself come in person to save Him." And as there appeared no rescue from heaven, they laughed loud and long at the utter helplessness of their enemy.

All the details of this torture had been described by the psalmist, saying: "All they that saw me have laughed me to scorn: they have spoken with the lips and wagged the head: let Him save Him, seeing that He delighteth in Him."[43] "Let Him now come down from the cross," shrieked the priests and the scribes, "and we shall believe Him."[44] Christ heard the challenge and stirred not; they concluded that His power was no match for that of the Sanhedrin.

For one to boast of divine power and then, in the time of testing, to prove utterly helpless, was a mark, so they argued, of folly. But had He been only foolish, He could have been ignored. But, in fact, He had proved Himself a dangerous fool. He had sought to delude and to bewitch the people with false ideals. He had shown a complete want of sympathy with their national aspirations and an indifference to their national pride. Had the nation

[43] Ps 22: 8–9.
[44] Mt 27: 42.

followed Him, it would have found itself in still direr slavery than that under which it had already groaned.

He had insinuated that they lay captive under a heavier yoke than that of Rome and that the messianic salvation they looked for consisted in liberation from this yoke, and not, as they judged, in shaking off the rule of Rome. He had implicitly stated that they were slaves—they, the children of Abraham! "We are the seed of Abraham," they had said to Him, "and we have never been slaves to any man, how sayest thou: You shall be free?"[45] In all this, He had shown Himself to be the enemy of His country and His people. Surely, as the high priest had said, "It was expedient that one man should die for the people, and that the whole nation perish not."[46]

Jesus hung powerless on the Cross because it was decreed "that He should die for the nation, and not only for the nation, but to gather together in one the children of God that were dispersed."[47]

"He saved others; Himself He can not save."[48] What a profound truth was, unawares, contained in the words of this taunt flung in the face of the dying Christ by His enemies: He might indeed have claimed the privilege due to His personal innocence and have descended from the cross. But He, Who enjoyed the nature of the Godhead, did not cling to the rights that belonged to Him as such, but He emptied Himself, taking the form of a servant.

Making Himself like unto fallen man in all things save sin, He consented to hang powerless on the cross as Head of the guilty race. And accepting the fate that was His because of this headship, "He humbled Himself; becoming obedient unto death, even to the death of the cross."[49] As Head of sinners He had not the right to save Himself.

[45] Jn 8: 33.
[46] Jn 11: 50.
[47] Jn 11: 51–52.
[48] Mt 27: 42.
[49] Phil 2: 8.

Sin was to be destroyed in the destruction of "Him who did no sin, neither was guile found in His mouth, who when He was reviled, did not revile, [but] who, His own Self bore our sins in His Body upon the tree, that we being dead to sin should live to justice." [50]

Christ's fate was to be a victim for sin. The lot of the victim is to be destroyed, not saved. The powerlessness of Jesus to save Himself was precisely the source from which sprang His power to save others. "At the end of ages He hath appeared for the destruction of sin, by the sacrifice of Himself: He suffered once to exhaust the sins of many." [51] In His death sin was destroyed and the empire of Satan overthrown.

A mysterious law of retribution runs right through the whole Passion considered as a sacrifice of expiation. Pride is at the root of all sin. Mankind in its Head had to be humbled utterly in order to expiate its wicked pride. Hence humiliations are heaped upon Christ during the Passion. He is the butt of mockery and derision. He does not open His mouth or complain because He sees in His sufferings the appropriate satisfaction for the sins of the race to which He had united Himself. That union with the race makes Him powerless to save Himself; because of that union it is decreed that He must die. But His powerlessness to save Himself was the very source of His power to save all others. The life of men issues from the death of the Son of man.

[50] 1 Pet 2: 22, 24.
[51] Heb 9: 26, 28.

CHAPTER NINE

Christ proved Himself obedient unto death, yea, unto the death of the Cross. Wherefore God hath exalted Him and given Him a name above all names.

—VERSICLE, LAUDS OF HOLY SATURDAY

Though a single act of homage on the part of the Man-God would have been sufficient to merit grace for all mankind, yet God decreed the superabundant satisfactions of the Passion.

THERE IS A CULPABLE self-indulgence involved in sin. It is fitting this self-indulgence should be atoned for by voluntary or involuntary suffering.[1] God ordained that such atonement for the crimes of humanity should devolve on Him Who was made to be, and accepted to be, the new Head of the race. Christ, as the New Adam, suffered to expiate the sins of the first Adam and all his descendants. "He was wounded for our iniquities. He was bruised for our sins. The chastisement of our peace was upon Him."[2] God, for reasons to us inscrutable, but which we know were prompted by incredibly merciful consideration for mankind, exacted of the Savior not only great sufferings, but even sufferings that should, in themselves, objectively bear some proportion to the magnitude of the guilty satisfaction involved in the totality of the sins of the race.

[1] St. Thomas writes: "That a guilty person be brought within the order of justice, it is necessary that such a person's will should be thwarted in what it desires. The chastisement is inflicted by making the culprit forego the good things which he would have or by making him endure harsh things from which he shrinks" (*Opusc.* 3, ch. 7).
[2] Is 53: 5.

"For God so loved the world as to surrender His only begotten Son."[3] It was this love of God for man and the divine zeal for man's interests that caused Christ's sufferings to touch the very limits of objective value. The torments endured during the Passion, being the torments suffered by Christ in His created nature, were necessarily finite. But, within the necessary limits of the created, they reached a certain species of infinitude. In their universality and intensity they attained a measure that baffles all finite conceptions.

The sufferings of Christ were universal. All classes and conditions of men combined to have a hand in His death.
Christ could not experience every kind of suffering, for one sort of pain can be incompatible with another. One cannot undergo at the same time the tortures of water and of fire. Neither could the Redeemer bear those ills which spring from defects in the bodily constitution and come from sickness and disease. But in another sense His sufferings were universal. All classes and conditions of men conspired to compass his destruction. The Savior was hounded to death by the pagans and by the people of God, by Gentile and by Jew. He suffered violence and insult from men and from women, from old and from young. The princes of the people stood against Him, and their servants vied with them in their hate and cruelty. The nobles and the rabble, priests and people, strangers and fellow citizens—every category in human society turned on Him.

His own intimates did not spare Him. He was abandoned by His disciples, denied by Peter, and sold by Judas.[4] This latter aspect of the sufferings of the Messiah had been foreseen and had been bewailed by the psalmist. "If my enemy hath reviled me, I would verily have borne with it. And if he that hated me had spoken great things against me, I would perhaps have hidden myself from

[3] Jn 3: 16.
[4] *Summa theologiae*, III, q. 46, a. 5.

him. But thou my other self, my companion and my familiar friend, who didst take sweet meats together with me: in the house of God we walked with the throng." [5]

Christ was condemned at three tribunals.
The three great fountains of evil are the concupiscence of the flesh, the concupiscence of the eyes, and the pride of life. All three clamor for the destruction of God. Caiaphas and the chief priests, in their malignant hostility to the enemy of the Most High, incarnated, as it were, the pride of life. "The chief priests, therefore, and the Pharisees, gathered a council and said: 'What do we, for this man doth many miracles? If we let Him alone so, all will believe in Him and the Romans will come, and take away our place and nation!' But one of them named Caiaphas . . . said to them. 'You know nothing, neither do you consider that it is expedient for you that one man should die for the people and that the whole nation perish not. . . .' From that day, therefore, they desired to put Him to death." [6] This is the judgment that in all ages the pride of life pronounces on Christ, in its insensate hatred of what He is and what He stands for. Men, in their pride, proclaiming the absolute independence of the human reason and disdaining any rule of conduct other than that dictated by their own will, labor to banish Christ's influence from the councils of the world. They thus hope to see the era of reason or of nature firmly established. [7]

Christ is dragged to the tribunal of Herod. He is mocked and condemned, not merely as a malefactor, but as a knave and a fool. "And Herod seeing Jesus was very glad, for he was desirous of a long time to see Him, because he had heard many things of Him, and he hoped to see some sign wrought by Him. And he questioned Him in many words. But He answered him nothing . . . and Herod with his army set Him at naught and mocked Him,

[5] Ps 55: 13–15.
[6] Jn 11: 47–53.
[7] See Billot, *De Verbo Incarnato*, 5th ed., pp. 479–480.

putting on Him a white garment, and sent Him back to Pilate."[8] The frivolous, shallow, and incestuous Herod personifies the concupiscence of the flesh.

Pilate, the worldling, ready to barter his conscience for position, clinging to the false worth that attaches to the favor of princes and the regard of the populace, aptly represents the antagonism of the concupiscence of the eyes. It, too, condemns the Christ.

The Savior suffers in every pulse of the human heart sensitive to pain. He suffers in soul and in body.

Nothing in the being of man capable of enduring agony was spared in the Passion. Christ suffered in the claims of friendship by the abandonment of his friends at the moment He stood most in need of their sympathy and their support. His reputation was outraged by the blasphemies uttered against Him. Dishonor and ignominy were heaped upon Him by the gibes, mockeries, and raillery of which He was the victim. Lots were cast for his garments, and He was thus stripped of the last vestige of his earthly possessions.

His soul was plunged into an abyss of desolation, verifying the words of the psalmist: "For the waters are come in even unto my soul. I stick fast in the mire of the deep, and there is no sure standing. I am come into the depth of the sea and a tempest hath overwhelmed me."[9] In this mental anguish Christ suffered both in the essence of the soul and in its faculties.

He suffered in every member of His body: in His head by the crown of thorns; in His hands and feet by the nails; in His face by the buffets and the blinding spittle. His body was one mass of wounds and was beaten almost shapeless by the cruel scourges.

He suffered in every bodily sense: in His sense of smell by the stench of the dungeon into which He was flung while awaiting crucifixion; in His sense of touch by the tortures to which He was subjected; in His sense of taste by

[8] Lk 23: 8–11.
[9] Ps 69: 2–3.

the bitter potion of gall and vinegar; in his sense of hearing by the chorus of jeers and blasphemies that fell on His ears as He lay dying; in IIis sense of vision by the sight of the tears and the agony of His Mother and the beloved disciple.

The sufferings of Christ, intense in themselves, were inconceivably bitter because of the extreme sensitiveness of Him Who suffered.

The exquisite sensibility of His sacred body added a peculiar intensity to the sufferings of the Savior. The finest and most delicately balanced nature we could imagine would be blunt of perception compared with the Christ. His body was fashioned by the hands of the Holy Spirit Himself to be the matter of the supreme sacrifice. It can be said that the body of Christ was made for suffering because expressly fashioned for sacrifice. "Sacrifice and oblation thou wouldst not, but a body thou hast fitted to me. Burnt offerings for sin did not please thee. Then said I, behold I come." [10] When one thinks of the thoroughness of the divine workmanship, awful in the extreme must have been the agonies experienced by Him Who was fashioned by God for the endurance of pain.

The Passion of Christ is a many-sided mystery.

But much as the penal aspect of the Passion strikes the imagination and stirs the feelings, it is not by any means the most important or the fundamental aspect. For the Passion is above all else a sacrifice. That is its dominant note. It is the unique sacrifice of mankind in the plan of redemption traced by God. It is the supreme act of religion on the part of the Second Adam.

The death of Christ on Calvary, though immediately due to the violence and injustice of his enemies, was a sacrifice in the strict liturgical sense of the term.

[10] Heb 10: 5–7.

Historically, the sufferings of Christ were the outcome of the circumstances created by His mission and the hostility to that mission on the part of the Jewish chiefs.[11] What He showed Himself to be, and what He stood for, was intensely antipathetic to their pride and fanaticism. They plotted His death on the cross and effectively brought it about. They pressed the pagan Romans into their service to achieve their ends. The Crucifixion was in one sense the result of the normal play of secondary causes. Jesus met the fate that had befallen many a prophet before Him, prophets whose monuments filled the land.[12]

Yet His death was a sacrifice in the strict, liturgical sense of the term. The Scriptures testify to this in no ambiguous terms. "Christ also," writes St. Paul, "hath loved us and hath delivered Himself for us, an oblation and a sacrifice before God for an odor of sweetness."[13] St. Thomas, asking himself if the Passion wrought our salvation, as being literally a sacrifice, replies in the affirmative and cites this text in support of his affirmation. The Council of Trent, voicing the whole of the Christian tradition, implicitly asserts the sacrificial character of Christ's death when it declares anathema against anyone who should hold that the sacrifice of the Mass is a blasphemy against, or is derogatory to, *the sacrifice of the Cross.*[14]

The undergoing of the death on Calvary was the crowning act of religion in Christ's earthly career. Sacrifice is intimately bound up with religion and is its most characteristic act. To understand its nature, it is necessary to have a clear concept of the essential nature of religion.

[11] See Rivière: *Le Dogme de la Rédemption,* 3d ed., p. 254.

[12] On one occasion Jesus thus apostrophized His countrymen: "Woe to you who build the monuments of the prophets, and your fathers killed them. Truly you bear witness to the doings of your fathers, for they indeed killed them and you build their sepulchers" (Lk 11: 47–49).

[13] Eph 5: 2; see also Heb 9–10, etc.

[14] Canon 4, sess. 22, Denz. 951.

Religion may be defined as the complex of the relations in which the creature stands to the Creator. In supernatural religion these relations are concerned with securing to men a destiny that transcends all created happiness and is, in fact, proper to God Himself. Historically, God created man in order to "divinize" man's soul by imparting to it a reality of a divine order. On God's side the whole economy of the dealings of God with man is governed by this purpose—that is, to infuse into the human soul divine realities that elevate it to a divine status and enable it to live a divine life: this divine life is lived initially here and, in full perfection, hereafter. This purpose of God cannot be realized unless man stands in the truth. To stand in the truth is, for man, to abide willingly and lovingly in the creature's necessary dependence on God, to acknowledge gladly that every thing that makes for his good comes to him from God, and, finally, to aspire to that perfect happiness which consists in union with God in the bliss of the divine life. The first fruits of happiness here, and its final consummation hereafter, are conditioned by man's freely, gladly, and lovingly holding himself in dependence on God and in practically acknowledging God as the origin and the consummation of his happiness.

Supernatural religion, then, must be considered from the point of view of the Creator and from the point of view of the creature. On God's side it is the purpose to divinize man and to ordain the means of divinization: on man's side it consists in fulfilling the conditions needed on his part if the process of divinization is to proceed to its issue. These conditions are nothing more than man's readiness to accept the divine benefits from God's hands, to use the means created by God to effect the divine transformation of the soul, and to look to God as the origin and the consummation of this happiness. Religion for man is to look to God as the source of all his good, to aspire to ultimate union with Him, and to order his human life and use the means of grace in such a way as to adapt himself effectively for that union.

Man may forget his own humanity and pretend to an angelic condition. God never forgets the humanity of man and the requirements of that humanity. The world of the supernatural is an intangible, invisible, super-sensible world. It is even, in a sense, super-spiritual, for even the pure spirits, left to their own resources, have no access to it and could have no proper knowledge of it. The realities of that super-sensible, supernatural world could be revealed to man only by means of palpable signs and symbols. That he should be alive to the divine realities in his soul and should be constantly alive to them, it is needful that such a revelation in sensible form should be continual while his soul was still developing itself in bodily conditions. Man is made aware of the inner invisible supernatural process by an external symbolic representation of it.

Hence, supernatural religion is a religion that moves in a realm of signs. God discloses the divine operations in the soul by means of a palpable symbol. In the days of innocence He walked in human form under the trees of paradise and unveiled the wonders of grace in human words and by the aid of apt imagery. In later times, He ordains that a cleansing with water accompanied by appropriate words should typify outwardly the inward cleansing and beautifying of the soul. The partaking of what, to the senses, should appear as the ordinary food of men was made to express visibly the soul's actual participation in the divine element, which causes it to wax strong in divine life. The sacraments are symbols ordained by God to reveal to men in a sensible manner the divine operations He accomplishes in their souls.

It befits man to reply in similar fashion. He, too, will use signs to manifest outwardly his readiness to cooperate with God in the accomplishment of the divine purposes. It has been pointed out how this cooperation is effected. Man must lovingly depend on God and recognize Him as the Author of his being, the source of all his good, and the consummation of his happiness. In the establishment of a religion that is supernatural, it was not left to man to determine the sign, or the dramatic gesture, by which he should signify his willing dependence on God. The Almighty reserved this determination to Himself. He arranged that man should take the material possessions that were God's gift to him and, by certain actions on them and words pronounced in regard to them, testify in symbolic manner his utter dependence on the Lord and the Lord's absolute dominion over him.

Nothing expressed this absolute dependence of the creature and the absolute overlordship of the Creator so eloquently as the destruction of something destined for human use—this destruction being carried out according to fixed forms and after the manner of a ritual. The thing made the object of this ceremonial is by the fact set apart, reserved, distrained from ordinary profane usage—in a word, it is made sacred. If man makes use of the sacred thing, the usage is not profane. If he eats of the sacred object, called the victim, it is not to nourish his body but to mark his desire to enter into participation with the divine by sharing what has been set apart for God.

But in no way could man's dependence on the Creator and his willingness to have his whole life subjected to Him, be expressed more powerfully and more dramatically than by the complete destruction of the matter of sacrifice, that is, of the victim. By the burnt offering man signified to God his utter "belongingness" to Him. Hence the burnt offering was the most perfect of all sacrifices. The sacrament was a sign of God's divine favor to man: sacrifice was a sign of man's desire for these favors and his readiness to fulfill the conditions required for gaining them. To keep in the truth (that is, to abide in his creaturehood) is all that God requires on man's part to dispose himself for the divine gifts. Sacrifice is man's dramatic gesture expressing this total dependence on God, his readiness to fulfill the divine will even if it cost his life, and his desire to attain his happiness through entering into the divine intimacy.

WHY THE CROSS?

Man was not created to be an isolated unit. He was created to be a cell, in organic, supernatural unity with all other human beings. As we have already said, in the supernatural plan mankind forms one Mystical Body, organically united by the bloodstream of sanctifying grace. Man submits to God, therefore, not as an isolated person. He submits to God and expresses that submission as part of a living body. It is that body that proclaims its willing dependence on God. It is the Mystical Body that sacrifices. Sacrifice is, in consequence, a social act, carried out by One Who represents the whole Mystical Body and accomplished according to a ritual arranged by God.

Calvary was the supreme sacrifice of humanity, represented in Christ its Head. Its greatness and its worth in the eyes of God did not depend directly on the dreadful nature of its tortures, but in its being a sublime gesture, testifying utter submission to the divine will. God had traced for His Incarnate Son a program of life that, in the circumstances, would bring death upon Him, unless the Son should use His divine power to ward it off. He was bidden to refrain, at a given moment, from using that divine power. Death was the inevitable result. That death was ordained to be the expiation of sin and the redemption of mankind. It was to promote the interests of God's glory and put eternal happiness within man's reach.

Christ obediently trod the path traced for Him by God's ordinance. He knew why He was bidden to tread it. God's glory and man's good were engaged therein. The path led Him to Gethsemane, the Praetorium, and Calvary. It was a path stained with His blood and marked at every step by inconceivable sufferings. God took no pleasure in these tortures. It would be blasphemous to think so. But He regarded with infinite complacency the heroic love-inspired obedience to which these sufferings bore testimony. To suffer pain or loss in the interest of the beloved is a sign of great love. That a man should sacrifice his life for the well-being of his friend is proof of the supreme love, on the testimony of the Master Himself:

"Greater love than this no man hath, that a man lay down his life for his friends." [15]

Christ went to death—and such a death!—the death of the Cross, out of devotedness to the glory of God and the welfare of man. The sufferings of the Passion were horrible in the extreme. In themselves they were abhorrent to God. But this horror was transformed into a thing of radiant beauty when transfigured by the devoted loyalty, heroic obedience, and utterly selfless love of which it was the outward expression.

Every act, every gesture, in that dolorous drama was, through the prescience of God, appointed with the exactitude of detail of a well-ordered ritual. The Passion was, in all its details, the unfolding of a liturgical rite. The words of Christ and His bearing in all the circumstances intimated that He was making the oblation of His life to honor God by His profound submission and to reconcile humanity with its Maker through that submission. In Christ, its Head, regenerate humanity was contained potentially. In His submission it submitted and so reentered into favor with God. "A true Sacrifice," says St. Augustine, "is every work done in view of adhering to God, establishing holy relations with Him, that is, every work that bears on the attainment of that ultimate Good which alone can beatify us." [16]

The Passion of Christ was infinitely agreeable to God as a most dramatic, ritualistic expression of humanity's loving acknowledgment of His supreme dominion over it and of its desire to enter into holy union with Him. For in Christ, its Head, humanity humbly expressed its submission to God. The Passion was a gesture of obedience and submission on the part of Christ as Head of the redeemed race contained potentially in Him. Hence it is that it is this aspect of obedience that the Church stresses during the Office of Holy Week, as being the predominant characteristic of the Passion. "Christ," she repeats at all the Hours,

[15] Jn 15: 13.
[16] Augustine, quoted by Aquinas, *Summa theologiae*, III, q. 48, a. 3.

"proved Himself obedient unto death, yea, unto the death of the Cross."

Calvary was, then, a true and most perfect sacrifice. It was a significant rite, ordained by God and testifying to man's loving dependence on Him and desire of union with Him. The wounds and death of Christ were the expressive, eloquent, visible sign of that willing dependence. The penal character of the Passion must not be lost sight of. It has its great importance. Calvary is a sacrifice of atonement. But the whole emphasis is not to be placed on "atonement." This is an element that enters into it because of sin. But the full wealth of meaning found in the concept of sacrifice could be realized without the inclusion of the notion of atonement. Sacrifice as a gesture of loving submission to, and dependence on, God would still be the essential act of religion on the side of the creature even if the Fall had never been.

When the Cross is stated to be a sacrifice of atonement, the emphasis should be on the word "sacrifice." The penal character of the Passion remains subordinate to the moral character. It is the moral aspect that gives the great tragedy its sublimity. The penal character is the vehicle of the moral character.

Essentially, Calvary was a magnificent act of obedience. The obedience was all the more glorious because of its cost. Christ's life was utterly poured forth in that grand act of submission. It was poured forth in obeying God. It was poured forth in the interests of God. It was poured forth to please God and not Christ Himself. "He did not please Himself." [17] On that rude altar Christ, as Priest and Head of Humanity and as its Mediator, offered Himself, His doings and His sufferings, His very life, as victim to Almighty God. Humanity, to be regenerated and contained potentially in Christ, by making its submission in this act of the Redeemer, was, after the long estrangement, reconciled with God. The sacrifice of atonement became a

[17] Rom 15: 3.

sacrifice of reconciliation—of newly established friendship with God. In the sacrifice on Calvary was sealed the new covenant, the New Testament.

The revolt of Eden was undone by the submission on Calvary.

Calvary is more clearly understood by placing it in contrast with Eden.[18] One is the antithesis of the other. On the first Adam was laid a solemn injunction, as on the second. The Lord God commanded him [the first man], saying: "Of every tree of Paradise thou shalt eat. But of the tree of knowledge of good and evil thou shalt not eat."[19] The words of Christ at a later time reecho these. "I lay down my life . . . I lay it down of myself. . . . This commandment have I received of my Father."[20]

The first head of the race was bidden to hold as sacred—that is, reserved for God and wholly set apart from profane use—the fruit of the tree of knowledge. This free and willing act of his in constituting that tree sacred (*sacrum facere*, to make sacred, or to sacrifice) was to be the sign daily renewed of his willing dependence on, and consequent "oneness" with, God. He refused to hold the fruit sacred. He refused to make sacrifice of it. With sacrilegious hand he snatched at it and turned it to profane use, to the satisfaction of his own bodily appetites. In the literal sense he "profaned" it and, in profaning it, disobeyed God and flouted His sovereignty. The taking of the fruit was a dramatic gesture, an outward and visible sign of revolt. It was an assertion of his independence of God—a denial of his dependence on Him. It was the negation of sacrifice. It was a crowning act of disobedience in which all human nature, then potentially in Adam, participated. "By the disobedience of one man, many were made sinners."[21]

[18] See P. Prat, S.J., *Théologie de Saint Paul*, p. 261.
[19] Gen 2: 16–17.
[20] Jn 10: 17–18.
[21] Rom 5: 19.

On Calvary Christ was bidden to hold His life sacred to God by not saving it for Himself but allowing the forces of evil to nail Him to the sacred tree. Christ did not seek to save His life and preserve Himself from torture and death. The Crucifixion was a dramatic gesture of obedience. The obedience of Calvary *"obliterated"* the disobedience of Eden. This is almost literally the expression used by St. Paul. "And you, when you were dead in your sins, he [God] hath quickened together with him [Christ], forgiving you all offenses, *blotting out the handwriting of the decree* that was against us . . . he hath taken the same out of the way." [22]

"So by the obedience of one, many shall be made just." [23] Every member of the new race, destined to have its origin in Christ in the rite by which it is regenerated, implicitly subscribes to Christ's great act of submission. "Know ye not," writes St. Paul, "that we who are baptized in Christ Jesus are baptized in his death." [24] Christ on Calvary stands sponsor for regenerated mankind and pledges submission to God on its behalf. Christians share in the risen life of Christ in the measure in which they share in the obedience unto death of Christ as exhibited on Calvary. To be subject to the will of God in union with Christ is to posit the condition of being deified by God. "For if we have been planted together in the likeness of his death, we shall be also in the likeness of his resurrection." [25]

The concupiscence of the flesh and of the eyes and the pride of life draw us into the spirit of revolt of our first parents and tempt us to sacrifice to our own satisfactions rather than to God. God cannot be completely submitted to, wholeheartedly obeyed, unless the concupiscences are crucified in us. "Knowing this, that our old man is crucified with him, that the body of sin may be destroyed, to the end that we may sin no longer." [26]

---

[22] Col 2: 13–14.
[23] Rom 5: 19.
[24] Rom 6: 3.
[25] Rom 6: 5.
[26] Rom 6: 6.

Why God should have decreed that the obedience of His Son should be expressed through the awful sufferings of the Passion, when it might have been expressed in a ritual act involving no such pain, is a secret of His inscrutable designs. All we can know is that the sacrifice of Calvary was decreed out of a merciful regard for man.

St. Thomas, while not pretending to solve this great mystery of pain, shows how, practically, the dreadful sufferings of Christ on Calvary aid man to profit by the salvation that these sufferings have merited for him. He points out that, though from the very beginning of His conception Jesus merited the divine life of grace for men, yet there remained obstacles to their profiting by the grace so won for them. The Passion was directed toward the removal of these obstacles.[27]

Calvary brings home to men in a vivid way the great gravity of sin and the terrible retribution that awaits it. The Passion, bringing home to the imagination, as well as to the mind, the loathsomeness of sin and the chastisement that it merits, acts as a powerful deterrent from evil. Calvary, by its example, encourages that heroism which is often demanded of men if they are to prove faithful to God in times of great trial and temptation. Above all, it moves men to the love of God, Who, in surrendering Himself to death on their account, gives such a convincing proof of His love for them. Love is, in final account, the great force in life, for love alone can inspire that sacrifice which is the price of unwavering fidelity to the Lord.

Every Christian who proves himself faithful to his vocation will deduce from his own experience the wisdom of the divine decree. He will learn by practical experience that it is only through contemplating with faith the sufferings of the Man-God that he nerves himself to abide in obedience to the Lord in spite of the hardships that such obedience so frequently entails. In a world that is ever at

---

[27] See *Summa theologiae*, III, q. 46, a. 3, and q. 48, a. 1, ad 2.

war with Christ and His ideals, there is a constant call for heroism if one is to persevere to the end in loyalty to God. The Cross is, for the Christian, the standard that rouses his courage to withstand bravely the assault of the concupiscences and, with Christ risen from the dead, "to walk in newness of life." [28]

> *Christ has traced for the Christian the path he must follow if he is to achieve himself and conquer happiness.*

The life of Christ on earth was a career of conquest, closing in the magnificent triumph of the entry into heaven on the day of the Ascension. The Christian who wishes to share in Christ's victory must be prepared to take active part in Christ's struggle. He must, in other words, display, in conflict with the adverse forces within and without himself, the moral and spiritual qualities of his Leader.

The great obstacles to final success in this welfare of the spirit are the concupiscence of the flesh, the concupiscence of the eyes, and the pride of life. If the Christian is to cleave his way to the peace that surpasseth all understanding and the happiness such peace gives, the concupiscences must be beaten down and reduced to a state of impotence. The poverty, chastity, and obedience of Christ are the weapons with which this result is achieved. These are the moral qualities of which Christ's life was the sustained expression.

The Christian will catch a reflection of Christ's noble distinction if he emulates Christ's grand independence of men and things, His contempt for purely fictitious glory, and His utter disregard for any honor except that which comes of God's approval bestowed on a man's life and actions. He will capture something of Christ's moral grandeur if, reproducing something of Christ's chastity, he attains to that mastery of spirit over matter which leaves the will free to expand in the purest love for God and

---

[28] Rom 6: 4.

man. He will clothe himself with a measure of Christ's serene sovereignty if, acquiring Christ's humility, he brings his nature to its highest by harmonizing it completely with the mind and will of its Creator and Sovereign Lord. In this lies the achievement of perfect truth: through this the Christian attains the excellence that comes of the flawless realization of the divine ideal of manhood. Undeniably, all this involves bitter suffering for man's fallen nature, but the follower of Christ must be ready to suffer with Him if he wishes "to be glorified with Him." [29]

---

[29] Rom 8: 17.

EPILOGUE

IN THE OFFICE OF HOLY SATURDAY, to the words "Christ proved Himself obedient unto death, even unto the death of the Cross" are added the following: "Wherefore God hath exalted Him and given Him a name above all names." It is not difficult to discern in this an echo of what the great prophet Isaiah had foretold when declaring the destiny of the Messiah: "If he shall lay down his life for sin, he shall see a long-lived seed." [1] Humanity was reborn in the death of Christ. The Lord of life died but to live. He could not impart life unless it were so. The reward of His sacrifice was that He should be empowered to send, from the altar on which He was slain, a vital flame enkindling to life every dead member of humanity touched by it. The reward of Calvary was the formation to Christ (as Head) of a Mystical Body, instinct with supernatural vitality and comprehending every soul willing to enter into union with Him. "Christ loved the church and delivered Himself up for it . . . cleansing it by the laver of water in the word of life, that he might present it to himself a glorious church, not having spot or wrinkle or any such thing, but that it should be holy and without blemish." [2]

Christ ended His earthly career only to resume it in another form. What seemed to men an ending was but a beginning. His death was not a corruption. "God would not give his holy one to see corruption." [3] In the living Church—the living Mystical Body that Christ formed to Himself as a result of His sacrifice—He continues on earth a real, though mystical, life. Christ lives in and through the Church, and that life of His, in His Mystical

[1] Is 53: 10.
[2] Eph 5: 25–27.
[3] Acts 2: 31; compare 2: 27; 13: 37; Ps 16: 10.

Body, reproduces the characteristic traits of His life in the flesh. There is one striking difference. The mortal body of Christ tasted death. The Mystical Body is indestructible. Another work will address the formative principles, the normal manifestations, and the characteristic expression of the earthly, yet unearthly, life of Christ perpetuated in and through the Christian.

INDEX

Adam
> Christ as Redeemer and, 138–39
> God's warning to, 131
> happiness lost in, 212
> happiness of, 224
> and his descendants, 136–38
> human nature in, 124–25, 137
> knowledge of, 131
> man and guilt of, 257
> man as child of, 112
> Mystical Body and, 122, 122–23 (n17)
> sin of, 132–34, 136 (n16), 138, 141, 142, 176

Agony of the Garden, 280–84
à Kempis, Thomas, 92–93
angels, 198, 206
angels of the Nativity, 56
animal life, 117–18 (n12)
animal nature, 129
Annas, 291
Apostles, 68, 89
Aquinas, Saint Thomas. *See* Thomas Aquinas, Saint
Aristotle, 219 (n17)
> endurance of life and, 41
> happiness and, 36–37, 237
> humility and, 254
> ideal life and, 36
> moral acts and, 114
> suffering and happiness and, 12

Ascension, 311
Augustine, Saint, 108
> living life so as not to die and, 43 (n7)
> man's will and, 110
> Original Sin and, 257
> philosophizing and, 237
> sacrifice and, 306

Baptism
> concupiscences and, 143, 159
> guilt of inherited sin and, 144
> human nature and, 150
> Original Sin and, 138–39

Barabbas, 269

beatific vision, 91, 223, 225–26, 228
beatitude, 78
> Christ's promises of, 83
> desired for man, 207
> Divine Beauty and, 116 (n10)
> grace and, 110
> human happiness and, 104
> life of thought and love and, 35
> Original Sin and, 133
> perfect, 80
> as realization of best of life, 226
> in state of innocence, 131–32
> temporal, 35–36, 35 (n12)
> verification of, 124–26

being, 112
believer, 93 (n26)
Blessed Trinity, 106, 169–70
Book of Wisdom, 25, 208
Bossuet, Jacques
> Christ and human race and, 181
> fear of death and, 42 (n4)
> God as life of soul and, 107 (n13)
> man's pursuit of greatness and, 177
> Original Sin and, 257

Caesar, 272 (n16)
Caiaphas, 286, 291, 298
Calvary
> Christ's path to, 305
> Christ's suffering at, 292
> conflict at, 265, 266
> object lesson of, 93
> reward of, 313
> *See also* Passion

catechism, 97, 98, 100, 115
Catholic Church, 24, 24 (n1), 140
> abuse of, 15–16
> Christ's teachings and, 70
> Christianity and, 10, 15–16
> economic evils and, 13–14
> essential function of, 15–16
> evils following revolt against, 23
> man and, 14
> Mystical Body and, 313
> wisdom of, 15

God
action on human spirit of, 193
Adam's sin and, 142
Agony of the Garden and, 283–84
artistry of, 228
Christ's contemplation of, 223–24
Christ's love of, 240–42
Christ's relations with, 141, 242–44
Christ's will and, 239–40
Christ as sacrifice for sin and, 274, 276
concupiscences and, 146–48, 148–50
conformity to will of, 52, 109–10, 116–17
continuity of plan of, 34–37
creation of man by, 96–102, 97 (n1), 110, 119–20, 126–27
cross of man and, 86–88
dishonoring of law of, 49
divine virtues and, 109 (n14), 157
education of man by, 191–92
evil and, 129, 167
faith and, 100
as First Cause, 101 (n3)
first experience of, 195–96
first parents and, 125–26
grace of, 86
happiness and, 79, 95, 103–5, 134, 159
humanity of man and, 303
human nature and, 102–3, 140, 159, 189–91
human vision of, 81
infinite happiness of, 80–81
intellectual creation of, 32 (n11)
Jews and, 60
knowing, 97, 98–100, 115
laws governing acceptance and rejection of, 61
love of, 193–94, 246
loving, 97–98, 115–16
loving purposes of, 109–10
man's activity and, 96–97
man's dependence on, 123–24, 304
man's pride and, 260–61
man's quest after, 186–87
man's taste of beatitude and, 35 (n12)
man's will, 111–12

man at cross purposes with, 58–59
mercy of, 53
messenger of, 196
as model, 72, 72 (n1)
morality and, 50
Mystical Body and, 122, 163–68, 173
ordinary things of life and, 187–89
Original Sin and, 128-129, 132–33, 135–36, 138, 144
Passion and, 296-297, 306, 310
personal knowledge of, 44
plan for man's happiness of, 33–34, 207–13, 221
power of, 163
preternatural gifts of, 119–22
purification and, 85, 89–91
purpose of, 302
realization of plan of, 124–25
rejection of, 71
religion as formalism and, 68–69
religious ideas of, 64–65
salvation and, 59, 61, 141–42, 163–68, 174, 278
service of, 98, 100, 113–16
sin and, 134, 267, 291
soul and, 105–6, 106–8, 107 (n12), 108–9, 196, 200
sovereignty of, 65, 246, 258–60, 265, 290–91
submission to, 195
tragic revelation of happiness by, 91
union with, 158, 206
unity and, 122 (n16)
vision of, 78–81, 79 (n13), 82, 83–84, 110
warning to Adam of, 131
wealth of, 180
will of, 110, 309
Word of, 29, 167
Golgotha, 291
Good Friday, 272, 274
gospel
aspects of, 58–59
fate of, 93 (n26)
happiness and Christ's, 71, 73–74, 77–78
humanitarian aspects of Christ and, 54
knowledge of, 51
man's adaption of, 57
paradox of, 88–89, 95

WHY THE CROSS?

as practical program for all men,
48–50
saints and, 48
Gospels, 203, 236
Christ's peace and, 227
Christ's sympathy for ills of man
and, 52–53
fallen human nature and, 59
misreading of, 50
rejection of Christ and, 60
story of, 204–5
grace
beatitude and, 110
Christ and, 56 (n26), 86, 138–39,
140, 143, 158
concupiscences and, 159, 171
divine, 25 (n2), 37, 44, 125
divine life of, 150–51, 179
eternal life and, 44–45
gifts of, 121–22
human nature and, 143
ideal life and, 37–38
intellect and, 25 (n2)
intimacy with God and, 155
life of, 155
nature and, 24–25
Original Sin and, 142
secret workings of, 193
soul and, 44, 104, 105–6, 152–
53, 171
tendency toward God and, 109
understanding of things of,
24 (n1)
will and, 25 (n2), 110
See also sanctifying grace
Greeks, 238
guilt, 51, 55, 267–68

happiness
Aristotle's definition of, 36–37,
219 (n17)
of Christ, 75–76, 221, 245
Christ's gospel and, 71, 73–74,
81
Christ's promise of, 77–78, 226–
27
Christ and man's path to, 311–
12
Christianity and, 39, 184
concupiscences and, 311
contemplation and, 222–25
Cross and, 95
crucifixion and, 89
divine, 103–5
economic reforms and, 62 (n7)

elements of human, 32, 125
experiments in ways of, 35–36
finiteness of human, 103
of first parents, 126
as goal of life, 38
God's plan for man's, 207–13,
221
God's purpose and, 302
God and, 79, 103–5, 159
health in life and, 29
ideal life and, 27, 33–34, 37, 44,
215–18, 245
infiniteness of God's, 103
as intellectual activity, 237
knowledge of, 29
of life of Christ, 222–26
likeness to God and, 86–88
man and, 40, 211–15
natural, 103–4
obstacles to, 64, 91–92
Original Sin and, 133
permanence and, 43–44
pleasure and, 44, 213–15, 245
purification and, 85–86
religion and, 33, 45–46
salvation and, 90
suffering and, 12, 40, 85–87,
224–25, 246
theory of existence and, 75–76
union with God and, 134
unity in human life of, 34–37
virtue and, 36
vision of God and, 95
See also unhappiness
health, 28–29
heresy, 29
Herod, 298
holiness, 65–66
Holy Spirit, 86, 151, 166, 300
Holy Thursday, 276
Homeric poems, 17
hope
concupiscences and, 144, 151
human soul and, 72 (n1)
re-creation of man and, 104
soul and, 106, 109
union with God and, 157
Humanism, 145 (n4)
humanity. See man
human life, 25 (n2), 27
belief in Christ and, 46–48
Catholics' improper use of, 31–
33
chaotic conditions of, 14
of Christ, 235

human life (*cont.*)
  Christ's Cross as theory of, 94–95, 94 (n28)
  Christ's theory of, 48, 50, 67–68, 87, 154, 158–59, 248–50, 272
  Christian theory of, 10, 16, 17
  confused issues of, 9–10
  contemplation and, 222–25
  cross of, 95
  cross of man and, 88–89
  dissatisfaction with, 21–23, 26–28, 38–39
  eternal significance of activities of, 56
  expression of, 41, 80
  faith and proper use of, 31–33
  God's plan for happiness in, 33–34
  God in ordinary things of, 187–89
  harmony between man and, 116–19
  imitation of Christ's life and, 152–54
  improper use of, 42
  Incarnation and, 186
  inner life of soul and, 200
  knowledge of how to live, 29
  love as great force in, 310
  organization of, 12
  Original Sin and, 128–32
  perfection of, 218–21
  purification and, 92–93, 154–56
  purpose of, 26–28, 28–29, 28 (n9), 39, 64, 96–97, 100
  quest after God of, 186–87
  reason and, 247–50
  removal of fear from, 42–43
  resources of, 178–84
  salvation and, 169–70, 176
  "secular" aspects of, 31
  suffering and, 246
  treasures in, 175–76
  unity of happiness in, 34–37
  use of ordinary activities in, 29–31
  See also concupiscences; divine life; human nature; ideal life
human nature
  appropriate satisfaction of, 176
  Baptism and, 138–39, 150
  characteristics of, 144
  Christ and, 170–73, 175–76
  Christianity and, 10

conformity to will of God and, 110
  divine element in, 36
  egoism and, 138
  evil tendency in, 260
  Fall and, 126, 308
  in first parents, 124–25
  God and, 102–3, 174, 189–91
  grace and, 143
  inherent weakness of, 120
  moral virtues and, 126
  Original Sin and, 127, 134–38, 136 (n16), 142, 150, 153, 170, 273, 285
  preternatural gifts and, 134–35, 139
  proneness to evil of, 53
  reactions of fallen, 59
  sameness of, 32 (n11)
  tendency toward God of, 159
  universality of, 64
  wounded state of, 143–45
  See also human life
humility, 157, 253–55, 261

ideal life
  accessibility of, 37–38
  Aristotle and, 36
  beatitude and, 80
  elimination of evils and, 33
  grace and, 37–38
  happiness and, 27, 33–34, 37, 44, 215–18, 245
  soul and, 157
  suffering and, 216–18
  See also human life
ignorance, 33, 132
ignoratio elenchi, 67
imagination
  of Christ, 231
  man's work and, 219
  natural literature and, 32 (n11)
  perfecting of, 220
  satisfactions of, 213
  in shepherds, 195
  in state of innocence, 131
  time and eternity and, 209–10
Immaculate Conception, 165, 169
immortality, 36, 127, 134
imprudence, 119
Incarnation
  Christ's position in creation and, 256
  Christ and man and, 277
  Christ and man in, 282–83

Jesus Christ (*cont.*)
      religion of, 38, 43, 45–47, 56,
          72–73
      removal of fear from human life
          of, 42–43
      resources of human life and,
          178–84
      restoration of man by, 141–42,
          143, 169–70
      revolt against, 23
      sacrificial death of, 169–70
      salvation and, 57, 141, 175
      sin and, 51, 58, 278
      social relations of, 238–39
      solidarity between man and, 277
      standard of, 17
      suffering of, 155, 207, 221, 246,
          268–69, 288–95, 297–300
      sympathy of, 53, 58
      teachings of, 278
      temptation of, 134
      theory of life of, 48, 50, 67–68,
          87, 94–95, 154, 158–59, 248–
          50, 272
      union with, 152–54
      as victim for sin, 279–80, 284–
          86, 295, 296–97
      vision of God and, 78–81, 83–84
      will of, 239–40
      works and, 68 (n19)
Jews, 93 (n26)
      false ideas about religion of, 63–
          65
      rejection of Christ by, 60
      as religious people, 59–60
      rooted prejudices of, 67
John, Saint, 252
      Christ's taking away of sins and,
          51
      concupiscences and, 143
      human nature and, 258
      life and duration and, 210
      Palm Sunday and, 270 (n14)
      salvation and, 90
Joseph, 201
joy, 50–51
Judas, 273, 280, 284, 291, 297
justice, 120
      of Christ, 278, 279–80
      Christ as sacrifice for sin and,
          275
      concupiscences and, 151
      man and, 113
      original, 137–38, 145
      Original Sin and, 137–38

Passion and, 267–68
peace and, 168–70
re-creation of man and, 104
reestablishment in, 277
restoration and, 152–53
knowledge
      acquisition of, 121
      of Christ, 231
      of God, 97–100, 115
      of good and evil, 132, 136
      of how to live life, 29
      of human happiness, 29
      intellect and, 102
      living and, 44
      love and, 244
      resemblance of God and, 103
      of self, 145
      service and, 100

Last Supper, 211, 277
law of existence, 26
Lazarus, 271
Lenin, Vladimir, 272 (n16)
Liberal Economics, 145 (n4)
Libermann, Francis
      belief in Christ and, 47 (n14)
      Christ's contact with man and,
          56 (n26)
      God's creation of man and, 101
      humility and, 253
      identification between Christ and
          man and, 282–83
      purpose of man's creation and,
          115
      soul and, 108
      union with Christ and, 152
      Word of God and, 167
life. *See* human life
love
      beatitude in life of, 35
      of God, 97–100, 193–94
      as great force in life, 310
      knowledge and, 244
      living and, 44
      primary characteristic of, 115–16
      service and, 100
      union with God and, 111
Luke, Saint, 88
      Christ's adherence to law and,
          49–50
      cross of man and, 83 (n1)
      expectation of Messiah and, 75
      story of shepherds in, 206
lust, 145–46

man
  Catholic Church and, 14
  Christ's death and, 295
  conflict with Christ of, 84–85
  creation of, 96–100, 110, 111,
    115, 119–20
  cross of, 83–84, 83 (n1), 86, 86–
    88, 88–89, 95
  at cross purposes with God, 58–
    59
  deafness to Christ's message of,
    50–51
  dependence on God of, 123–24,
    304
  desire for greatness of, 176–77,
    177–78, 184
  destiny of, 164
  as divine idea, 96–97
  divine life and, 110
  divine nature and, 126–27
  dual birth of, 85, 144
  education of, 191–92
  eternal values and, 24–26
  fallen, 9, 25, 159
  fear of moral nothingness of, 40–
    43, 56
  freedom and, 110
  God's hiddenness from, 189–91
  God's plan for happiness of,
    207–13, 221
  God's plan for salvation and,
    163–65, 278
  gospel and, 48–50, 57
  happiness and, 73–74, 75–76,
    81, 82–83, 211–15, 311–12
  harmony with his nature and,
    116–19
  humanity of, 303
  indefinite perfectibility of, 257–
    58
  intellect of, 237
  intelligence of, 219–20
  joy and, 50–51
  justice and, 113
  mortality of, 130–31
  natural, 32 (n11)
  natural good of, 24
  nature's revolt against, 129–30
  obstacles to happiness of, 91–92
  Original Sin and, 128–32
  perfect life for, 27 (n6)
  personality of, 185
  pride of life, 260–61
  pride of life and, 148–50
  purpose of, 27 (n7), 96–97, 100

  purpose of creation of, 97–100
  quest after God and, 186–87
  reason and, 24, 113, 129 (n3),
    231–32
  rebirth of, 313
  religion and, 64–65
  restlessness of, 21–23, 40
  restoration of, 141–42, 143, 167
  reversibility of choice in, 141
  salvation and, 59, 71, 84, 175
  service of God and, 113–16
  sin of, 278
  solidarity between Adam and,
    136–38
  solidarity between Christ and,
    277
  sovereignty of God and, 290–91
  spiritual decline of, 12
  spiritual transformation of, 71
  suffering and, 54, 61, 87, 145
  supernatural good of, 24
  supernatural ideal and, 139–40
  temporal well-being of, 32
  temptation and, 127
  treasure in life of, 175–76
  unhappiness and, 34
  universal suffering of Christ and,
    297–98
  vision of God and, 81, 83–84,
    95
  will of, 111–12
  will of God and, 110
  Word of God and, 167–68
  wounded nature of, 143–45
  See also human nature
Mark, Saint, 83 (n1), 88
Mary, 195, 201, 242
  Immaculate Conception of, 165–
    66, 169
Matthew, Saint, 83 (n1)
memory, 109
Modern Painters (Ruskin), 99 (n2)
morality, 50, 73
moral virtues
  acquisition of, 120–21
  concupiscences and, 151
  human nature and, 126
  re-creation of man and, 104
mortality, 28
  conditions of, 40
  distresses inherent to, 9
  of man, 130–31
mortal sin, 134
mortification, 156
Moses, 106, 194 (n16)

Satan

   Christ's death and, 295

   envy of first parents of, 146

   false words of, 129

   revolt of, 141

   temptation of man by, 126, 127, 132, 149

   truth and, 261

Scholastic philosophers, 68 (n19)

science, 127, 131, 134, 231, 237

Scripture, 133, 190–92, 208, 209, 301

senses

   appeal to man of, 139–40

   conflict with reason of, 116–17

   man's work and, 219

   preference for, 271 (n16)

   satisfactions of, 213

   in shepherds, 195

   tendencies of, 135

sensibility, 117, 117 (n12), 120–21

Sermon on the Mount, 158

service of God, 97–100, 113–16

shepherds

   faith of, 201–3

   God's grace and, 193–94

   holiness of, 194

   instructions given to, 196–98

   lesson of story of, 203–4

   life of, 230

   qualities of, 197

   spiritual life of, 199–200

Simeon, 85

sin

   Adam's prevarication and, 266

   baptism and, 144

   chastisement of, 131

   Christ's attitude toward, 58, 251

   Christ's death and, 267–68, 273–77, 286, 295

   Christ's taking away of, 51

   as Christ's uncompromising enemy, 285

   Christ and man's, 278

   conflict with God of, 267

   disunion and, 122 (n16)

   egoism and, 138

   estrangement from, 47 (n14)

   as a force of disintegration, 128

   forgiveness of, 55

   God's chastisement of, 291

   God's creation and, 163

   God's plan and, 164–65, 207–13

   mortal, 134

   Original Sin and, 132

   Passion and, 310

   pride and, 291, 295

   against rational nature, 119

   self-interested view of religion and, 51–53

   as sin of nature, 142

social evils, 15–17

Solomon, 228

soul

   charity and, 107, 123

   of Christ, 175

   Christ's healing of, 56 (n26)

   Christianity and divinization of, 90

   concupiscences and, 159

   divine happiness and, 105–6

   divine life and, 116, 119–20

   divine virtues and, 144

   divinization of, 121

   faith and, 107

   free will and, 164

   God and, 102, 106–8, 107 (n12), 108–9, 180, 196, 200

   grace and, 44, 105–6, 152–53, 171

   greatness and growth of, 185

   hope and, 106

   ideal life and, 157

   inner life of, 198–201

   intellect and, 102

   intuitive knowledge of, 44

   likeness to God of, 95, 104

   man's pursuit of greatness and, 176

   Original Sin and, 154

   powers of, 103

   purification and, 89–91, 156, 196

   revelation of God and, 190

   in shepherds, 195

   suffering and, 85, 156

   supernatural life and, 171

   two lives in, 88

   union to Christ of, 47 (n14)

   union with God of, 125

   vision of God and, 79 (n13), 95

   vitality of, 104

spirituality, 12, 51, 195

spiritual life, 157, 158, 199, 203

spiritual literature, 54

suffering

   of Christ, 155, 207, 221, 246, 268–69, 288–95, 297–300

   Christ and human, 55–56

   Christianity and, 9

   conflict with well-being of, 54